A workbook that helps you master the skills you will need to be successful in your courses . . . and beyond.

Containing many questions written in a similar format as on the licensing exam, *Connecting Core Competencies: A Workbook for Social Work Students* includes 300+ assessment questions.

Each chapter covers one of CSWE's 10 core competencies and includes:

- A detailed explanation of the competency
- Assessment questions that help you master the skills in the competency with multiple choice, short case vignette, and reflective essay questions.

**Students: If your text did not come bundled with this printed workbook, you can purchase it at:
www.mypearsonstore.com**

MySocialWorkLab will help you develop the skills you'll need as a professional social worker.

Features include:

- **NEW! Hundreds of assessment questions**—multiple choice, case vignette scenarios and reflective essay—to help you monitor your progress in mastering the skills you will need as a social worker. And, they are written in a similar format as you will find on the licensing exam.

- Complete **eText** with audio files and **chapter tests**

- **Numerous videos** of real scenarios that you are likely to encounter as a social worker.

- **75 case studies** to help you apply theory to practice

- A **Gradebook** that allows you to monitor your progress on all assessment questions on the site

- **MySearchLab**—a collection of tools that help you master research assignments and papers

- And much more!

If your text did not come packaged with MySocialWorkLab, you can purchase access at: www.MySocialWorkLab.com

Professional Identity

2.1.1 Identify as a professional social worker and conduct oneself accordingly.

Necessary Knowledge, Values, Skills

- Social workers serve as representatives of the profession, its mission, and its core values.
- Social workers know the profession's history.
- Social workers commit themselves to the profession's enhancement and to their own professional conduct and growth.

Operational Practice Behaviors

- Social workers advocate for client access to the services of social work;
- Social workers practice personal reflection and self-correction to assure continual professional development;
- Social workers attend to professional roles and boundaries;
- Social workers demonstrate professional demeanor in behavior, appearance, and communication;
- Social workers engage in career-long learning; and
- Social workers use supervision and consultation.

Ethical Practice

2.1.2 Apply social work ethical principles to guide professional practice.

Necessary Knowledge, Values, Skills

- Social workers have an obligation to conduct themselves ethically and engage in ethical decision-making.
- Social workers are knowledgeable about the value base of the profession, its ethical standards, and relevant law.

Operational Practice Behaviors

- Social workers recognize and manage personal values in a way that allows professional values to guide practice;
- Social workers make ethical decisions by applying standards of the National Association of Social Workers Code of Ethics and, as applicable, of the International Federation of Social Workers/ International Association of Schools of Social Work Ethics in Social Work, Statement of Principles;
- Social workers tolerate ambiguity in resolving ethical conflicts; and
- Social workers apply strategies of ethical reasoning to arrive at principled decisions.

Critical Thinking

2.1.3 Apply critical thinking to inform and communicate professional judgments.

Necessary Knowledge, Values, Skills

- Social workers are knowledgeable about the principles of logic, scientific inquiry, and reasoned discernment.
- They use critical thinking augmented by creativity and curiosity.
- Critical thinking also requires the synthesis and communication of relevant information.

Operational Practice Behaviors

- Social workers distinguish, appraise, and integrate multiple sources of knowledge, including research-based knowledge, and practice wisdom;
- Social workers analyze models of assessment, prevention, intervention, and evaluation; and
- Social workers demonstrate effective oral and written communication in working with individuals, families, groups, organizations, communities, and colleagues.

Diversity in Practice

2.1.4 Engage diversity and difference in practice.

Necessary Knowledge, Values, Skills

- Social workers understand how diversity characterizes and shapes the human experience and is critical to the formation of identity.
- The dimensions of diversity are understood as the intersectionality of multiple factors including age, class, color, culture, disability, ethnicity, gender, gender identity and expression, immigration status, political ideology, race, religion, sex, and sexual orientation.
- Social workers appreciate that, as a consequence of difference, a person's life experiences may include oppression, poverty, marginalization, and alienation as well as privilege, power, and acclaim.

Operational Practice Behaviors

- Social workers recognize the extent to which a culture's structures and values may oppress, marginalize, alienate, or create or enhance privilege and power;
- Social workers gain sufficient self-awareness to eliminate the influence of personal biases and values in working with diverse groups;
- Social workers recognize and communicate their understanding of the importance of difference in shaping life experiences; and
- Social workers view themselves as learners and engage those with whom they work as informants.

Human Rights & Justice

2.1.5 Advance human rights and social and economic justice.

Necessary Knowledge, Values, Skills

- Each person, regardless of position in society, has basic human rights, such as freedom, safety, privacy, an adequate standard of living, health care, and education.
- Social workers recognize the global interconnections of oppression and are knowledgeable about theories of justice and strategies to promote human and civil rights.
- Social work incorporates social justice practices in organizations, institutions, and society to ensure that these basic human rights are distributed equitably and without prejudice.

Operational Practice Behaviors

- Social workers understand the forms and mechanisms of oppression and discrimination;
- Social workers advocate for human rights and social and economic justice; and
- Social workers engage in practices that advance social and economic justice.

Research Based Practice

2.1.6 Engage in research-informed practice and practice-informed research.

Necessary Knowledge, Values, Skills

- Social workers use practice experience to inform research, employ evidence-based interventions, evaluate their own practice, and use research findings to improve practice, policy, and social service delivery.
- Social workers comprehend quantitative and qualitative research and understand scientific and ethical approaches to building knowledge.

Operational Practice Behaviors

- Social workers use practice experience to inform scientific inquiry; and
- Social workers use research evidence to inform practice.

Human Behavior

2.1.7 Apply knowledge of human behavior and the social environment.

Necessary Knowledge, Values, Skills

- Social workers are knowledgeable about human behavior across the life course; the range of social systems in which people live; and the ways social systems promote or deter people in maintaining or achieving health and well-being.
- Social workers apply theories and knowledge from the liberal arts to understand biological, social, cultural, psychological, and spiritual development.

Operational Practice Behaviors

- Social workers utilize conceptual frameworks to guide the processes of assessment, intervention, and evaluation; and
- Social workers critique and apply knowledge to understand person and environment.

Policy Practice   2.1.8 Engage in policy practice to advance social and economic well-being and to deliver effective social work services.

Necessary Knowledge, Values, Skills	Operational Practice Behaviors
• Social work practitioners understand that policy affects service delivery and they actively engage in policy practice. • Social workers know the history and current structures of social policies and services; the role of policy in service delivery; and the role of practice in policy development.	• Social workers analyze, formulate, and advocate for policies that advance social well-being; and • Social workers collaborate with colleagues and clients for effective policy action.

Practice Contexts
2.1.9 Respond to contexts that shape practice.

Necessary Knowledge, Values, Skills	Operational Practice Behaviors
• Social workers are informed, resourceful, and proactive in responding to evolving organizational, community, and societal contexts at all levels of practice. • Social workers recognize that the context of practice is dynamic, and use knowledge and skill to respond proactively.	• Social workers continuously discover, appraise, and attend to changing locales, populations, scientific and technological developments, and emerging societal trends to provide relevant services; and • Social workers provide leadership in promoting sustainable changes in service delivery and practice to improve the quality of social services.

Engage, Assess, Intervene, Evaluate   2.1.10 Engage, assess, intervene, and evaluate with individuals, families, groups, organizations, and communities.

Necessary Knowledge, Values, Skills	Operational Practice Behaviors
• Professional practice involves the dynamic and interactive processes of engagement, assessment, intervention, and evaluation at multiple levels. • Social workers have the knowledge and skills to practice with individuals, families, groups, organizations, and communities. • Practice knowledge includes - identifying, analyzing, and implementing evidence-based interventions designed to achieve client goals; - using research and technological advances; - evaluating program outcomes and practice effectiveness; - developing, analyzing, advocating, and providing leadership for policies and services; and - promoting social and economic justice.	**(a) Engagement** • Social workers substantively and affectively prepare for action with individuals, families, groups, organizations, and communities; • Social workers use empathy and other interpersonal skills; and • Social workers develop a mutually agreed-on focus of work and desired outcomes. **(b) Assessment** • Social workers collect, organize, and interpret client data; • Social workers assess client strengths and limitations; • Social workers develop mutually agreed-on intervention goals and objectives; and • Social workers select appropriate intervention strategies. **(c) Intervention** • Social workers initiate actions to achieve organizational goals; • Social workers implement prevention interventions that enhance client capacities; • Social workers help clients resolve problems; • Social workers negotiate, mediate, and advocate for clients; and • Social workers facilitate transitions and endings. **(d) Evaluation** • Social workers critically analyze, monitor, and evaluate interventions.

CSWE's Core Competencies Practice Behaviors Coverage in this Text

Practice Behavior	Chapter
Professional Identity (2.1.1)	
Social workers advocate for client access to the services of social work;	
Social workers practice personal reflection and self-correction to assure continual professional development;	9
Social workers attend to professional roles and boundaries;	4
Social workers demonstrate professional demeanor in behavior, appearance, and communication;	2
Social workers engage in career-long learning;	
Social workers use supervision and consultation.	1, 3, 8
Ethical Practice (2.1.2)	
Social workers recognize and manage personal values in a way that allows professional values to guide practice	3
Social workers make ethical decisions by applying standards of the National Association of Social Workers Code of Ethics and, as applicable, of the International Federation of Social Workers/International Association of Schools of Social Work Ethics in Social Work, Statement of Principles	5
Social workers tolerate ambiguity in resolving ethical conflicts	
Social workers apply strategies of ethical reasoning to arrive at principled decisions	8
Critical Thinking (2.1.3)	
Social workers distinguish, appraise, and integrate multiple sources of knowledge, including research-based knowledge, and practice wisdom	2, 9
Social workers analyze models of assessment, prevention, intervention, and evaluation	1
Social workers demonstrate effective oral and written communication in working with individuals, families, groups, organizations, communities, and colleagues	3, 7
Diversity in Practice (2.1.4)	
Social workers recognize the extent to which a culture's structures and values may oppress, marginalize, alienate, or create or enhance privilege and power	
Social workers gain sufficient self-awareness to eliminate the influence of personal biases and values in working with diverse groups	6
Social workers recognize and communicate their understanding of the importance of difference in shaping life experiences	
Social workers view themselves as learners and engage those with whom they work as informants	
Human Rights & Justice (2.1.5)	
Social workers understand the forms and mechanisms of oppression and discrimination	
Social workers advocate for human rights and social and economic justice	8
Social workers engage in practices that advance social and economic justice	5

CSWE's Core Competencies Practice Behaviors Coverage in this Text

Practice Behavior	Chapter
Research Based Practice (2.1.6)	
Social workers use practice experience to inform scientific inquiry	
Social workers use research evidence to inform practice	4, 6, 7
Human Behavior (2.1.7)	
Social workers utilize conceptual frameworks to guide the processes of assessment, intervention, and evaluation	
Social workers critique and apply knowledge to understand person and environment.	
Policy Practice (2.1.8)	
Social workers analyze, formulate, and advocate for policies that advance social well-being	
Social workers collaborate with colleagues and clients for effective policy action	
Practice Contexts (2.1.9)	
Social workers continuously discover, appraise, and attend to changing locales, populations, scientific and technological developments, and emerging societal trends to provide relevant services	5
Social workers provide leadership in promoting sustainable changes in service delivery and practice to improve the quality of social services	
Engage, Assess, Intervene, Evaluate (2.1.10(a)–(d))	
A) ENGAGEMENT	
Social workers substantively and effectively prepare for action with individuals, families, groups, organizations, and communities	
Social workers use empathy and other interpersonal skills	6
Social workers develop a mutually agreed-on focus of work and desired outcomes	
B) ASSESSMENT	
Social workers collect, organize, and interpret client data	7
Social workers assess client strengths and limitations	
Social workers develop mutually agreed-on intervention goals and objectives	
Social workers select appropriate intervention strategies	
C) INTERVENTION	
Social workers initiate actions to achieve organizational goals	
Social workers implement prevention interventions that enhance client capacities	4, 9
Social workers help clients resolve problems	
Social workers negotiate, mediate, and advocate for clients	
Social workers facilitate transitions and endings	
D) EVALUATION	
Social workers critically analyze, monitor, and evaluate interventions	

CONNECTING CORE COMPETENCIES **Chapter-by-Chapter Matrix**

Chapter	Professional Identity	Ethical Practice	Critical Thinking	Diversity in Practice	Human Rights & Justice	Research Based Practice	Human Behavior	Policy Practice	Practice Contexts	Engage, Assess, Intervene, Evaluate
1	✔		✔							
2	✔		✔							
3	✔	✔	✔							
4	✔					✔				✔
5		✔			✔				✔	
6				✔		✔				✔
7			✔			✔				✔
8	✔	✔			✔					
9	✔		✔							✔
Total Chapters	6	3	5	1	2	3	0	0	1	4

UPDATED SIXTH EDITION

Field Instruction

A Guide for Social Work Students

David Royse
University of Kentucky, Lexington

Surjit Singh Dhopper
University of Kentucky, Lexington

Elizabeth Lewis Rompf
University of Kentucky, Lexington

Pearson Education

Boston Columbus Indianapolis New York San Francisco Upper Saddle River
Amsterdam Cape Town Dubai London Madrid Milan Munich Paris Montreal Toronto
Delhi Mexico City São Paulo Sydney Hong Kong Seoul Singapore Taipei Tokyo

Editorial Director: Craig Campanella
Editor in Chief: Dickson Musslewhite
Executive Editor: Ashley Dodge
Editorial Product Manager: Carly Czech
Director of Marketing: Brandy Dawson
Executive Marketing Manager: Jeanette Koskinas
Senior Marketing Manager: Wendy Albert
Marketing Assistant: Jessica Warren
Media Project Manager: Felicia Halpert

Production Manager: Kathy Sleys
Editorial Production and Composition Service:
  Chitra Ganesan/PreMediaGlobal
Interior Design: Joyce Weston Design
Creative Director: Jayne Conte
Cover Designer: Kristina Mose-Libon/
  Karen Salzbach
Cover Image: Vetta Collection/iStockphoto

Credits appear on Page 239, which constitutes an extension of the copyright page.

Library of Congress Cataloging-in-Publication Data

Royse, David D. (David Daniel)
Field instruction : a guide for social work students / David Royse, Surjit Singh Dhooper, Elizabeth Lewis Rompf.—Updated 6th ed.
   p. cm.
Includes bibliographical references and index.
ISBN-13: 978-0-205-02224-3
ISBN-10: 0-205-02224-3
 1. Social service—Fieldwork.   I. Dhooper, Surjit Singh.   II. Rompf, Elizabeth Lewis.   III. Title.
HV11.R67 2012
361.3'2—dc23

2011020682

10 9 8 7 6 5 4 3 2 1   15 14 13 12 11

Student Edition
ISBN-10: 0-205-02224-3
ISBN-13: 978-0-205-02224-3

Instructor Edition
ISBN-10: 0-205-20324-8
ISBN-13: 978-0-205-20324-6

à la Carte Edition
ISBN-10: 0-205-02278-2
ISBN-13: 978-0-205-02278-6

Contents

6. Client Systems: The Recipients of Service   123

Preface

If you are about to begin your first practicum, this book was written for you. It is a "survival manual" or "consumer's manual" designed for students. Although we had undergraduates primarily in mind, the material is also applicable for graduate students—especially those who come into social work from some other discipline.

Most students find the practicum to be a valuable experience that confirms they have made the right career choice. Still, being placed in an unfamiliar agency and being assigned real clients make some students a little anxious and unsure of themselves. Even confident students have questions prior to and during their field experiences. By offering practical advice for some commonly raised questions, we hope to reduce your anxiety so that you can maximize your learning and development as a social work professional.

We have attempted to provide the type of advice that students will find useful even though social work programs vary greatly in the way they are structured and administered. Few programs supply students ahead of time with information about the problems most commonly encountered in the field. It is our hope that in some small way this book will make for a better field instruction experience for all those involved—students, instructors, clients, and supervisors. Field instruction is a significant part of social work education. It is not simply a "volunteer" activity or a chance to escape the classroom. The practicum is an opportunity for tremendous learning and refinement of skills. At the same time, students have enormous responsibilities whenever they serve clients as representatives of social services agencies and institutions of higher learning.

Please note that in reading this book we have used the terms *field instruction, field work, field education, practicum,* and *internship* interchangeably. Similarly, persons supervising students in the field can be known as agency supervisors, field supervisors, intern supervisors, or field instructors. Of these, *agency supervisors* and *field instructors* are used most often and are treated as equivalent terms. Finally, faculty supervisors, field coordinators, seminar instructors, faculty advisers, faculty consultants, field professors, or faculty field liaisons are always referred to as faculty field liaisons.

We hope that this text will prove to be useful to you as you guide students going into their practica. Should you find topics that we have missed or that ought to be included, please feel free to contact me or one of the other authors.

Connecting Core Competencies Series

The new edition of this text is now a part of Pearson Education's *Connecting Core Competencies* series, which consists of foundation-level texts that make it easier than ever to ensure students' success in learning the ten core competencies as stated in 2008 by the Council on Social Work Education. This text contains:

▸ **Core Competency Icons** throughout the chapters, directly linking the CSWE core competencies to the content of the text. **Critical thinking questions** are also included to further students' mastery of the CSWE standards. For easy reference, page vi displays which competencies are used in each chapter, in a chapter-by-chapter matrix.

- **An end-of-chapter Practice Test,** with multiple-choice questions that test students' knowledge of the chapter content.
- **Assess your competence** at the end of each chapter by evaluating your mastery of the skills and competencies learned.
- **Additional questions pertaining to the videos and case studies found on MySocialWorkLab** at the end of each chapter to encourage students to access the site and explore the wealth of available materials. If this text did not come with an access code for MySocialWorkLab, you can purchase access at: www.mysocialworklab.com.

Acknowledgments

We wish to acknowledge the help of Nancy House, JD; John H. Rompf, Jr., JD; and Elizabeth Rompf Bruen, JD, for their contributions to portions of this book. We would also like to extend our appreciation to the reviewers of this edition: Susan Bowers, Northern Illinois University; Sharon A. Smith, The Richard Stockton College of New Jersey; Allen R. Stata, Eastern New Mexico University; and Helle Thorning, New York University.

David Royse
droyse@uky.edu

Surjit Singh Dhooper
dhooper@uky.edu

Elizabeth Lewis Rompf
sprrompf@uky.edu

1

Field Instruction and the Social Work Curriculum

Core Competencies in This Chapter (Check marks indicate which competencies are covered in depth)				
✓ Professional Identity	Ethical Practice	✓ Critical Thinking	Diversity in Practice	Human Rights & Justice
Research-Based Practice	Human Behavior	Policy Practice	Practice Contexts	Engage, Assess, Intervene, Evaluate

OVERVIEW

This introductory chapter provides the historical and current context for understanding the requirement of field instruction in social work programs. It also begins to answer questions about student preparation, supervision, and the coordination of field instruction within the larger educational program.

WHY FIELD INSTRUCTION?

As professionals in the making, social work students attend classes to learn practice principles, values and ethical behaviors, a body of specialized knowledge, and the scientific basis for practice. In field instruction, students apply, under supervision, what they have been learning in the classroom to real situations. Thus, the preparation to become a social work professional is composed of formal learning as well as practical experience—sometimes known as field instruction, field placement, field work, practicum, or internship. Such training experiences are not unique to social work but are common to most of the helping professions.

A career in social work requires many abilities. Social workers must have competence in relating to individuals, families, small groups, organizations, and communities; in assessing needs and problems; and in planning and intervening appropriately. Social workers have to be skilled in carrying out various helping roles such as advocate, broker, educator, group leader, mediator, clinician, community planner and organizer, administrator, and so forth. While students may not be able to acquire expertise in each of these roles during a single practicum, placement in an agency allows them the opportunity to observe other professionals and to learn from their actions. Students can learn from any of the staff around them—all play a role in helping students to become more proficient.

Students not only acquire practical experience from the field, but they also are socialized into the professional subculture. There are two important aspects of this socialization: acceptance of individuals into a professional group where common expectations are held of all members, and the development of a professional self-concept consistent with role models. During field instruction, interactions with clients, colleagues, and the professional community help students master the culture, norms, and values of social work. Field instruction assists students in making the transition from passive learners to active professionals.

The new educational policy and accreditation standards (EPAS) from the Council on Social Work Education emphasize competency-based education. "Competencies are measurable practice behaviors that are comprised of knowledge, values, and skills. The goal of the outcome approach is to demonstrate the integration and application of competencies in practice with individuals, families, groups, organizations and communities" (CSWE, 2008, p. 3). Students must acquire the following core competencies. They

The new educational policy and accreditation standards from the CSWE emphasize competency-based education.

1. identify themselves as professional social workers and conduct themselves accordingly;

2. apply social work ethical practice principles to guide professional practice;

3. apply critical thinking to inform and communicate professional judgments;

4. engage diversity and difference in practice;
5. advance human rights and social and economic justice;
6. engage in research-informed practice and practice-informed research;
7. apply knowledge of human behavior and the social environment;
8. engage in policy practice to advance social and economic well-being and to deliver effective social work services;
9. respond to contexts that shape practice; and
10. engage, assess, intervene, and evaluate with individuals, families, groups, organizations, and communities. Field education is considered the signature pedagogy in social work. "Signature pedagogy represents the central form of instruction and learning in which a profession socializes its students to perform the role of practitioner" (CSWE, 2008, p. 8).

Field instruction allows students to test whether social work is the best career for them. The choice of a career is a major decision, and not everyone is suited to be a social worker. Because students are closely monitored and evaluated, agency supervisors can help students identify their strengths and weaknesses and determine whether social work is the best choice for them. Occasionally, faculty field liaisons must recommend that students address personal issues before entering their field placements.

Case Example

John has changed college majors four times in the past three years. He entered as an English literature major, then changed to accounting. In his sophomore year, he tried both geography and Russian. After one year of Russian, he dropped out of school to "get his act together." He worked as a bartender and joked about how easily drunks can be shortchanged and their drinks watered down. When a DUI conviction caused him to lose his driver's license, John took a couple of social work courses and did well in them although several of his friends say they have smelled alcohol on his breath during class. Last week John was fired from his job for stealing from his employer. He claims the charges are not true and plans to go to school full time next semester to become a social worker because, he says, "It's easy work—all you have to do is talk."

Questions

1. Is John ready to become a social worker?
2. What questions could you ask to help John examine his motivations for becoming a social worker?
3. Why, in your mind, should a person choose the career of social work?
4. What characteristics make a good social worker? A poor one?

WHAT IS THE ROLE OF THE FACULTY FIELD LIAISON?

The primary job of the faculty field liaison is to see that students' practicum experiences are educational. That job covers all aspects of a student's experience from placement in the field agency to the final evaluation of his or her total performance. Note, however, that in some programs the field education director is responsible for placing students in agencies, training agency field instructors, and monitoring students' experiences. Faria, Brownstein, and Smith (1988) identify ten liaison responsibilities that they divide into six roles and four functions. The faculty field liaison functions are commonly the following:

- ▶ *Placement*—selects field agencies and field instructors and matches them with students.
- ▶ *Linkage*—interprets school policies, procedures, and expectations of field agencies and assesses the fit between school curriculum and educational experiences provided by the agencies.
- ▶ *Administration*—ensures completion of placement forms (e.g., students' evaluation of agencies, field instructors, and faculty field liaisons).
- ▶ *Evaluation*—evaluates students, field instructors, and agencies; assigns students' grades; and makes recommendations for continued use of agencies and field instructors (more on the evaluation of students in Chapters 2 and 4).

In the performance of their functions, you should see faculty liaisons in the following roles:

- ▶ *Adviser*—provides assistance to students in planning for practicum.
- ▶ *Monitor*—assesses agencies, field instructors, and students' learning experiences.
- ▶ *Consultant*—assists field instructors in developing supervisory skills and provides course outlines and other materials.
- ▶ *Teacher*—assists students with the integration of course work and practicum and serves as a role model to students.
- ▶ *Mediator*—assists in resolving problems between students and field instructors or other agency personnel.
- ▶ *Advocate*—provides relevant information to academic review committees (when necessary) to evaluate students' field and academic performances.

In many programs, faculty field liaisons conduct seminars to provide students with a regular occasion to share their learning and to ask for information or assistance when difficult problems arise. In addition, students may be expected to submit weekly papers or logs of their field experiences and plan individual conferences with their faculty field liaisons. These seminars and conferences provide opportunities for faculty to get to know students, to guide them when necessary, and to help them with integrating theory and practice.

WHAT IS THE HISTORY OF FIELD INSTRUCTION IN SOCIAL WORK?

Field instruction has always been a major part of social work training. Its history goes back to the days of the Charity Organization Societies in the last quarter of the nineteenth century when students learned social work by apprenticeship. Through "applied philanthropy" students obtained firsthand knowledge of poverty and adverse social conditions. With this *apprenticeship model,* training emphasized doing and deriving knowledge from that activity.

By the end of the nineteenth century, social work was moving away from the apprenticeship model.

The first training school for social work was a summer program that opened in 1898 at the New York City Charity Organization Society. In 1904, the Society established the New York School of Philanthropy, which offered an eight-month instructional program. Mary Richmond, an early social work practitioner, teacher, and theoretician, argued that although many learned by doing, this type of learning must be supplemented by theory.

At the 1915 National Conference of Charities and Corrections, presenters emphasized the value of an educationally based field-practice experience, with schools of social work having control over students' learning assignments. This idea put schools in the position of exercising authority over the selection of agencies for field training and thus control over the quality of social work practice to which students were exposed.

Early in social work education, a pattern was established whereby students spent roughly half of their academic time in field settings (Austin, 1986). This paradigm was made possible by the networking that emerged from the early organizational efforts of social work educators. For instance, in 1919 the organization of the Association of Training Schools for Professional Social Work was chartered by 17 programs. Thirteen of the original 17 schools were associated with universities or colleges at the postbaccalaureate level by 1923. The American Association of Schools of Social Work, in its curriculum standards of 1932, formally recognized field instruction as an essential part of social work education (Mesbur, 1991).

During the first part of the twentieth century, psychoanalytic theory dominated social work education. This influence tended to focus the attention of students and social work educators on a client's personality rather than on the social environment. The Depression of the 1930s and the enactment of the Social Security Act of 1935 brought about major changes in the United States' provision of social services and need for social workers. Subsequent amendments to this act created several social welfare programs and social work roles.

From about 1940 until 1960, an *academic approach* dominated social work education. This approach emphasized students' cognitive development and knowledge-directed practice. Professors expected students to deduce practice approaches from classroom learning and translate theories into functional behaviors in the field (Tolson & Kopp, 1988).

Educational standards for field instruction were refined in the 1940s and the 1950s, and field work became known as field instruction. The American Association of Schools of Social Work took the position that field teaching was as important as classroom teaching and demanded equally qualified teachers and definite criteria for the selection of field agencies. In 1951, the Hollis-Taylor report on the state of social work education in the United States asserted that "education for social work is a responsibility not only of educators but equally of organized practitioners, employing agencies, and the interested public. Widely accepted by the profession, this assertion became the cornerstone of all subsequent developments" (Kendall, 2002).

Social work education is a responsibility shared by educators, practitioners, and agencies.

In 1952 the Council on Social Work Education was established and began creating standards for institutions granting degrees in social work. These standards required a clear plan for the organization, implementation, and evaluation of both in-class work and the field practicum. Interestingly, it was not until 1970 that field work was made a requirement for undergraduate programs affiliated with the Council.

The *articulated approach* characterized the third phase in the history of social work field instruction (from about 1960 to the present). This method integrates features from both experiential and academic approaches. It is concerned with a planned relationship between cognitive and experiential learning and requires that both class and field learning be developed with learning objectives that foster their integration. It does not demand that students be inductive or deductive learners but expects that knowledge development and practice will be kept close enough together in time to minimize these differences in learning style (Jenkins & Sheafor, 1982).

Students may not be aware of the tensions and strong disagreements that have existed in previous years over the purpose of field education. When social work programs were housed in other disciplines, academically minded social scientists sometimes argued that the function of field instruction was to allow students to observe and collect data on poverty and social conditions first hand. The emphasis was often on the *study* of social problems. Students were *not* expected to provide services or assist clients. Agencies, of course, wanted students to roll up their sleeves and pitch in and help with the work that they were doing. As social work has matured as a unique discipline, a view of field education has emerged that blends both the academic and experiential perspectives.

The 2008 Educational Policy and Accreditation Standards highlight the role of field education as "to connect the theoretical and conceptual contribution of the class room with the practical world of the practice setting" (CSWE, 2008, p. 8). Both classroom and field are of equal importance for the development of the requisite competencies of professional practice. Social work programs are free to use creativity in ensuring that their students develop the required competencies. Therefore, there may be differences in the design, coordination, supervision, and evaluation of students' field experiences.

WHAT ARE THE CURRENT STANDARDS FOR FIELD INSTRUCTION?

The Council on Social Work Education requires that undergraduate programs provide each student with a minimum of 400 hours of field instruction. Graduate programs must arrange a minimum of 900 hours. The Council mandates that every program "specifies policies, criteria, and procedures for selecting field settings; placing and monitoring students; maintaining field liaison contacts with field education settings; and evaluating student learning and field setting effectiveness congruent with the program's competencies" (CSWE, 2008, p. 9).

Critical Thinking

Critical Thinking Question: If your agency does not provide you with the conceptual framework to guide your assessments and intervention, how might you go about developing one?

Case Example

Betty thinks that the requirement of 400 hours in an unpaid field placement is too much—mainly because it takes away from time she could be on the tennis court. Tennis is easily the main interest in her life and is always the major topic in any conversation she starts. Betty has the potential to become a professional tennis player and make more money than she ever would as a social worker, but wants the Bachelor of Social Work (BSW) to fall back on.

Her supervisor's schedule does not overlap with every hour Betty is supposed to be in the agency. Halfway through the semester Betty confides in you that she has slipped out two or more hours early each day her supervisor wasn't in and also lied about the number of hours that she was supposed to be in the library doing a search for literature.

Questions

1. What is your reaction to Betty's confiding in you?
2. Does Betty have the characteristics that make a good social worker?
3. Does 400 hours of field experience seem an excessive amount of time to prepare you to be a social worker?

ARE THERE DIFFERENT TYPES OF FIELD PLACEMENTS?

Social work programs can organize the required field instruction in different ways as long as degree programs are educationally directed, coordinated, monitored, and meet the requirements of the Council on Social Work Education. The most common types of field placements are block and concurrent. Under the *block* placement arrangement, a student is placed in a social service agency with an approved learning plan for a block of time—for example, a whole academic term, two full terms, or a summer term. The students devote full time (four or five days per week) to experiential learning in the agency. Under a *modified block model,* students participate in field instruction in a social service agency four days each week while the fifth day is reserved for taking courses.

Under the *concurrent placement,* the students' time is divided between classroom learning and field work experiences. (Typically, students are expected to be in the agency for two or three days per week and to take classes for two or three days.) The exact proportion of time devoted to each set of learning experiences varies, depending on the type of academic term, the number of academic credits, and whether the students are undergraduates or first- or second-year graduate students.

Social work programs across the United States have mixed and matched these two types of placements to create models of field instruction. Sometimes first-year graduate students do a concurrent placement (two days per week for two semesters), and second-year students complete a block placement (for 15 weeks at five days per week). Larger schools may offer as many as three models of field practicum for students: the *standard model*—two years of concurrent placements for 28 weeks each year at three days (21 hours) per week; the *extended model*—two years of concurrent placement for 42 weeks each year at two days (14 hours) per week; and the *reduced field instruction model*—one year of placement for 33 weeks at four days (28 hours) per week. Students who work and go to school may have preferences for one model over another. Educationally, all these models are considered sound. For example, in a recent study, Theriot, Johnson, Mulvaney, and Kretzschmar (2006) evaluated the impact of block versus concurrent field placement on the professional development and emotional well-being of students in a BSW program. They found no differences in measures of professional competence, depression, assertiveness, and self-esteem in the two field models.

HOW ARE STUDENTS PREPARED FOR FIELD INSTRUCTION?

At the undergraduate level, social work programs must prepare students for beginning *generalist* social work practice with individuals, families, small groups, organizations, and communities. To reach this objective, most programs follow a three-step graduated approach. At step 1, students enroll in an introductory course in social work and may need to make application to the program.

Step 2 is the completion of basic core courses—social work practice, human behavior and the social environment, social welfare policy and services, and social work research. Step 3 is the placement of students in their field practicum. Faculty field liaisons assign students to social welfare agencies so they can acquire new skills and further refine their existing skills. In many programs, the practicum is scheduled for the senior year.

As an undergraduate student you can expect to spend between one-and-a-half to two days a week in the field agency during a typical semester if there is a two-semester field sequence. The Council on Social Work Education requires a minimum of 400 clock hours in the field, although it is not unusual for programs to require a few more hours than this.

HOW ARE STUDENTS IN FIELD PLACEMENT SUPERVISED?

Field instructors are considered members of the extended faculty.

Professional Identity

Critical Thinking Question: If your field instructor is not helping you to learn advocacy skills, how might you use supervision and consultation in the agency to acquire these skills?

In most programs, students are placed in a public service agency under the day-to-day supervision of a field instructor who is a social worker employed by the agency. It is the responsibility of the field instructor to provide students with opportunities for contact with various client systems and to oversee students' performance with assigned tasks. Field instructors are considered members of the extended teaching staff of the school and may be granted faculty privileges such as the use of the university library facilities or discounts at the university bookstore.

Field instructors should be well aware of the social work program's philosophy, the content and sequence of courses, and the expected level of student performance. Often there are special training sessions for new field instructors—this ensures that assignments given to students are consistent with students' abilities and the program's expectations. In addition to the supervision students receive from field instructors, social work programs usually assign faculty members as advisers to students and as liaisons between the agency and the school.

Social work programs vary considerably from school to school (and sometimes even within a school) in the level of student monitoring that field liaisons do. Some faculty field liaisons will meet with their students weekly, but others may meet at the beginning, at the midpoint, and at the end of the term. Other faculty field liaisons may meet only for an evaluation at the end of the term. Some faculty will monitor students' progress by requiring written or oral assignments (e.g., case presentations, planned observations, or interviews); others do not. Even though your field instructor may be asked for a recommendation on the grade you earned in your practicum, the assignment of the grade is most often the responsibility of the faculty field liaison.

Sharing relevant information benefits everyone.

HOW ARE CLASSROOM LEARNING AND FIELD INSTRUCTION INTEGRATED?

The very nature of field instruction fosters integration with classroom learning—particularly when students meet regularly to discuss what they have been learning. Students are often amazed at how much knowledge they have acquired when taking turns to describe their interesting or problematic cases.

Social work programs have also employed a variety of approaches to nurture integration of theoretical content and field instruction. Some have developed close relationships with agencies and may provide consultation or occasional in-service training to the staff in host agencies. Field instructors may also serve on advisory boards to provide feedback on the social work program's field education component. Whenever the faculty and the staff of field agencies meet and discuss mutual concerns, opportunities arise to explore ways to integrate students' field experiences with classroom learning.

Efforts to achieve integration can also be more purposive, as when agency field instructors supervising students for the first time are required to attend seminars on field instruction. These sessions facilitate the integration of field and classroom experiences as field instructors are given access to syllabi, course outlines, bibliographies, curriculum statements, field manuals, newsletters, and other relevant documents.

Most social work programs place the major responsibility on the faculty field liaison for the integration of classroom learning and field instruction. As discussed earlier, the faculty field liaison may use methods such as holding field seminars, commenting on students' logs, or holding conferences with students to increase the integration of classroom and field experiences.

The students' role, too, should be recognized. Students can enrich their learning by sharing relevant information that they have come across and by making a point to bring into the classroom their interesting field experiences, discussions, cases, and learning from their agencies. Equally valuable is the habit of reflecting on what is learned in the field. Students should periodically ask themselves questions such as, What knowledge, skills, or values am I learning in the field? How workable are the theories that I have been learning? How do situations encountered with real clients mesh with what I have learned in class? Because our families can influence our attitudes about life and how we view others (e.g., with punitive, condescending, or accepting attitudes), we also need to think about how our own life experiences contribute to our ability to recognize, appreciate, and affirm clients and their efforts, courage, and strengths.

The use of a professional log can be invaluable for recording your reflections about interventions, clients, and the agency, as well as what you might be learning about yourself. Perhaps you will identify areas where you need to acquire information or instruction. Your log can also include narratives of key events, problems, feelings, impressions, lists of things to do or learn, as well as reflections on your reading and questions you want to ask your field instructor or field liaison. Such reflection, practiced from time to time, not only helps you integrate classroom content and field education but also promotes your growth as active, responsible, self-directed learners.

WHAT IS THE PURPOSE OF FIELD SEMINARS?

As a part of the practicum requirements, many social work programs require students to participate in weekly seminars. A *seminar* is a group of students engaged in a special study under the guidance of a professor. The basic assumption underpinning seminars is that each person in attendance has important information to share or contribute. By contrast, in lecture courses the assumption is that the professor has the most knowledge and will be the prime communicator of ideas.

Usually, field seminars are conducted by faculty field liaisons, although they may be directed by field instructors or even students themselves. Faculty field liaisons or seminar leaders make arrangements for the time and place of the meeting, and they determine the frequency of the seminars as well as the focus of each session. In addition, it is their responsibility to see that the discussions are relevant to students' current experiences in their practicum placements. Many see their seminar leadership role as helping students (1) to understand their cases in terms of applicable theories and (2) to integrate discoveries in an area (e.g., practice) with content from another (e.g., policy or research implications).

Seminars may be highly structured, as when students are given specific reading assignments or are asked to make presentations. Or seminars may be loosely structured, as when students take turns relating significant experiences or problems that recently occurred in the field. In structured seminars, it is likely that the faculty field liaison will choose the topics and carefully focus student discussion. Similarly, the faculty field liaison may give specific directions for seminar presentations. Here are a few suggestions if you are required to make a presentation:

1. Keep within the time limit (organize your thoughts and rehearse your presentation).
2. Begin with a brief introduction of what you intend to cover.

3. Limit your main points to three or four, and support these with illustrations.

4. Summarize your main points at the end of your presentation.

5. Stimulate discussion by looking at each person as you speak.

6. Use visual aids to clarify ideas.

7. Anticipate questions, and to encourage discussion, ask several questions of your own.

Whether their seminars are structured or unstructured, most faculty field liaisons prefer that all students contribute to seminar discussions. Informal exchanges can help students feel comfortable with the way their interventions are proceeding. Learning that your peers have had similar experiences or even that they would have handled the problem the same way you did can be very reassuring. In the best seminars, students can feel free to raise questions with the faculty member or other students—to ask for resources or help with a special situation or problem.

To get the most out of an unstructured seminar, prepare ahead of time by reflecting on the past week's important events. Rank order them when time is limited, so that the most pressing matters can be discussed first. Try not to monopolize the group's time. In some instances, it may be necessary to continue the discussion with your faculty field liaison after the seminar or to make an appointment for this purpose.

In seminars, you are expected to be a good listener when others are speaking, to stay alert, and to interact with others in the group. A seminar works well only when everyone takes part of the responsibility to make it interesting by raising questions and sharing information that may not be common knowledge.

DO STUDENTS WITH UNDERGRADUATE FIELD INSTRUCTION GET CREDIT WHEN THEY WORK TOWARD A MASTER'S DEGREE IN SOCIAL WORK?

Yes. Most Master of Social Work (MSW) programs allow applicants with Bachelor of Social Work (BSW) degrees from schools accredited by the Council on Social Work Education to apply for *advanced standing* status. If given this status, students are usually granted a waiver allowing them to receive credit for undergraduate field experience. Depending upon the program, students with BSWs from accredited programs may be allowed to waive one or two semesters of coursework.

CSWE's Educational Policy and Accreditation Standards (2008) require that "BSW graduates entering MSW programs are not to repeat what has been mastered in the BSW programs. MSW programs describe the policies and procedures used for awarding advanced standing" (pp. 11–12).

Although the basic qualification for advanced standing is graduation from an accredited undergraduate social work program, most programs also insist that applicants earn at least a B average in their social work courses. A written examination covering foundation course material may be required, as well as a personal interview.

IS IT POSSIBLE FOR A STUDENT TO HAVE A FIELD PLACEMENT WHERE HE OR SHE IS ALSO EMPLOYED?

The answer is a qualified yes. Although this option is not routinely available to undergraduates, programs do occasionally allow students to be placed in the same agencies where they are employed. Because certain conditions must be met, not all employment situations qualify as field sites. Students are to be employed in agencies meeting all field instruction and other program standards and expectations. Other requirements often include having responsibilities different from those customarily performed, having a MSW supervisor different from the regular supervisor, and receiving permission from the employing agency for release from paid duties during regular business hours in order to be a student.

The best rationale for requesting a practicum in the agency where one is employed is the availability of unique educational experiences—exposure to a clientele or intervention not available at any other agency. Some agencies also encourage their employees to "cross-train" so that they have a pool of better qualified and experienced staff on which to draw. These agencies may be willing to provide release time for student-employees to learn different skills within the agency. The concern that most faculty field liaisons have with allowing students to have a practicum with an employer is that it may be difficult to view the students as "learners" by the student-employee's colleagues. Because of their knowledge of the agency and its programs, these students may be given so much responsibility that they are unable to read, study, or reflect on their new practice experiences. As a result, these students may be so busy (especially if not given release time) that they are unable to differentiate between hours spent as a regular employee and time spent as a student intern.

In our experience, large agencies (such as hospitals) provide the best models for situations where students could be both employees and students. For instance, Sue could be a hospital social worker assigned full time to the maternity unit. If a practicum within the psychiatric unit could be worked out, she would have different responsibilities and supervision. When working in the maternity unit, it would be clear that Sue was functioning as an employee; when working in the psychiatric unit, Sue would be functioning as a student.

SUMMARY

This introductory chapter has provided the historical and current context for understanding the requirement of field instruction in social work programs. It has also provided students with information about their preparation, supervision, and the coordination of field instruction within the larger educational program.

Making the Right Career Choice

1. Choosing one's profession is not a decision to be made too quickly. Every profession has somewhat different demands and stresses, and advantages and disadvantages. What are three reasons why you want to pursue a career in social work.

   a. _____

   _____

   b. _____

   _____

   c. _____

   _____

2. As you think about your particular talents, abilities, or knowledge, what qualities do you have that would help you to be a good social worker?

   a. _____

   _____

   b. _____

   _____

   c. _____

   _____

3. The opposite of strength is weakness or limitation. What challenges do you think you will face as a social worker?

   a. _____

   _____

   b. _____

   _____

   c. _____

   _____

4. What roles that social workers perform interest you most? Why?

   a. _____

   _____

   b. _____

   _____

   c. _____

   _____

5. What are your long-term career goals? What would you like to do once you finish this degree?

a. _____

_____

b. _____

_____

c. _____

_____

6. Where do you see yourself working ten years from now? What will you be doing? Who will be your primary clients?

_____

_____

_____

_____

_____

_____

7. Reflect on your responses to these questions, and discuss how your responses may inform about what you need to learn in a field education experience. For instance, what skills might you need to learn? What activities/responsibilities could be built into your learning contract to prepare you for your long-term career goals? What agency or agencies would be beneficial to host settings? Is there anything special you would need to negotiate with your field instructor or faculty liaison?

_____

_____

_____

_____

_____

_____

_____

_____

_____

_____

Altruism as a Foundation for Social Work

Your instructor may ask you to complete this exercise individually or, alternatively, pair you with another student. If this exercise is employed as an ice-breaker, you will be asked to interview someone you don't know and that person will then interview you. This exercise can help you get to know your classmates.

1. Have you previously volunteered for a charity or nonprofit organization? If so, which one, and what did you do for that organization? What would you say was the most important thing you learned from volunteering?

_____

_____

_____

_____

_____

2. Have you ever helped someone (e.g., an elderly person or a person with a disability with chores) not for pay, but because you just wanted to help? If so, whom did you help, and how did you help that person? Was this a one-time activity, or was it ongoing for a while?

_____

_____

_____

_____

_____

3. Have you ever seriously considered becoming

   a. a Big Brother/Big Sister?

   b. a Peace Corps volunteer?

   c. a blood donor?

4. Give an example of when you shared something of value with another individual. What did you learn from that experience?

_____

_____

_____

_____

_____

5. Name persons in your life who have been role models because of their "giving attitudes"? Who would you say is the person most responsible for influencing you to consider a social work degree? Why?

_____

_____

_____

_____

_____

6. At what jobs have you worked? What lessons did you, as an employee, learn about helping others? Did any of your previous positions help you become more altruistic? Why or why not?

_____

_____

_____

_____

_____

7. Review your responses to the earlier questions, and conclude something about your altrusim aptitude. If you consider that altruism might be measured on a continuum from low to high, where might you fall on that continuum?

_____

_____

_____

_____

_____

_____

_____

_____

_____

Obtaining a Historical Perspective

Go to the library or the social work program's Web site to see if you can find the answers to the following questions:

1. When was your college or university founded? By whom?

_____

_____

_____

2. When did the social work program at your college begin? (Note: If you are attending a university that offers both undergraduate and graduate social work programs, you may want to obtain information only on the program in which you are enrolled.)

_____

_____

_____

3. Identify any social service agencies you can find that were involved in the start of the program.

_____

_____

_____

  a. Are they still in existence and serving clients?

_____

_____

  b. Are they still vitally involved with the social work program? List two ways in which social service agencies are involved with your program.

_____

_____

4. Has the social work program changed in the last five years or so? (Note: You may want to examine the materials your program has submitted for re-accreditation to the Council on Social Work Education. These materials should be available in the library. Alternatively, you could interview a student who is farther along in the program than you, an alumnus of the program, or a faculty member.)

_____

_____

_____

_____

_____

The source of my information was _____.
I also learned that:

_____

_____

_____

_____

_____

5. Reflect upon the historical evolution of social work and your social work program. Is change inevitable? What changes might you expect in the future? Why?

_____

_____

_____

_____

_____

_____

_____

_____

_____

_____

_____

Succeed with PEARSON mysocialworklab

Log onto **www.mysocialworklab.com** to access a wealth of case studies, videos, and assessment. (*If you did not receive an access code to* **MySocialWorkLab** *with this text and wish to purchase access online, please visit* www.mysocialworklab.com.)

1. **Read the MySocialWorkLibrary case study "Mikki's Story."** The social worker admits to having "practitioner arrogance" noting that her work was disempowering the client, that her goal of independence and self-sufficiency was not what the client most desired. How does a social worker guard against making this kind of mistake?

2. **Read the MySocialWorkLibrary case study "Stephanie and Rose Doer."** How does the worker show the importance of cultural competence in working with clients and educating other professionals?

PRACTICE TEST
The following questions will test your knowledge of the content found within this chapter.

1. Which of the following purposes of field education was not discussed in this chapter?
   a. Students' exposure to different clients/client systems.
   b. Students' exposure to professional interventions and roles.
   c. Students' socialization into the professional culture.
   d. Students' learning how social workers act ethically in agencies.

2. The functions of the faculty field liaison do not include which of the following?
   a. Advising students in planning their practicum.
   b. Monitoring students' learning experiences and progress.
   c. Resolving students' problems with their field instructor/other personnel.
   d. Supervising students' day-to-day activities.

3. In self-reflecting on what is being learned in the agency, the topic of least importance is:
   a. Professional knowledge, skills, and values being acquired.
   b. Application of human behavior and social organization theories.
   c. Keeping my field instructor pleased with me.
   d. Relevance of cultural contexts and life experiences in understanding clients.

4. Which statement was not discussed as a valid reason for not placing students in the agency of their employment?
   a. Agency is not meeting the social work program standards.
   b. Experiences that the student needs are not available.
   c. The student cannot keep the employee and student roles separate.
   d. The student or agency may exploit the situation for non-educational purposes.

Short Answer Question:
A college student from another department in the university asks why it is necessary to have field instruction in social work. "Why can't you learn what you need to know from scientific papers and books?" she asks. Using you best critical thinking skills and your identity with the profession, how would you respond?

ASSESS YOUR COMPETENCE
Use the scale below to rate your current level of achievement on the following concepts or skills associated with each competency presented in the chapter:

1	2	3
I can accurately describe the concept or skill.	I can consistently identify the concept or skill when observing and analyzing practice activities.	I can competently implement the concept or skill in my own practice.

_____ Analyze models of assessment, prevention, and intervention to guide my practice.

_____ Use supervision and consultation to acquire needed skills.

Answers

Key: 1) d, 2) d, 3) c, 4) d

2

The Partnership with Social Service Agencies

Core Competencies in This Chapter (Check marks indicate which competencies are covered in depth)				
☑ Professional Identity	☐ Ethical Practice	☑ Critical Thinking	☐ Diversity in Practice	☐ Human Rights & Justice
☐ Research-Based Practice	☐ Human Behavior	☐ Policy Practice	☐ Practice Contexts	☐ Engage, Assess, Intervene, Evaluate

OVERVIEW

The intent of this chapter is to answer basic questions about social service agencies and field instructors who host and supervise social work students during their field instruction.

WHY DO AGENCIES ACCEPT STUDENT INTERNS?

Social service agencies rarely receive direct financial incentives from colleges and universities to provide field experiences to their students. However, these agencies like being affiliated with teaching institutions—the training of students is stimulating and enriching for both the agency staff and the students involved. And there are secondary benefits. Most social service agencies are tremendously underfunded and have too many clients and too few staff. When there are not enough staff in an agency, students provide important and valued help. By using students' assistance, social work staff can focus on more problematic cases or begin projects that have been put aside for lack of time. You should expect that the tasks assigned to you will be helpful to the agency. Additionally, the assignments given to students normally introduce them to the variety of tasks performed by social workers in the practicum setting.

Most social service agencies have a strong commitment to the training and development of future social workers. As well as helping to increase the number and quality of social work professionals, the agency finds that providing placements for students has two other advantages: First, the agency can screen, orient, train, and evaluate potential job applicants with a minimal investment in personnel costs. (It is not unusual for student interns to be offered employment by the agency when they have done a good job and when staff positions become vacant.)

Second, even if the agency cannot offer employment, it benefits by having a pool of future social workers in the community who are knowledgeable about the agency's services. Even though practicum students take jobs in other agencies, they will likely make referrals back to the practicum agency and, in general, will be better informed about the agency.

Beyond these reasons, staff within an agency may want to be field instructors because they enjoy teaching. They may find that their own practice skills are sharpened as they discuss with students various aspects of their practice. Furthermore, working with students can expose the agency staff to new developments in social work and help relieve job fatigue.

HOW ARE FIELD AGENCIES CHOSEN?

A human service agency may become a field instruction site for social work students in several ways. A faculty member, a social work practitioner in the community, or a student may recommend an agency. An agency may contact a social work program and request students. Or agencies may be approached directly by a faculty field liaison. Generally, agencies are expected to provide information on their programs, the learning experiences available to students, and the qualifications of the personnel available to supervise students. Faculty field liaisons look for agencies with such assets as: competent staff to provide effective supervision and professional learning; a commitment to social work ethics, values, and the training of social work professionals; diverse and broad programs compatible with the school's educational objectives; and adequate physical facilities (e.g., desk space and telephone access) to accommodate students.

Even agencies that have these qualifications may not become field agencies. Often, other factors such as an agency's reputation in the community, its leadership or innovation, and its climate (whether it is conducive to student learning) are considered. Some of the agencies that meet these general criteria may become particularly attractive as field instruction sites because of considerations such as method of intervention, problem area of practice, population served, or availability of stipends for students.

After an agency has been found suitable for field instruction, the school and the agency frequently enter into a formal contractual agreement governing placement of students. Contained in the contract are the conditions, expectations, and terms of agreement that will be in effect during a student's practicum.

Some social work programs recommend that each field agency develop an outline for field instruction detailing important orientation items, assignments, and learning opportunities. Most social work programs maintain files on frequently used agencies for students' reference.

Colleges and agencies frequently enter into formal contracts regarding students in field education.

HOW ARE FIELD INSTRUCTORS SELECTED?

Although agency executive directors may recommend certain staff as supervisors for students, the faculty field liaison ultimately has the responsibility for determining who is qualified to supervise students. Criteria often include a master's degree from an accredited social work program, two to three years of postgraduate professional experience in a given practice area, and a social work license. It is also desirable that the field instructor have at least six months of experience within the particular agency. In some settings, the field instructor may be an experienced BSW. Beyond these primary requirements, the faculty field liaison looks for field instructors who have an interest in teaching and who are supportive of students. Field instructors must be knowledgeable and flexible individuals. They need to make time for overseeing students and for coordinating with faculty field liaisons. Field instructors tend to be among the most competent and energetic of an agency's staff. They incorporate the values and ethics of the profession and usually make excellent role models for students.

In order to know that field instructors meet the minimum requirements, social work programs usually ask for their résumés and maintain a file. However, just meeting the minimum requirements does not make a good field instructor. Field instructors who give students too little of their time, make unrealistic demands, or in other ways show themselves unable to assist students in their educational endeavors may not be used again.

Case Example

Marcie's supervisor, Leesa, is the head of the social services department at a large hospital. Besides supervising 18 full-time and 12 part-time employees, the field instructor has a private practice. On three occasions Marcie's scheduled supervision time has been interrupted by emergency calls from Leesa's clients or other hospital business. However, Leesa has continued to give Marcie new admissions to follow. Marcie has been assigned 12 patients, but after one month has yet to receive any meaningful constructive feedback on her performance. Yesterday Leesa announced that she had been called to be an

Happiness: the outcome of good social services.

expert witness in a court case that could last several weeks. When Marcie asked if she could have another supervisor in Leesa's absence, Leesa laughed and said that Marcie should be "less compulsive."

Questions

1. Is Marcie's request unreasonable?
2. What options should Marcie explore?
3. Should this field instructor continue to be used?

HOW ARE AGENCIES AND STUDENTS MATCHED?

Frequently, students will have a preference for specific practicum settings. Some students know that they want to work with older adults when they graduate and desire to begin refining their skills with this population. Other students know that they want to work with children or in a medical setting. We believe that most faculty field liaisons try to place students in a practicum consistent with the students' first or second choice. However, what is paramount is that the experience be educational—that the student have opportunity for new learning and growth. In most programs, faculty field liaisons make the final decision.

Assuming that you have a preference (e.g., a mental health setting) and that your faculty field liaison will attempt to find you a practicum within this general area, what additional considerations are important? In our experience, faculty field liaisons give first consideration to the student's educational and learning needs. Faculty field liaisons must assess each student's specific needs and familiarity with the field of social work. Students who are knowledgeable or experienced in one area or type of agency should expect that they will be exposed to new activities (e.g., case management or advocacy) to help them become well rounded. Students who want to dedicate all of their practicum

*The first practicum
usually exposes students
to a broad array of
diverse clients.*

experience to a specific population (e.g., psychiatric outpatients in a private practice clinic) may find that not every program will support their specialization. Philosophically, many faculty field liaisons believe that at least the first practicum ought to expose the student to a broad array of diverse clients. This is particularly true in undergraduate practicums.

Students who either have been employed in social service agencies or have extensive volunteer experience will generally be placed where greater responsibility, knowledge, or judgment are required. Students who have had little or no exposure to social services will often be assigned to agencies where lack of previous experience will not be a disadvantage or a disservice to clients.

Less-experienced students are not necessarily placed in situations where there will be limited exposure to client systems. These students can still expect significant contact, but in settings where there will be ample structure and supervision (e.g., assisting in a day treatment program for the chronically mentally ill). More experienced students will be able to function in situations where there is less structure or direct supervision. An example would be a respite program for senior citizens where (after a brief orientation period) students would be expected to travel to clients' homes to conduct assessments for the program.

In making assignments to agencies, faculty field liaisons also consider the individual student. A student considered unorganized or immature will most likely be placed in a less-challenging practicum than a student considered organized, mature, and responsible. Of course, other traits or characteristics may also influence the faculty field liaison's decision. For instance, a confident and assertive student might be placed in a setting such as a locked psychiatric ward of a large hospital before a timid student would be.

Other factors that can affect the field placement include the student's unique learning style, characteristics, or disability and can involve the faculty field liaison's contacts in the community. A faculty field liaison who is well known in the community may receive requests for students from local social service agencies. These requests can be rather specific. An agency with a shortage of male therapists might request a male student who enjoys working with adolescents. An after-school or day-treatment program for children might request a student who is athletic and able to participate in strenuous sports such as swimming and backpacking. If a student then comes along with prior experience in scouting, recreational programming, or camping, the faculty field liaison could see him or her as a solution to meeting the agency's request. Faculty field liaisons know it is important to find students who meet social service agencies' needs so the training opportunities afforded by these agencies will continue to be available to future social work students. Such considerations may be responsible for students not getting their first, but a second or third, choice of a practicum.

WHAT SPECIFICALLY ARE SOCIAL SERVICE AGENCIES LOOKING FOR IN STUDENT INTERNS?

When interviewing students who are seeking practicum placements, agency supervisors tend to look for four characteristics: First is a strong desire on the part of the student to help others. Second is the student's interest and ability to deal with specific knowledge and skills pertinent to particular problem areas. Third is emotional maturity. And the fourth is honesty. Each of these will be briefly discussed.

A Strong Desire to Help Others

Most agency supervisors believe that the basic quality practicum students must have is a burning desire to help others. This desire should be a driving force in students' lives—they must feel it enough to keep trying even when it appears that a client wants to fail. Students must have a high tolerance for frustration. Social work can be discouraging, and students must be strongly motivated by the belief that clients want to help themselves. One agency supervisor explained:

> It is crucial to have the ability to be empathic with clients—to genuinely believe that clients are good people. Students must believe that clients love their children, that parents want to do what is best, and want to be appreciated. Without these beliefs, there is no way to make a social worker out of a student.

Agencies are looking for students who are determined, enthusiastic, and have genuine empathy for people. When a student displays attitudes that show condescension, you can be sure empathy is lacking. Students with empathy are easy to talk with, are good listeners, and are not cynical. They understand the client's world and the meaning it has for the client, both cognitively and emotionally.

Interest and Ability to Function in a Particular Setting

Agency interviewers seek students with genuine interest in the problem areas with which their organization deals. For example, an interest in addiction treatment is best displayed by a genuine desire to understand the human experience of addiction. Social service agencies do not want students who are fascinated by the complexity of clients' problems and who lack real interest in wanting to help them. Agencies want a student whose concern for a fellow human being is motivated by *both* an intellectual curiosity about the problem and a compassionate desire to help.

Particularly at the graduate level, agency supervisors may look for knowledge and skills in specific areas. For instance, a substance abuse treatment agency may expect students to already understand the disease model of alcoholism. Students seeking a macro or administrative placement may be expected by some agencies to have acquired knowledge of their clientele by having previously worked directly with these clients.

Maturity

Many agency supervisors try to assess the intellectual and emotional maturity displayed by a practicum applicant. Intellectually and emotionally mature individuals have achieved a balance between self-directed activity and a knowledge about the limitations of their competence. This is frequently displayed when applicants have formulated some clear objectives and are willing to seek advice and ask questions—even to say, "I don't understand."

Honesty

More and more agencies are fingerprinting new employees and running background checks with the police. If you have been arrested, this may or may not be a problem with your practicum agency depending on the type of offense and

Professional Identity

Critical Thinking Question: What characteristics should you demonstrate in the agency in order to have a professional demeanor in appearance, behavior, and communication?

the length of time that has passed. Honesty is usually the best policy in these matters, and maturity is demonstrated when you are able to reveal this type of information rather than leading agency personnel to believe you have never been in trouble with the law. If you have been arrested for a serious offense, you should discuss this with your faculty field liaison before going for interviews. Note that in some states you might be refused employment or a social work license if you commit a felony or are classified as a habitual criminal.

Although agencies can have certain expectations about the qualities students need to possess before beginning an internship, the enthusiasm and interest they bring may have a strong influence. Also, it is often important to get ready for your interview by jotting down a few ideas about why you want to work with a particular group of clients, how you have prepared yourself for the practicum, and examples demonstrating past responsibilities you have had. See also Chapter 3 "How Do I Prepare for the Practicum Interview?"

WHAT IS THE DIFFERENCE BETWEEN PUBLIC AND PRIVATE AGENCIES?

The social welfare system is a vast and complex array of programs that provide services and benefits. Both public and private agencies are involved in those programs. Differences between the two types of agencies can be viewed in terms of their origin, purpose, sanction, funding, activities, and clientele. However, increasingly many of those differences are becoming less marked. We are dividing those differences into the following three categories (1) historical, (2) fading, and (3) persisting.

Historical Differences

Public agencies are (1) established by law; (2) at all levels of government—federal, state, county, and city/town; (3) owned by the government; (4) funded by tax dollars; and (5) run by government employees. They represent the bulk of the social welfare programs and services. However, these agencies are primarily responsible for residual or means-tested programs (Colby & Dziegielewski, 2001). These programs perform a safety net function and serve essentially the poor and those who need temporary assistance in dealing with their problematic situations. The quality of services of these agencies, particularly at the state and local levels, varies considerably. The quality, which is associated with the employment of professionally trained personnel and presence of good work conditions, depends on the availability of adequate funds. The importance given to social services by the government concerned determines the allocation of needed funds.

Private agencies are (1) created by voluntary groups or individuals, (2) local in their origin but often branch out and become regional and national organizations, (3) owned by people or such entities as churches, (4) supported primarily by private contributions and service fees, and (5) run by persons who are not government employees. They come into existence in response to a specific social problem or a set of needs and provide services different from those of public agencies. These agencies are generally nonprofit. Some of the private agencies use volunteers for providing most of their services. Those volunteers may or may not have professional qualifications for the work they do. Other private agencies employ appropriately trained professionals and ensure that their clients receive high-quality services.

Fading Differences

The differences in the sources of funds for the two types of agencies are not clear-cut anymore. Funding for the services of the two overlaps. Many private agencies actively seek public, that is tax-supported, funds for their programs. They get government grants for their work and charge on a contractual basis for specialized services they provide to the clients of public agencies (Colby & Dziegielewski, 2001). On the other hand, public agencies look toward private sources such as philanthropic foundations for funds for experimental and innovative programs. Services provided by the two do not fall clearly into public welfare and private professional categories. Sometimes, states and other government entities privatize some of their social services (see, e.g., Flaherty, Collins-Camargo, & Lee, 2008). Service models of public and private partnership are appearing in the professional literature and are being tried across the United States. Social workers and other professionals in both public and private agencies are guided by the same standards of practice and codes of ethics. For example, both public and private child welfare agencies are accredited by the Council on Accreditation of Services for Families and Children. Both types of agencies are equally faced with the demand for cost-containment and quality assurance.

Social workers in both public and private agencies are guided by codes of ethics.

Persisting Differences

Public and private agencies are different in the types of images they create in the minds of people. Some communities have little confidence and faith in voluntary associations, and they put their trust in the hands of public agencies. On the other hand, citizens in other communities may not regard public agencies very favorably. Private agencies are less saddled by bureaucratic structure and demands and are/can be more creative and innovative. There may be significant differences in the management practices. When public agencies that are staffed by professionally trained and credentialed personnel are compared with private agencies with similar staffs, the latter are sometimes found to be better than the former. For instance, Harlan (2004) studied compassion fatigue in social workers with master's level working in public and private mental health agencies. Compassion fatigue, also called secondary traumatic stress, results from work with survivors of abuse, natural disasters, torture, violent crimes, and other trauma. She found that those in a public agency are at a greater risk for potentially developing compassion fatigue.

HOW DO STUDENTS GATHER INFORMATION ON POSSIBLE PRACTICUM AGENCIES AHEAD OF TIME?

Many sources of information about social service agencies are available to you as a student. Several are suggested next.

Start with your field education office. It is possible that your social work program keeps on file (either paper or electronic) a list of approved agencies. This listing will likely contain a brief description of whom the agency serves, the programs that are provided, and the address and phone number of the contact person. Sometimes listings show dates when students were last placed there and the names of their field instructors.

Critical Thinking

Critical Thinking Question:
What information should
you gather to prepare
yourself to be successful
in a new practicum
agency?

Larger agencies may have their own Web sites that provide helpful information in identifying the type of client population and problems with which they deal.

Your adviser or other faculty in your social work program may be able to provide valuable consultation. Sometimes faculty serve on agency boards and may have knowledge about new programs or developments. Sometimes they have worked with employees in agencies who are involved in a particular line of research or who especially like to supervise students.

Another idea is to ask students who have recently completed practicums about the strengths and weaknesses of the agencies where they were placed. One of the most important features of a good agency is a field instructor who not only makes time for students but also involves them in important agency work. You might want a field instructor who can answer your questions, when they arise, and one who is kind and knowledgeable. Students are sometimes better sources of this information than written descriptions.

Lastly, well before the academic term in which you will be placed in an agency, you should be reading the newspaper to keep abreast of any articles written about agencies in your community. Have any been recognized for outstanding or innovative services? You might want to do an electronic search of the local newspaper's archives once you have three or four agencies in mind as possible practicum sites. Any agency under investigation or one that seems to be having trouble keeping staff is *not* likely to provide a good educational experience for a student. If you are new to the community and have very little idea about what agencies may be available to host students in practicum, you may have to open up the telephone book's yellow pages and browse under the topic "Social Service Agencies" or do an Internet search.

SUMMARY

The intent of this chapter is to answer basic questions about social service agencies and field instructors who host and supervise social work students during their field instruction.

Investigating Social Service Agencies in the Yellow Pages

Social service agencies range from large, complex governmental organizations to small, nonprofit organizations. They also vary tremendously in the scope of their mission, the kinds of services they provide, and the number of clients they serve annually. Find in the yellow pages of your phone book where social services agencies are listed.

1. Social services agencies are listed under the following headings:

   a. _____

   b. _____

   c. _____

   d. _____

2. By just reading the names of the agencies, is it easy to identify the public from the private agencies? Why or why not?

   _____

   _____

   _____

3. As you look at the long list of social service agencies, write down the names of agencies that you are most familiar with or know something about. Are these agencies primarily local, state, or national organizations? What do you conclude about this?

   _____

   _____

   _____

   _____

   _____

   _____

4. As you look at the names of these social service agencies, identify one that you think is affiliated with a national organization. Try to find the following information about it on the Internet.

   The agency's name is: _____

   a. What is the agency's mission?

   _____

   _____

   b. What population does the agency primarily serve?

   _____

   _____

c. Who founded the agency? In what year?

_____

_____

d. In how many states does the agency have branches or offices?

_____

_____

e. How is the agency funded?

_____

_____

f. About how many clients are served each year?

_____

_____

g. About how many programs and staff are there?

_____

_____

5. Based on what you have learned about this agency, do you feel that it is attuned to issues of diversity? Why or why not?

_____

_____

_____

_____

_____

_____

Students' Experience with Interning

Going to a library or surfing the Internet to find out information about social service agencies provides one type of knowledge, but an altogether different kind of awareness and insight into an agency can come from interviewing students who are currently interning or just finishing their internships in a human service agency. Interview a student who can help you understand what it would be like to be a social work intern in an agency where he or she just served or is serving as an intern. Here are some sample questions to get you started, but you will likely think of others that you may want to ask as well.

1. Where did/do you perform your internship?

   _____

   _____

   _____

2. What types of clients did/does the agency serve?

   _____

   _____

   _____

3. Did/do you have your own clients to work with? If yes, how many did/do you have?

   _____

   _____

   _____

4. What roles did/do you perform, and what skills did/do you need most?

   _____

   _____

   _____

5. What was/is the hardest part of the internship?

   _____

   _____

   _____

6. How friendly and helpful were/are the staff at the agency?

   _____

   _____

   _____

7. What did/do you like most about doing your internship?

   _____

   _____

   _____

8. Did/do you get good supervision?

_____

_____

_____

9. How often did/do you meet with your supervisor?

_____

_____

_____

10. What one thing should new interns know before they come into the agency where you were/are placed?

_____

_____

_____

Learning about Social Service Agencies from the Field Education Office

Most social work programs keep information on human service agencies in which their students are placed. In many programs, faculty evaluate the quality of the placements provided by those agencies. Oftentimes, records are also kept regarding students' experiences so that new students preparing to go into a field setting can read what former students said about what they learned and encountered.

Go to the field education office affiliated with your social work program and, after looking over the database of material, identify two agencies where you think you might want to do an internship in the future. Compare these agencies on the following criteria.

	Agency A (Agency Name)	Agency B (Agency Name)
Interesting clientele	_____	_____
Amount of contact with clients/caseload	_____	_____
Opportunity to learn new skills	_____	_____
Adequacy of supervision	_____	_____
Helpfulness of staff	_____	_____
Availability of evening/weekend hours	_____	_____
Ease in reaching/proximity to public transportation	_____	_____
Suitability for a beginning (first-semester) student	_____	_____
Placement of more than one student in the agency	_____	_____
Basically favorable evaluations of the agency	_____	_____
Other criterion (identify)	_____	_____

It is likely that each agency is better than the other on some criteria and worse on others. What criteria will be the most important to you, and why?

_____

_____

_____

Desirable Traits in Social Workers (and Human Beings in General!)

This chapter discusses several characteristics that social service agencies often seek in their student interns. This exercise is for your own self-reflection and development of self-awareness.

1. Strong Desire to Help Others—When have you demonstrated this characteristic? (Give an example.) What risks or sacrifices did it require of you?

_____

_____

_____

2. Maturity—How would someone know that you are a responsible person? In what ways have you shown your maturity?

_____

_____

_____

3. Honesty—Give several examples to attest to your honesty.

_____

_____

_____

4. Enthusiasm—How do you show enthusiasm? How do you act when you are not interested in something?

_____

_____

_____

5. Willingness to Learn—When you are really interested in learning something, what do you do? How do you act?

_____

_____

_____

6. Handling Mistakes Constructively—As a new student you might unintentionally create a problem or make a mistake. Your supervisor may need to give you information to keep you from making the same mistake again. If you are overly sensitive to criticism, you might have your feelings

hurt. How have you handled mistakes in the past? How well do you receive advice and supervision? How *should* you handle them as an intern in a social service agency?

_____

_____

_____

_____

_____

7. Dealing with Destructive Criticism—How can you tell the difference between constructive criticism and destructive criticism? What could you do if you felt that you were being criticized too harshly or unfairly?

_____

_____

_____

_____

_____

8. Look at your responses to the items in this exercise. If this information were elicited during a placement interview, what would the interviewer likely conclude about you? What else might the interviewer want to know?

_____

_____

_____

_____

_____

9. Is there some area where you would like personal self-improvement? For instance, do you get angry too quickly or tend to be impulsive and act without thinking through things? Do you tend to be shy and quiet when others are expecting you to talk?

_____

_____

_____

_____

_____

Succeed with PEARSON mysocialworklab

Log onto **www.mysocialworklab.com** to access a wealth of case studies, videos, and assessment. (*If you did not receive an access code to* **MySocialWorkLab** *with this text and wish to purchase access online, please visit* www.mysocialworklab.com.)

1. **Read the MySocialWorkLibrary case study: "Mrs. Smith and Her Family."** Managed care has affected the way hospitals provide services, and social workers in these settings have to consider ways to minimize costs. How are social workers to do this without violating their professional ethics?

2. **Read the MySocialWorkLibrary case study: "Carrie."** The case mentions her dealings with insurance and managed care companies. If employed as a medical social worker, what could you do to advocate for appropriate treatment for a client?

PRACTICE TEST The following questions will test your knowledge of the content found within this chapter.

1. Which reason was not provided as to why agencies accept students for internships?
   a. Agency is training potential job applicants.
   b. Students keep agency's staff abreast of professional developments.
   c. Agency's involvement with a college raises its prestige.
   d. Students add to the agency's manpower.

2. Which of the following characteristics of excellent field instructors is not included in the discussion in this chapter?
   a. Expertise as a social work practitioner
   b. Commitment to educating future social workers
   c. Willingness to give students the necessary time and energy
   d. Willingness to learn from involvement with students

3. Which of the following characteristics that field agencies are looking for in students is not included in this chapter?
   a. Desire to help others and empathy
   b. Robust common sense and practicality
   c. Intellectual and emotional maturity and honesty
   d. Interest and ability to function in the agency

4. Among the suggestions for gathering information on possible field agencies provided in this chapter, which one of the following is not included?
   a. Read the school's file on practicum agencies and talk with faculty.
   b. Speak to students who have done placements in agencies of interest.
   c. Learn from the Internet, local phone book, and newspaper.
   d. Use your own imagination and creativity.

Short Answer Question:
Marcy has been interviewing for a practicum at local agencies. So far she has been interviewed at four different agencies, but none of them have invited her to be an intern with them. Without knowing her at all, what advice might you give to help her have a professional demeanor in appearance and behavior?

ASSESS YOUR COMPETENCE Use the scale below to rate your current level of achievement on the following concepts or skills associated with each competency practice behavior presented in the chapter:

1	2	3
I can accurately describe the concept or skill.	I can consistently identify the concept or skill when observing and analyzing practice activities.	I can competently implement the concept or skill in my own practice.

_____ Present a professional demeanor in appearance, behavior, and communication.

_____ Distinguish, appraise, and integrate multiple sources of information to inform my practice.

Answers

3

Getting Started

Core Competencies in This Chapter (Check marks indicate which competencies are covered in depth)				
✓ Professional Identity	✓ Ethical Practice	✓ Critical Thinking	☐ Diversity in Practice	☐ Human Rights & Justice
☐ Research-Based Practice	☐ Human Behavior	☐ Policy Practice	☐ Practice Contexts	☐ Engage, Assess, Intervene, Evaluate

OVERVIEW

Most students want their practicum experiences to be instructive, exciting, and gratifying. But before the practicum can start, the student often must be interviewed in the agency. Even if an interview is not required, the student is likely to be a little nervous about getting off on the right foot and making a good impression. This chapter provides some suggestions for students preparing to go into an agency for the first time.

HOW DO I FIND AN AGENCY THAT MEETS MY NEEDS?

The amount of student input allowed in the choice of a practicum agency varies immensely. On one end of the continuum, students are permitted to contact agencies and interview on their own. Students in these programs often talk to other students and faculty members about the agencies that provide the best learning experiences. If, for some reason, you are unable to secure a placement in one of the agencies most often recommended (possibly because they already have their quota of students), you may want to look through the yellow pages of your phone directory (or even the directories of neighboring counties if travel time isn't an issue). Under such headings as "Counselors," "Social Service Organizations," "Marriage Counseling," "Mental Health Services," or "Alcohol Abuse and Addiction," you are likely to find more agencies than you had imagined. In addition, your local United Way will have a list of agencies it funds, and it may produce a directory of community resources. Such a publication would likely contain more information about individual agencies than you would find in the yellow pages. Check in the reference section of your library.

In programs at the other end of the continuum, students are assigned an agency and have little choice. Most programs allow students to state preferences even if they are not actively involved in the selection process. Correspondingly, most agencies want to interview prospective students before offering them a placement.

Even if your program does not allow you to choose your practicum agency, there are several important topics to consider as you plan for a practicum. Occasionally students or agencies have special requirements, and discussing them with your faculty field liaison will result in a better learning experience. Here are a few examples.

Transportation

Getting to and from the agency can be a problem for students without a car. Students need to consider how close the agency is located to where they live and attend class. Many agencies are located near college campuses and are easy to reach. Others are some distance away and require access to a car or public transportation, or arrangements for car pooling with other students or employees.

If you have a car or access to one, some agencies may ask you to use your car to transport clients or make home visits. Other agencies have cars available for student use. If you are required to drive an agency car, ask your agency supervisor about the extent of insurance coverage needed to protect you in case of an accident. If you drive your own car, check with your insurance agent about your liability coverage.

Scheduling

Agencies differ regarding hours of operation, from those open only a few days per week (this is often the case with new agencies or those that operate almost entirely with volunteers) to those that provide intervention 24 hours per day, seven days per week.

Some students can be very flexible as they plan their agency time. Others must work around job responsibilities and family commitments and are far less adaptable. Agencies are aware of these differences, and although some are able to accommodate students' schedules, others simply cannot. Students whose schedules are restricted must find agencies that are open at times they can work.

Even if your schedule appears to have no complications (e.g., your classes are on Tuesdays and Thursdays and the agency agrees to accept you as a student on Mondays, Wednesdays, and Fridays), be alert to potential problems such as staff meetings on Tuesday afternoons—a day when you are not scheduled to be in the agency. This circumstance would probably necessitate that you consider a different agency because staff meetings are an important experience in professional socialization. In staff meetings, students can observe how the agency operates and how professionals interact with one another, and they can learn what problems are facing the agency and how the problems will be resolved.

Supervision

Some students want agency expectations laid out in clear and behaviorally specific terms. They want to know what to do, when to do it, and how to do it. They do not like wondering whether they are meeting agency expectations. One student explained:

> Prior to my first day at work, I was surprised to find that I was feeling anxious. My anxiety was based on a fear that there might be little or no structure, that I might have to roam aimlessly, searching for assignments and feeling generally uncomfortable with my new situation.

Other students want a setting in which they can observe for a while, determine what they would like to do, and then begin to use all of their creative and problem-solving capabilities in a task of their choosing.

When selecting an agency, it is important to consider the amount of supervision you require. The next step is to share this preference with your faculty field liaison. From prior experience with other students, your faculty field liaison will know which agencies allow employees, students, and volunteers the most freedom and which agencies provide greater supervision. At a minimum, the Council on Social Work Education requires that all students meet with their supervisors for at least one hour per week.

Placements vary a great deal in the amount of supervision that they provide students. Consider these three examples.

One undergraduate student, who was placed in an unstructured environment with little supervision, arrived at a day-care center for high-risk children and was told that 15 toddlers were in the next room. She was instructed to go and assist in any way she could.

A second undergraduate working in an agency that distributed food to 16 outlying food pantries was given a detailed questionnaire and asked to interview one social worker at each site to gather information on anticipated food requirements.

Still a third undergraduate, in a very structured setting, walked into her agency supervisor's office and was given a schedule of training sessions to be held that week for all hospital student interns. She was assigned specific areas of the hospital in which to work, specific tasks to complete, deadlines by which to accomplish the assignments, and a schedule of supervisory conferences. She was told to begin reading hospital policies and logs of former students. Later, she viewed a video on the hospital's history and its projected future.

These examples show how problems might develop for students who want a lot of supervision and who do not get it, or who like to work on their own but whose agency supervisors closely observe and direct their activities. It is important to communicate your preference concerning the degree of supervision, or problems may quickly arise and continue throughout the placement. What you want in a supervisor is a supportive, enthusiastic, knowledgeable person who is interested in helping you to have a good learning experience. A good supervisor will not abandon or ignore you, will find interesting assignments for you, and will be available to answer your questions.

Critical Thinking

Critical Thinking Question:
What would go into your "ideal" learning contract?

Agencies vary widely regarding what they will allow students to do. Some schedule immediate contact with clients; others do not allow students to have client interaction without supervision until the second semester. One graduate student told a class of undergraduates going into the field for the first time, "Be prepared for the possibility of spending the initial weeks in your agencies doing nothing but observing." She noted that as a second-year graduate student, with six years of social work experience and one graduate practicum completed, she was told by her new field instructor that for the first month her only assignment was to observe others at work. The second month she could interview clients but only with another social worker present. Finally, at the start of her third month, assuming things went to the supervisor's satisfaction, she could practice alone.

Most agencies are not this stringent in their supervision of students and present students with opportunities to interact with clients early in their internships—sometimes even in the first week. This occurs at both the graduate and undergraduate levels. The variation in students' direct contact with clients can be explained by many factors, among them the staff–client ratio, the complexity of the students' tasks, and the consequences of students making poor judgments.

Populations, Problem Areas, and Networking

Ideally, students should find placements where they can learn about populations and problem areas that excite them. The agency they select should capture their interests and challenge them to become actively involved. Although it is possible to learn something in any placement, students are most energized when they can immediately immerse themselves in a setting where they easily relate to the primary client group present (e.g., preschoolers, adolescents, elderly) or are curious about the problems with which the agency deals (e.g., chemical dependency, teenage runaways, spouse abuse, juvenile offenders, the terminally ill). Especially before the first placement, students should reflect on their primary areas of interest and the age groups they interact with the best.

Agencies that do more networking are more interrelated with other agencies and thus provide a broader practicum experience. Students who want to learn about other social service organizations and the interactions among them should consider how much networking a particular agency does. For example, a family counseling agency that works almost entirely with middle-income families may have little cause to work with other agencies in the community. On the other hand, an agency that works with pregnant teens will make connections with social insurance agencies, county or state social service departments, health departments, hospital social service departments, childbirth education organizations, legal services, and residential facilities. Students interested in maximizing their knowledge about other agencies and community resources would receive more of this type of learning in the latter example.

Agency Value Base

Another area for students to consider is an agency's value base. Once students identify the core values of a potential field agency, they should decide whether it creates a conflict with their own. For example, a student who believes that abortion is morally wrong will have a difficult time working in a setting where clients are often referred for abortions. Likewise, a student whose religious ethic is opposed to divorce may have difficulties in a setting where persons are frequently supported in leaving their spouses.

Often our clients' values may not be the same as ours. As professionals, we learn to accept individual clients as worthwhile persons although we may not condone their every behavior. Although it is important to know our strongly held values and to examine them from time to time, it is also worth remembering that values are not permanently fixed. Many people, particularly those acquiring college degrees, are continually updating the facts that form the foundation for their opinions and values. A 19-year-old undergraduate may strongly believe in the death penalty, thinking that certain incarcerated individuals deserve this punishment. With this value, that student may not be very successful in some criminal justice placements. However, a short time later, the same student may have learned that the poor and minorities have a much greater likelihood of ending up on death row. Seeing the evidence of racism within the legal system, the student may come to view the death penalty quite differently.

In the process of obtaining a social work education, students become aware of their own basic values and the values of the profession, and they are challenged to understand the impact of their values on their interactions with others. Personal and professional growth occurs when we examine our values and the stereotypes we hold. However, students should not be forced to act against their basic principles. In such a situation or at any time when you cannot be objective, you should inform your field instructor and discuss transferring or referring the case. If this poses any problem, a three-way meeting with your faculty field liaison, field instructor, and you should be convened.

Professional Identity

Critical Thinking Question: What characteristics of an agency supervisor would best help you to develop as a social worker?

Anticipate questions you
might be asked.

HOW DO I PREPARE FOR THE PRACTICUM INTERVIEW?

Anticipation of the initial interview with a prospective agency supervisor can produce anxiety. One undergraduate student recalled:

> I phoned the executive director of the agency and arranged for an interview. In the day or two before I was to see her, I unexpectedly discovered that I was feeling quite nervous. Upon examining my feelings, I found that I feared such things as: They won't like me. I won't like them. They will find my dress too casual. I will find them too snooty. All of these fears could be categorized under a basic "fear of the unknown."
>
> To my surprise, the interview went very well. The director talked about the agency and its purpose and her ideas about students' roles. She asked me about my background and interest in social work and she shared some personal experiences about her own agency work. Before I knew it, an hour had passed. It was a relief to know rapport had definitely been established between us.

Not all first interviews go nearly as well. One student recalled how she was caught totally off guard:

> When I was interviewing for a practicum placement last semester, I was asked what would seem to be a simple question. However, the manner in which the question was asked intimidated me. The interviewer, a stern looking clinical social worker, folded her hands, looked me straight in the eye, and asked, "Yesterday I interviewed another student. Tell me why I should choose you over other students?" I remember frantically trying to think of a good reason. I'm sure my voice was shaking when I asked her to repeat the question (I wanted to stall for time). I ended up giving

her two or three reasons, none of which sounded very convincing to me. From then on I was unnerved. When I left the interview, that question was about the only thing I could remember!

Although no way exists to guarantee that your first interview with a potential agency supervisor will be a fun experience, a few steps can be taken to increase the likelihood of a positive experience. Many people find it hard to speak extemporaneously about their strengths, weaknesses, qualifications, career goals, skills, and abilities. For example, some students may find it difficult to answer the following questions:

- What led you to social work?
- Why do you think you are qualified to be a student intern at this agency?
- How would you describe yourself?
- What talents do you have?
- What do you plan on doing five or ten years from now?
- What skills can you bring to our agency?
- Why should we consider you as a student intern?
- What problems do you think will be most difficult for you to deal with in this agency setting?

Yet these questions and others may be asked during your interview. Fortunately, you can prepare for questions such as these.

Making a detailed self-assessment is one way to prepare for an interview. You should be able to describe traits and skills that contribute to your uniqueness. You might begin by compiling a list of flattering adjectives that characterize you (e.g., ambitious, trustworthy, reliable, compassionate, intellectual). Next, narrow the list to three or four items that summarize your personality. Use examples to illustrate particular attributes (e.g., one undergraduate described himself as "committed" and then explained how he continued working for a summer youth camp during a three-week period when funding shortages meant he did not receive any pay). Once you have specific attributes and examples in mind, it is fairly easy to respond to the request, "describe yourself."

Making a detailed self-assessment is one way to prepare for an interview.

Trace skills (e.g., the ability to work in stressful situations) to concrete, specific experiences. Describe a particular experience to show how you have used this skill (e.g., you managed an office for two weeks by yourself while other office personnel were on leave). You should be deliberate in describing a strength relative to the position sought (e.g., knowledge of medical terminology when seeking a practicum within a hospital setting). As attorneys do in a courtroom, you want to "build a case," that is, present "evidence" that you actually possess the traits and skills you say you have.

WHAT CAN I DO TO DEEMPHASIZE LITTLE OR NO WORK EXPERIENCE?

Both graduate and undergraduate students worry that they will be asked about their lack of practical experience. This anxiety sometimes blocks the memory of experiences that are related to the demands of the desired practicum. To avoid overlooking relevant experiences, consider your significant past activities before the interview. Perhaps you did volunteer work, were employed in a family business, or were a member of a community service or school organization.

Next, make a list of the skills you needed to complete assignments in those settings. You are now ready to link your past with what the current agency needs.

Begin by telling the interviewer what you have done in the past. Next, use a transitional statement to link the past to the present. An undergraduate student gave the following example:

> As leader of my daughter's Girl Scout troop for two years, I coordinated group activities for eight- and nine-year-olds. I found I was organized and creative. I think I would be able to build upon this experience when working here in the after-school program.

Even jobs that are not related to social work (e.g., working in a supermarket) show that you have learned how to balance schoolwork and other responsibilities and, more likely than not, you picked up valuable skills in working with people.

Case Example

A student in one of your classes begins to share some personal material with you. She was a victim of severe child abuse and reared by foster parents. Although she has never received any individual counseling, she now wants to do a practicum that will place her on a treatment team for children who have been sexually abused. Previously, other students who have completed a practicum with this agency have told you how intense and stressful their placement was. The student who wants to go to this agency hints that such a field experience will be "therapeutic" for her.

Questions

1. Do you think her plan for a practicum is a good one?
2. Would you advise her to choose a different practicum?
3. On what might your decision depend?
4. Would it be a good idea for the student to inform her field instructor and faculty field liaison of her prior history?

IS IT WISE TO ADMIT MY WEAKNESSES?

In an interview, agency supervisors may ask potential student interns to describe their weaknesses. Questions such as these are asked:

What weaknesses do you have?

What aspect of this placement do you think will be the most difficult?

What is the biggest hindrance you will have to deal with if we select you as a student intern? To prepare for these types of questions, consider any potential weaknesses you may have and then rehearse a response using one of the following approaches.

One method is to accentuate the positive. One student remembered:

> When asked what my weaknesses were relative to the placement, I knew that I did not want to focus on any anticipated problems; so I said that I thought my organization, willingness, and flexibility would enable me to handle any difficult situations I might encounter.

A second approach is to state a weakness and then reframe it into a trait that is positive. One student did this in an interview by saying, "Some people would say that I push myself too hard but I like to think of myself as someone who strives for excellence." As another example of reframing, a student said, "People may think I do not grasp things quickly enough, but I spend a lot of time trying to completely understand. I find this often helps me to save time in the long run."

A third way to deal with the subject of weaknesses is to explain how you are working on a particular liability and illustrate specific instances in which you have been encouraged by progress. During a practicum interview, a student explained that she gets very nervous speaking in front of a group. She is working on this by taking a public speaking course.

Occasionally, students have questions about whether medical diagnoses should be mentioned during an interview at an agency. A student with epilepsy informed his faculty field liaison of this, and together they were able to find a placement where staff were well prepared if the student had a seizure. Had the agency supervisor not known that the student's medical condition was the reason for his reluctance to do certain work (e.g., transporting clients), the supervisor might have thought the student was uncooperative.

If you are presently in counseling for an emotional problem, or have been in the recent past, it may be wise to share this information with the faculty field liaison so that the two of you can decide on the best placement for you. It is generally not advised, for instance, for victims of incest or sexual abuse to begin counseling others with the same problem until considerable progress has been made in their own treatment. Similarly, students from alcoholic families should be pretty far into their own recovery before seeking to work intensively with alcoholic clients. Sharing this type of information with the faculty field liaison does not indicate any weakness on your part; it shows maturity and good judgment in dealing with a sometimes painful reality.

How much personal information about students should be shared with agencies is a thorny dilemma for faculty field liaisons. For example, if a student has a criminal record, fails to inform the agency of this, and then violates the law again (e.g., harming clients, putting clients at risk, or causing the agency bad publicity), the issue of liability is raised. Disclosing certain types of information will undoubtedly induce some agencies to reject a student. Many require a criminal records check. Agencies must take reasonable precautions to protect their clients.

In general, students should advise their faculty field liaisons of medical conditions or other situations that could affect their agency work or have repercussions for the agency. The faculty field liaison and the student can then jointly decide whether and to what degree to inform the agency. There are no simple rules on this matter; the advantages and disadvantages of revealing personally sensitive information must be weighed in each individual situation. It is always a delicate issue, but it can be handled successfully with adequate planning.

Consider the following example of how to inform an agency about these matters:

> A student who was on medication for bipolar disorder discussed this with her faculty field liaison, and the two of them decided on an agency where she would learn needed skills and also receive supervision from an understanding and perceptive agency supervisor. No exceptional information was given to the agency supervisor ahead of time. The student went through the interview the same as any student would, and she and

the agency supervisor developed good rapport during the interview. As the interview was drawing to a close, the agency supervisor announced that he was favorably impressed and informed the student that she could begin a placement with the agency. At that time, the student revealed her medication needs but added that she felt secure this would not present a problem to the agency. The supervisor asked a couple of questions for clarification. The student did not go into a detailed history, but answered factually regarding her behavior when she was acting symptomatically and reassured the supervisor that over the past 18 months she had been functioning well—missing fewer days of school than others. The supervisor thanked the student for her honesty and began discussing when the student would be available to start the practicum.

In this example, information was not given ahead of time in order not to bias the supervisor against the student. Since the interview had gone well, the student felt comfortable in disclosing. Had the student felt that the interview was not going well and that it was unlikely that she would be invited to join the agency for a practicum, then the faculty field liaison and the student would have agreed that disclosure was not necessary.

HOW SHOULD I RESPOND TO QUESTIONS ABOUT MY EDUCATIONAL PREPARATION?

In a practicum interview, you may be asked to explain how your classroom learning will apply to the particular agency setting. Although you cannot foresee every specific question that might be asked, you can prepare by anticipating related questions and mentally reviewing your educational preparation. The following example shows how a little preparation can give you poise and confidence:

A graduate student tried to locate a placement that would improve his counseling skills. He contacted an acquaintance at a local community mental health center and inquired about the possibility of an internship. The acquaintance, the director of the agency, seemed interested and supportive but suggested that the student attend the next "team" meeting at the center and make the request at that time. Not wishing to seem impolite, the student wondered why he would have to make the request a second time but did not seek further explanation. Since he and the director already knew each other from membership in a local organization, the student assumed that the way was smoothed for him to become an intern—only the details would need to be worked out.

On the appointed day, the naive student arrived bright and early but was made to wait outside of the meeting room until "agency business" was concluded. When the meeting ran late, the student began to suspect that team members were arguing about the merits of accepting him as an intern. Finally, after waiting 40 minutes, the student was invited to enter the meeting.

The director made the initial introductions and indicated that the student wanted to become an intern. Then he said, "Tell us something about yourself and your program." The student patiently spoke of his career goals, hobbies, and so on. Somehow this did not seem to be what the team wanted. The student had thought that by now he would be at the end of the interview. However, one of the team members then said, "No, we want to know what theoretical approaches you use when you counsel?" The student's mind raced. Systems theory, reality therapy, Gestalt, and psychoanalysis came to mind. He wondered if he really knew enough about any of them. After several false starts, the student said, "I think I'm eclectic."

The point of this illustration is that students should give prior thought to the types of things (e.g., their training or counseling frame of reference) that may interest the interviewer or interviewing staff in the prospective agency.

Interviewers ask questions about educational backgrounds for many reasons. They may be trying to assess intellectual abilities, breadth and depth of knowledge, or special interests or training. To get ready for any questioning along this line, think about your educational experience and then write down two or three courses that were valuable preparation for this specific practicum placement. Next, think of theories or concepts discussed in these courses, and write down why you think each would be helpful. This exercise will enable you to go into the interview mindful of important concepts and theories. Interviewers will not expect you to recite an entire course syllabus. However, being able to recall two or three major theories and explain how they relate to the work of the agency would impress many interviewers.

What if the general questions are, "What kind of program do they run there at your university? Is it a good one?" To answer these questions, think about two or three aspects of your social work program that have given you good preparation. For example, some programs incorporate a social work course that requires students to perform a few hours of agency volunteer work each week. This educational experience helps a student know what to expect and what to do in a practicum and could be described as a program strength.

Be positive in describing the valuable learning acquired from your educational experience. An educational program that is described chiefly in negative terms may be seen by some interviewers as inadequately preparing you to function in their agency—as a student or as an employee.

Be positive in describing the valuable learning acquired from your educational experience.

How Should I Dress for the Practicum Agency?

As with many things in life, it is best to avoid extremes. Whether going for the first interview or reporting for work on the first day, you should not plan to make a fashion statement. Provocative dress will not be acceptable and may result in losing a placement that you desired. Generally speaking, dress conservatively, but neither too formally nor informally. If possible, visit the agency beforehand and observe what other staff members are wearing. If the staff dresses informally (men in sports shirts without ties; women in slacks and casual tops), then dress similarly. Do not wear jeans on the first interview. Later, if you become an intern there and learn that jeans are typical dress because of the agency population or setting (e.g., assisting clients in a sheltered workshop), then it is usually permissible to wear jeans. Some agencies have policies against staff and students wearing nose pierces or extreme tattoos. Plan your dress to avoid getting "noticed," and always ask ahead of time if you have questions about what's appropriate. When in doubt, dress up a little more than you normally would for class.

How Do I Make a Good Impression?

Most initial interviews will last only 30 to 60 minutes. Use this time to make a positive impression by remembering a few simple but important details. First, plan to arrive 10 to 15 minutes early. It is always better to be early for an important appointment than to be late. If you plan to arrive early, then even unexpected delays can be absorbed without major problems.

Second, when you meet the prospective agency supervisor, look the person in the eyes and offer a firm handshake. Smile and show a genuine interest in the person. Take care to pronounce the supervisor's name correctly (if you are unsure, ask). Be prepared to spend the first few minutes making small talk. If you have not been keeping up with current events, read the local newspaper and a national magazine prior to your meeting. This can help to give you topics for discussion should the conversation move past your credentials. This could easily happen, for example, if your interview was scheduled for 11:15 A.M. and the agency supervisor invites you to lunch.

Third, be observant. Look around the office or room, and note anything of particular interest to you. One student noticed a guitar sitting in a corner and quickly engaged the supervisor in a discussion about their shared interest in classical guitar. Meeting strangers is always a little difficult at first. By facilitating conversation with the interviewer, you can demonstrate a skill that will later be required with clients. You will leave a better impression if both you and the interviewer can speak comfortably than if you appear frightened and hesitant to talk.

Fourth, show enthusiasm. One way to do this is to ask questions. Do not be completely passive and think your role is only to wait for questions. Ask questions about the agency, the staff, the clientele, how long the supervisor has been with the agency, and so on. You can ask what formal training is given to students, how student performance is appraised, and what student responsibilities are. Furthermore, you can inquire about the staff you will be working with, the primary functions of the office, and the expected working hours.

Students can usually generate interesting discussion if they have acquired some basic information about the agency before the interview, such as:

- The relative size of the agency (Has it added or lost staff recently?)
- Its organizational auspices (Is it a private or public agency? From where do most of its funds come?)
- The array of services provided to clients (Who is the "typical" client?)
- Recent news pertaining to the organization (Have there been any recent newspaper articles?)

During the interview, show congruence between your verbal and nonverbal communication. Modulate your voice to maintain the interviewer's attention, and be sure to keep appropriate posture. Try to avoid saying what you will not do (e.g., "I will *never* work past 4:30"); rather, emphasize your congeniality and flexibility.

Finally, keep in mind that many agency supervisors ask questions in the hopes of answering the following:

- What can you do for the agency?
- How long will it take you to become productive?
- What do you want from the agency?
- Can you handle stress?
- Can you get along with others?

By anticipating questions that interviewers are likely to ask and by knowing the "hidden agenda," there is a better chance that you will leave a good impression than if you go unprepared.

A day or two after your interview, it is a good idea to drop the potential field instructor a brief thank-you note in the mail expressing appreciation for interviewing you. If you schedule three or four interviews, and each agency offers you the opportunity to be an intern, it is always expected that as soon as you have made a decision you will call and inform the other agencies. They may be waiting to hear from you before committing to other students. Also thank these agencies for their interest and assistance.

GETTING ORIENTED—WHAT CAN I EXPECT ON THE FIRST DAY?

Agencies prepare for and use students in enormously different ways. Two accounts illustrate this:

> The first day in one of my graduate practicums, another student and I were handed a scrapbook of clippings about the agency and instructed to familiarize ourselves with the agency's range of activities. We carefully pored over the scrapbook and about 45 minutes later returned it to our supervisor and asked what we should do next. With a look of surprise he informed us that he thought the activity would have taken us most of the day. He actually had made no other plans for us on the first day, and said that we could go home. Looking back on this experience now, I realize that very little planning had gone on prior to our arrival.

Another student experienced something quite different:

> I participated in a training session aimed at familiarizing new students with various facets of the agency. The director, codirector, two experienced volunteers, and one agency worker conducted the seminar. Several topics related to agency operations were discussed, such as the importance of confidentiality, agency policies, forms, and procedures.

The atmosphere created by the staff in the latter example enabled the student to feel comfortable about making comments and asking questions. A large part of the training was devoted to role playing by the staff. They acted out several typical cases, demonstrating a variety of likely occurrences. In summary the student commented:

> At the end of the session, we were given the opportunity to assess the worth of the training. I offered my positive comments and left the meeting feeling I had been treated with respect, appreciation, and a genuine concern. The staff seemed to provide me with the knowledge necessary for a productive learning experience.

These examples illustrate differences in orientation. Ideally, the first day and perhaps the first week should be closer to the second example. Your orientation should include an introduction to the agency (e.g., its mission and services), the staff, and the physical layout of the facility, and an explanation of pertinent agency policies and procedures. However, agency staff members may be pulled away to take care of client emergencies or to attend to other crises within an agency. Occasionally, agency supervisors simply have not planned or do not have the time to provide activities that will be meaningful or fully involve students on their first day. One student expressed her frustration this way:

> My first day in the practicum my supervisor had gone to a workshop and had forgotten that I was coming. I lost three days that I had planned on working there because he was unavailable. His secretary offered to give me some filing to do, but I decided to come back the following week. I've done secretarial work, I wanted to learn how to be a social worker.

The best field instructors thoughtfully anticipate and plan experiences for students to gain new perspectives and insights into the social work profession while helping with the work that needs to be done. And although it is not uncommon for "disasters" to occur during a student's initial orientation to an agency, settings where there is too little planning, insufficient supervision, and too much chaos do not provide students with the necessary structure. If these terms characterize your placement, you should address this problem by speaking with your faculty field liaison.

On your first day, you may feel slightly overwhelmed with how much there is to know. For instance, if you are in a large hospital, it may take a while to learn your way through the labyrinth of corridors and buildings. The staff may be using so many new medical terms and abbreviations that your head spins. And, you may encounter so many new people that you worry about whether you'll ever be able to remember all their names.

Be reassured that you *will* learn your way around, that gradually you'll acquire a new vocabulary of terms and jargon that the staff use, and that you'll soon learn everyone's name. Because you are the new student (or may be one of a group of them), staff won't expect you to know everything right away. In fact, they're probably very accustomed to giving directions and explaining things to students. As long as you are pleasant and try your best to learn, you'll find that most people will be helpful. Fight the temptation to hide in your office because you are the least experienced one on the floor or in the agency. Instead, be assertive. Take the time to introduce yourself and to ask questions of staff that you encounter. If during the first several days you don't have that much to do, offer to help others who look like they need assistance. If you do, you'll be surprised how many people will remember *your* name.

HOW DO I DEVELOP A LEARNING CONTRACT?

You will probably be given the opportunity to develop contracts with clients in your practicum. To become familiar with the use of contracts, most social work programs will expect you to prepare a learning (or educational) contract of your own—one that outlines your responsibilities in the practicum. This three-way agreement involves you, the field instructor, and the faculty field liaison and generally states what you hope to learn from the practicum (i.e., your goals), the responsibilities or tasks that will be given to you, the amount or extent of supervision you will receive, and the hours or days that you will be in the practicum agency. Usually, the three parties will sign and receive a copy of the contract.

The learning contract minimizes the possibility of misunderstandings and provides a basis for accountability. The contract helps students keep in mind what they have committed themselves to, provides a sense of progress and satisfaction as portions of it are completed, and helps students to plan their time in the agency. The learning contract supplies necessary safeguards to ensure the integrity of the practicum as an educational experience and to discourage the use of students as substitute employees.

Start working on the learning contract by familiarizing yourself with the practicum requirements of your program and the agency's expectations of you. (Sometimes, all the students in a given agency are expected to meet certain learning goals, and these may already be stated for you.) Read the practicum syllabus or manual. For example, how many days or hours are you expected to be in the agency each week? Compare your learning needs and career goals with the educational opportunities that will be afforded to you in this placement. Then, draft a set of goals and objectives that you hope to achieve in this practicum.

Note that a distinction has been made between goals and objectives. *Goals* provide a general sense of direction—the target for which you are aiming. For instance, you might have the goal of learning how to make differential psychiatric diagnoses. Or, you might write a goal to develop skills to work with adolescents in groups.

Objectives follow from your goals and may be thought of as stepping stones, that is, activities that help you reach your goals. Objectives should always be expressed so that it is easy to monitor whether they were accomplished. Therefore, objectives need to be both measurable and attainable. It is helpful to use action verbs, to specify a time or date within the objective when a task should be accomplished and, if possible, to identify quantities (i.e., the number of psychosocial assessments to be conducted).

After you have listed your goals for the practicum, think of each active step, activity, or responsibility that you will have to undertake or perform. These will suggest to you the objectives that should fall under each learning goal. Of these tasks or activities, choose the ones that are most directly observable. For each objective ask, "How will my field instructor know that I have achieved this objective?"

Identify the goals that you would like to work toward and two or three related objectives for each goal. Each objective achieved should help your field instructor know that you have made progress toward reaching a goal. If it will be difficult or impossible to know when you have completed an objective, then the objective is not useful; it needs to be rewritten in more behavioral terms. Finally, consider how much time it will take you to achieve the objective. If it will take more time than is available to you, then you must discard it. You should have a mixture of a few objectives that can be met within the first several weeks of the practicum, and others that will not be completed until the last several weeks.

When you are satisfied with the rough draft of your learning contract, share it with your field instructor and faculty field liaison. The three of you can then make any necessary revisions. After incorporating the revisions and retyping the document, you are ready for signatures. Each one of you should receive a copy of the final agreement. There are three sample practicum learning contracts provided for your reference in Figures 3.1, 3.2, and 3.3, respectively.

There is no single best approach to contract development. However, the SPIRO model (Pfeiffer & Jones, 1972) provides a good set of guidelines that emphasize the following critical characteristics of a contract: *specificity, performance, involvement, realism,* and *observability*.

Ethical Practice

Critical Thinking Question: When you experience a struggle between your personal and professional values with a client, how do you resolve the dilemma?

GEORGE GOODSTUDENT

Placement Agency:	Rogers County Mental Health Services
Address:	1414 Evans Drive, Zanesville, Ohio
Phone:	(513) 555–5000
Field Instructor:	Mary Ann Mobbie, M.S.W
Hours in Placement:	Tuesday: 8:00 A.M. to 5:00 P.M. Friday: 8:00 A.M. to 5:00 P.M.
Supervision Time:	Tuesday: 8:30 A.M. to 10:00 A.M.

GOAL 1: TO IMPROVE ASSESSMENT SKILLS

Objective 1:   To search Medline and PsycInfo for current literature on assessing sexual abuse.
Objective 2:   To read at least seven articles from the literature search.
Objective 3:   To observe five interviews conducted by agency staff during the second week.
Objective 4:   To conduct at least 12 interviews with clients by the end of the semester.
Objective 5:   To write at least 12 psychosocial assessments.

Evaluation: Field instructor will observe an interview at mid-term and an interview at 14 weeks for competence in assessing clients' problems at initial intake.

GOAL 2: TO LEARN THE COMMUNITY'S SOCIAL SERVICES

Objective 1:   By midsemester to visit United Way's Information and Referral Center and interview two staff members about services available.
Objective 2:   To read 20 recently closed cases by the seventh week to identify referrals that were made.
Objective 3:   To attend at least five case conferences by the end of the semester.

Evaluation: Field instructor will review a random sample of completed assessments to see if those not appropriate for treatment were referred to appropriate community resources.

GOAL 3: TO LEARN HOW TO CONDUCT GROUP THERAPY

Objective 1:   To observe for three weeks the incest survivors' support group.
Objective 2:   To attend the scheduled four hour in-service entitled "Working with Groups."
Objective 3:   To cofacilitate a new time-limited support group for male sexual abuse victims (eight weeks).
Objective 4:   To write accurate progress notes for each of the group meetings.

Evaluation: Field instructor will watch video tapes of two different group therapy sessions to assess student's expertise in conducting the groups and will read the progress notes for accuracy and completeness.

Student _____   Date _____

Field Instructor _____   Date _____

Faculty Field Liaison _____   Date _____

Figure 3.1
Sample Practicum Learning Contract

Specificity demands that your learning goals be specific rather than general or global. For instance, "To learn how to be a better social worker" is much too general, as is, "To learn how to respond to clients in a professional manner." An evaluation of what you should be learning at any point in the

---

MARY RODRIGUEZ

Placement Agency: Alzheimer's Association

Hours in Placement: Mondays and Wednesdays 8:30 to 5:00, Fridays 8:30 to noon

Objective 1: Learn fund-raising skills by involvement in a significant fund-raising activity.

Tasks: 1. Read relevant literature as assigned by field instructor such as: *Principles of Professional Fund-Raising.*

      2. Discuss with the agency director the Association's plans/strategies for fund-raising.

      3. Study the agency's records of fund-raising activities including grant applicants.

      4. Research possible sources of grant funding for the agency's programs.

      5. Select one grant-funding source and work on/participate in preparing a grant proposal.

Evaluation: 1. The supervisor's assessment of the student's mastery of the grant-writing process and the quality of his or her effort.

      2. Submission of a grant application by April 30.

Objective 2: Learn program development skills through involvement in a Safe Return Program.

Tasks: 1. To conduct a literature search for information on how to develop a new program.

      2. Contact Alzheimer's Associations in other communities that have such programs and gather information on those programs.

      3. Discuss the specific program literature and findings from other agency contacts with the director and other staff.

      4. Contact the appropriate personnel in the police department and meet with them.

      5. Develop a Safe Return Training program for the local police force.

      6. Assist in preparing for the training session.

Evaluation: The supervisor's assessment of the quality of the training materials and the training itself.

Figure 3.2

Sample Practicum Learning Contract

academic term is facilitated by a more specific goal: "To learn how to screen clients for substance abuse."

By making your learning goals *performance* oriented, all three parties should have a good idea of the activities, duties, assignments, or responsibilities to be completed for you to meet your goals. For instance, if your goal is to learn interviewing, the next step is to specify objectives or tasks. For instance, a student who wants to learn how to conduct substance abuse evaluations might list below that goal the following objective: "To conduct at least ten substance abuse evaluations during the practicum placement."

Involvement ensures that the contract spells out the extent to which you, the field instructor, and the faculty field liaison will be involved in helping you reach your learning goals. Obviously, if the field instructor and faculty

---

Goal 1: To learn how the state's General Assembly makes legislation.

Strategies:

1. To read daily the newspaper coverage on the state legislature.
2. To read the legislature's Web page each week.
3. To interview local legislators regarding their positions on health coverage for the underinsured.
4. To observe one meeting each of the House and Senate and one meeting of the Health and Education Subcommittee.
5. To interview at least one staff member from the Legislative Research Commission.
6. To track the progress of a particular bill through the legislature.

Measurement:

1. Student will present weekly to the seminar a one-page summary of legislative activities relevant to health care insurance and coverage of the underinsured.

Goal 2: To advocate for improved health coverage for the underinsured.

Strategies:

1. To contact local health departments for needs assessment data that would convince legislators of the extent of the problem within the tri-county area.
2. To meet with two local groups that advocate for the impoverished.
3. To provide testimony or participate in a legislative committee hearing, if possible.
4. To participate in at least three different lobbying activities.

Measurement:

1. A report will be prepared demonstrating the extent of the problem of the underinsured and portraying actual people's stories about troubles getting health care.
2. Letters will be written to ten key legislators asking for their support; reports will accompany each report.
3. At least two letters will be written for the editorial page of the newspaper.

Figure 3.3
Sample Practicum Learning Contract

field liaison approve of you learning how to screen for substance abuse, then you will have to be assigned enough clients for the objective to be achieved.

Your learning contract might also specify when the faculty field liaison will visit the agency and when you will receive supervision from your field instructor. (This makes the contract more than just a one-sided agreement.)

The element of *realism* is a reminder that your learning goals and associated objectives need to be realistic and attainable within the limits of the agency's educational resources, the time you will be in the practicum, and your personal assets and limitations.

Observability "demands that results be defined in a measurable form so that it is obvious whether or not the specific goal has been achieved" (Abbott, 1986, p. 61). For example, although the absolute number of substance abuse screenings to be completed may not always be critical, it is important that an impartial observer be able to determine whether you have completed your objectives.

Try to strike a balance between ambitiousness and practicality in your learning contract.

Try to strike a balance between ambitiousness and practicality in your learning contract. Discussion with your field instructor and faculty field liaison will help you identify areas where change or modification is needed.

Note in these learning contract illustrations that in some programs the terminology may vary slightly. Goals might be called objectives, for instance.

Sometimes objectives are divided into *strategies* (for achieving your goals) and *outcomes* (or measurements) for assessing what the student accomplished.

POINTS TO REMEMBER ABOUT THE LEARNING CONTRACT

Contracts should indicate the following:

▶ The days and hours you will be in the agency
▶ Your supervisor (with telephone number or e-mail address)
▶ Learning goals (in broad terms)
▶ Objectives (in concrete, measurable terms)
▶ Your responsibilities, activities, or assignments (be as specific as possible. For example, state the number of groups to be led, number of assessments to be conducted, and any important deadlines or target dates for accomplishment.)
▶ Date when drafted (because there may be later revisions)

Case Example

You have a friend, Heather, in the social work program. Heather always seems to be too busy for her own good. Typically, she runs a day or two late in turning in major assignments. She is working full time and is also going to school full time. She seems to be getting only four or five hours of sleep each night. Still, she is active in several volunteer organizations around town. Heather tells the faculty field liaison that she is working only part time on weekends.

Possibly because she failed to note it on her calendar, Heather missed a day she was scheduled to work at her practicum agency. The next time she appeared, her field instructor inquired whether she had been too ill to call in. Heather was momentarily flustered as she tried to recall what she had been doing. Not wanting the field instructor to know that she was really working a full-time job, Heather made up a flimsy excuse.

Heather also had a problem turning in required agency paperwork within the deadlines her field instructor gave. Now, at the midterm evaluation, the field instructor is suggesting to the faculty field liaison that Heather be terminated. Heather is confused, hurt, and angry. She has been trying her best, she thinks, although she dislikes the clients she has to work with.

Questions

1. What do you consider to be Heather's biggest problem?
2. What could Heather have done to improve her situation in the agency?

HOW WILL THE AGENCY EVALUATE MY PERFORMANCE AS A STUDENT INTERN?

Although the evaluation procedures used by different agencies and social work programs vary widely, you can expect that your field instructor will be looking at your progress during the internship. Field instructors often use prepared forms or scales to rate students on their knowledge, skills, and social work values. These forms may be supplied by the students' faculty field liaison or may have been developed at the agency. Field instructors generally discuss their written evaluations with students or give students the opportunity to review their comments and respond. In some programs, faculty field liaisons attend the evaluation session. During your orientation to the agency or to the field practicum, you may be given a copy of the evaluation form that will be used. If a copy is not supplied, ask for one so that you can be familiar with the areas in which you will be expected to show improvement. (More discussion of this topic is provided in Chapter 4.)

In addition to the skills and knowledge you are expected to acquire, certain other qualities are necessary. Foremost are good attendance and being on time for your appointments and scheduled days. You may be considered unreliable if your attendance is poor (even if you have valid excuses). Other qualities that agencies like in student interns include a pleasant disposition, willingness to work (sometimes expressed as interest in helping others when not busy with your own assignments), a sense of humor, sensible (businesslike) appearance, and sincerity in learning. Furthermore, agencies want students who are in control of their emotions, who are calm and objective (even under stressful conditions), who have good judgment, and who are appropriately assertive.

Most field instructors will rate more highly those student interns who have qualities that would make them good employees once the practicum is finished. As suggested earlier, these would be individuals who get along easily with their coworkers and clients, and who are hardworking, conscientious, and responsible. Student interns who are willing to help out no matter what the task, and those considered to be an asset to the agency (perhaps because they have developed a special expertise or have found a niche for themselves in the agency), are favored by field instructors and agency administrators.

Here are other guidelines to help you get along with your field instructor and other staff within the agency:

Listen carefully the first time any instructions are given, and make notes if necessary.

- ▶ Do not try to impress agency workers with vocabulary that you have just learned.
- ▶ When you communicate in writing, use good grammar and spelling and try to write legibly. (If you can't spell well, don't guess—always use a dictionary or spellchecker.)
- ▶ Listen carefully the first time any instructions are given to you, and make notes if necessary. Do not make a practice of going back to the agency supervisor on multiple occasions to ask for information that has already been given to you. However, if you need further instructions or information to complete your assignments, then it is more responsible to ask for help than to finish an assignment incorrectly.
- ▶ Do not give your field instructor the impression that you are picky about the assignments you will take. If you are not given enough work, don't be afraid to ask for additional duties.
- ▶ Once you have been given responsibility for something, carry it out. Do not draw out tasks; do not forget assignments.
- ▶ Be on time and keep appointments.
- ▶ If you borrow something, return it. Show consideration to others. Do not leave a mess for others to clean.

- If there are personality clashes or personnel problems within the agency, try not to get involved. Avoid agency gossip or discussion that you perceive to be about the faults or flaws of selected agency employees.
- If you develop a significant problem with a coworker within the agency, then share this information with your faculty field liaison as soon as possible. Conform to the National Association of Social Workers' Code of Ethics (1999)—do not engage in unethical behavior.
- Keep a positive attitude. Even if the agency does not conform to your ideal image, considerable learning can occur in every practicum. If you have decided (or even if you and your faculty field liaison have decided) that a different placement is necessary next semester, do not adopt the attitude that you will do just enough to get by. (One worthwhile reason to try your best is that you might want your field instructor to write a good letter of reference for a future job.)

If you truly want to learn and help the clientele of your agency, you will almost certainly meet most of the agency's performance standards and receive a positive evaluation.

WHAT DO I DO IF THE FIELD INSTRUCTOR BECOMES INCAPACITATED?

Occasionally, events such as accidents, illnesses, or planned absences may mean that your field instructor is unable to continue with your supervision. Your field instructor and faculty field liaison should have enough time to make alternative arrangements for planned absences (e.g., vacations). However, your faculty field liaison may not always know when your field instructor is unavailable to supervise you because of unplanned absences such as an accident or illness. In this situation, it is your responsibility to inform your faculty field liaison of such absences—particularly when it is likely that more than one supervisory session will be missed.

SUMMARY

Students want their practicum experiences to be instructive, exciting, and gratifying. But before the practicum can start, students often must be interviewed by the agency. Even if an interview is not required, the student is likely to be nervous about getting off on the right foot and making a good impression in the agency. This chapter has provided some suggestions for student interns preparing to go into an agency for the first time.

Further Researching Social Service Agencies

In addition to information about social service agencies that may be available from former students, faculty evaluations, and organizational profiles in the field education office, another way to learn about an agency is to go for an interview there. Not only will the staff ask you questions, but also you will have an opportunity to quiz them. Before you think about what questions you might want to ask the agency staff, see what information you can obtain about the agency on the Internet.

1. Using a search engine (e.g., Google), type in the name of the agency and perhaps a city. For example, "Red Cross, Indianapolis." You may also want to go to the local newspaper's electronic archives to see what stories have appeared about the agency in the last three years. Has it been involved in any controversy? How would you describe the news coverage? Basically favorable or unfavorable?

   AGENCY NAME: _____

   _____

   _____

2. What questions do you want to ask the staff at the social service agency when you go for an interview? Prepare yourself by listing your questions here:

   a. _____

   _____

   b. _____

   _____

   c. _____

   _____

   d. _____

   _____

   e. _____

   _____

   f. _____

   _____

Thinking Like an Agency Supervisor

Social service agency supervisors and staff may have limited slots for interns but many students to choose from.

1. If you were an agency supervisor, what qualities would you look for in a student? As you think about those qualities, how would you rate yourself?

Qualities Needed for a Good Intern	My Self-Rating (Low/Medium/High)
_____	_____
_____	_____
_____	_____
_____	_____
_____	_____

2. Imagine that you are going for an interview at a social service agency where you most want to do your internship. What questions might the agency supervisor ask you?

a. _____
   _____

b. _____
   _____

c. _____
   _____

d. _____
   _____

e. _____
   _____

f. _____
   _____

3. How would you respond if the agency supervisor asked you a question such as, "Thinking about your education to date, what have you learned that would help you if you are chosen to be our intern?"

a. From my practice class or classes:

   _____
   _____

b. From my human behavior class:

   _____
   _____

c. From my policy class:

_____

_____

d. From my research class:

_____

_____

e. From my elective or liberal arts classes:

_____

_____

4. What would you say if the agency person interviewing you asked this question, "Give me one reason why we should choose you over the other candidates"?

_____

_____

_____

_____

_____

5. Make a list of your potentially applicable life experiences, work experiences, skills (computer knowledge), or areas of the curriculum where you feel particularly strong.

_____

_____

_____

_____

_____

_____

_____

More Questions You May Be Asked in an Initial Interview

How will you answer the following questions?

1. How would you describe yourself?

_____

_____

_____

_____

2. What skills can you bring to our agency?

_____

_____

_____

3. Be honest. Do you think you can you work with

child abusers?

substance abusers?

persons who are developmentally challenged?

the mentally ill?

the physically challenged?

felons?

women seeking an abortion?

demented/confused elderly?

4. What life experiences have helped to prepare you for an internship with our agency? In what ways have they prepared you?

_____

_____

_____

_____

_____

Orientation/First-Day Information

During your orientation a lot of information will be given to you, and you'll be expected to remember key events (like days when staff meetings are held, days when your supervision is scheduled, etc.). It is a good idea to write down specifics that you'll need to know later. If some of the following topics don't come up during your orientation, you might want to ask about them anyway.

My agency and location where I will be placed is: _____

The agency phone number is: _____

I can park _____ or take bus/train _____

My supervisor is: _____

My supervisor's phone number is: _____

My supervision will begin on: _____

I will be in office number: _____

The telephone number in my office is: _____

Other students in the agency are: _____

Other key staff I will work with are: _____

My faculty field liaison is: _____

His or her telephone number is: _____

Do I need to complete a time sheet?   Yes   No

Do I need a criminal background check?   Yes   No

Do I need to complete any health screening?   Yes   No

Is there a dress code?   Yes   No

Staff meetings are held on: _____

My personal supervision time is: _____

Drafting a Learning Contract

Sometimes all of the social work interns in an agency follow the same "master" learning contract with just a little variation. However, most students have to create their own learning contract. Use the following space to help you get a good start on developing a learning contract.

1. List at least three goals that will serve to generally organize your learning at the agency:

   a. _____

   _____

   b. _____

   _____

   c. _____

   _____

2. List two or three objectives for each goal that you hope to achieve during your internship.

   Goal A, Objective 1: _____

   _____

   Objective 2: _____

   _____

   Objective 3: _____

   _____

   Goal B, Objective 1: _____

   _____

   Objective 2: _____

   _____

   Objective 3: _____

   _____

   Goal C, Objective 1: _____

   _____

   Objective 2: _____

   _____

   Objective 3: _____

   _____

As a final check, read over your objectives to determine if they are measurable. That is, will the faculty person overseeing your practicum be able to conclude at the end of the semester or quarter that you completed your objectives? After reading them again, you may want to revise any ambiguous objectives to make them more clear.

	Objective Clearly Stated (Yes/No)	Completion of Objective Easily Determined (Yes/No)
Goal A, Objective 1	_____	_____
Objective 2	_____	_____
Objective 3	_____	_____
Goal B, Objective 1	_____	_____
Objective 2	_____	_____
Objective 3	_____	_____
Goal C, Objective 1	_____	_____
Objective 2	_____	_____
Objective 3	_____	_____

Log onto **www.mysocialworklab.com** to access a wealth of case studies, videos, and assessment. (*If you did not receive an access code to* **MySocialWorkLab** *with this text and wish to purchase access online, please visit* www.mysocialworklab.com.)

1. **Watch the Core Competency video: "Professional Roles and Boundaries."** In this video, social worker Sarah Harden clarifies her role, and we learn that part of professional demeanor is learning to explain roles and boundaries without being defensive or apologetic. What would keep you from being combative and losing your cool?

2. **Watch the Core Competency video: "Demonstrating Effective Oral and Written Communication."** We learn that written communications must be clear, succinct, and without error. As you think about your oral and written communication competencies, which one needs further development and what will you do to improve?

PRACTICE TEST The following questions will test your knowledge of the content found within this chapter.

1. The learning contract should include:
   a. Specific learning goals
   b. A map of your agency's location
   c. Concrete, measurable objectives
   d. Plans for an incapacitated field instructor

2. The most important professional behavior is:
   a. Dressing appropriately
   b. Keeping confidentiality
   c. Being on time
   d. Avoiding trying to impress agency staff

3. Occasionally, students have questions about whether to share information concerning their medical diagnoses and/or emotional problems. What is recommended?
   a. Share all the detail you can.
   b. Choose clients with your same problems.

   c. Avoid sharing personal information.
   d. Be well into recovery before intervening.

4. The agency will evaluate your performance based upon:
   a. Improvement in practice areas
   b. How quickly you accomplish tasks
   c. Limiting endeavors to very compelling opportunities
   d. Learning complex practice vocabulary

Short Answer Question:
Ava's field instructor is probably the busiest person in the whole agency and, unfortunately, she has, in the first two weeks of the academic term, had very little time to meet with Ava. However, Ava's faculty field liaison is insisting that Ava begin developing a learning contract. What suggestions could you give Ava about how to address this problem by beginning to draft a contract?

ASSESS YOUR COMPETENCE Use the scale below to rate your current level of achievement on the following concepts or skills associated with each competency practice behavior presented in the chapter:

1	2	3
I can accurately describe the concept or skill.	I can consistently identify the concept or skill when observing and analyzing practice activities.	I can competently implement the concept or skill in my own practice.

_____ Aware of and can manage my personal values when they conflict with clients' values.

_____ Devise a learning contract that effectively communicates my work in the practicum agency.

_____ Use sessions with my agency supervisor to improve my skills as a social worker.

Answers

Key: 1) c, 2) b, 3) d, 4) a

4

The Student Intern: Learning New Roles

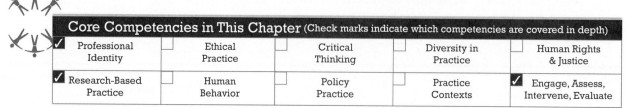

Core Competencies in This Chapter (Check marks indicate which competencies are covered in depth)				
✓ Professional Identity	☐ Ethical Practice	☐ Critical Thinking	☐ Diversity in Practice	☐ Human Rights & Justice
✓ Research-Based Practice	☐ Human Behavior	☐ Policy Practice	☐ Practice Contexts	✓ Engage, Assess, Intervene, Evaluate

OVERVIEW

Whether you are a new employee or a new student just beginning in an unfamiliar agency, you will likely have questions about the expectations others will have of you. Who will supervise and oversee your efforts? Will the work be difficult or easy? How will your program evaluate your work with clients and all that you have been learning? This chapter will examine the new role of being a student in a professional setting and answer questions related to making use of supervision, being evaluated, and handling the stress of juggling multiple roles.

HOW MUCH WILL I BE EXPECTED TO ACCOMPLISH?

The amount of work assigned to students in practicum is not standardized. Students who possess more maturity, intelligence, competence, and prior experience will probably end up with larger caseloads than students who lack one or more of these traits. Even if you are easily the most mature person you know, some agencies may require you to spend the first semester observing and listening before being given responsibilities involving clients in the second semester.

In most agencies, a rough rule of thumb is that student interns might expect to carry four to seven cases at a time. Two or three cases are too few, and ten or more are often too many unless a student is in a block placement and working 30 hours or more a week in the agency. Four or five cases will keep a student reasonably occupied—especially if these have distinctive problems that require background or additional reading.

It is true that four or five cases will not keep a student completely occupied if he or she is placed in an agency for 20 hours per week or so. At a minimum, students should expect to be involved in some type of professional activity at least half of the time. In addition to managing their own cases, students often can assist with client intake assessments, participate in case conferences or staff meetings, accompany other staff who make home visits, and observe group or family therapy sessions. By planning ahead, students can request to participate in a particular type of session (e.g., termination with a client) that they will need to handle by themselves later in the academic term.

Because agencies vary markedly with regard to their clientele, some students may have few clients initially, but these are ongoing or long term; whereas students in other agencies may have many more clients over the academic term, but these involve briefer contacts. Actually, a combination of both short- and long-term clients would be ideal. Optimally, a student should receive clients at intake and work with them until the clients terminate services.

As a student, it is to your advantage to learn as much as possible about the agency and its methods of serving its clientele. If you feel that you are being underutilized, talk with your field instructor. He or she may agree to your taking on other assignments within the agency. Perhaps you could assist with a research or evaluation project. It may be possible, for instance, to contact former clients to determine if they require additional intervention from the agency.

Learn as much as possible about the agency and its methods of serving its clientele.

Another educationally meaningful activity is to update the agency's community resource directory. Most agencies maintain a file of health and human resources they use when referring clients. Often these files are loosely organized, with penciled notes and brochures that may not be current. By contacting some of these programs yourself and becoming familiar with these resources, you can learn what services are available, their eligibility requirements, and how they can be accessed by your clients.

Talk with your field instructor to find out if any agency personnel are engaged in such activities as planning and creating new resources. It is not uncommon for agency-based social workers to be involved with task forces, coalitions, or community planning groups that may be conducting needs assessments or trying to document the need for new programs in the community. Such groups may have special projects that could use your assistance.

Still another useful educational strategy is to interview staff with whom you have not worked. Ask them what knowledge they think is important to do their jobs well. Be assertive in meeting other staff members as you attempt to get more involved in the agency. If after a week or two you still feel that too much of your time is being wasted, it is appropriate to inform your faculty field liaison. Problems you encounter during your field instruction are the mutual responsibility of three parties: the faculty field liaison, the field instructor, and you. All three must be involved to ensure the integrity of the field instruction.

If you feel that you are being treated more like an employee than a student and given too much responsibility for the time you are in the agency, you'll probably begin to feel stressed. If you are hard-pressed to complete your paperwork or assignments on time, and if you are tense and feeling too much pressure, you may need to remind your field instructor that you are only a student. It is important that you learn how to advocate for yourself if you are to be an effective advocate for your clients. However, if the agency's demands on you do not let up, you will need to speak to your faculty field liaison.

Case Example

Eileen decided to return to college after her children finished high school. At 45, she is the oldest student in her integrating seminar. Because of her maturity and good judgment, Eileen is placed in a very active social work department in a large metropolitan hospital. Very soon after her orientation, she is treated as a regular staff member—possibly because of an unfilled vacancy and the pregnancy leave of another social worker. Eileen is kept so busy in her practicum that she is often too busy to reflect or discuss with her agency supervisor what she has learned. On average, Eileen is working one or two hours extra each day she is in her practicum.

Usually, although not always, Eileen and her agency supervisor are able to find an hour once a week to talk. Eileen is beginning to resent having so much responsibility and so little time to study, read, and reflect as some of her classmates are finding time to do. Her supervisor has hinted that she knows Eileen is being given too much to do, but they are going to be shorthanded for at least another four weeks. And, there is the possibility of a permanent job opening up for Eileen even while she is going to school. Eileen is torn between wanting to be considered for the vacant position and wanting to be treated as a student and not given quite so much responsibility.

Questions

1. Should Eileen ask her field instructor to sit down with her to discuss her learning contract?
2. Does Eileen need to involve her faculty field liaison?
3. Could Eileen be a good intern and still cut back on her hours?
4. How would you cope in such a situation?
5. How do you cope with stress?

HOW MUCH WILL I BE SUPERVISED, AND BY WHOM?

A qualified social work supervisor (field instructor) should be regularly accessible within the agency where you are placed. If your immediate agency supervisor does not hold a social work degree, then another person with social work credentials will be asked to provide your formal or official supervision at least once a week. In a few instances where a program or an agency does not employ any social workers but where rich learning opportunities are available, a social work faculty member may be asked to be your field instructor.

Your agency supervisor will be responsible for giving you duties or assignments and monitoring your performance. He or she will be in charge of you, and unless you are informed to the contrary, this is the person to whom you should turn if you have any questions or problems while carrying out your assignments.

A major difference between the type of supervision you will receive as a student and other nonprofessional supervision that you may have experienced in paid employment or volunteer work is that the field instructor has a major teaching role. Field instructors attempt to introduce students to a wide range of activities performed by social workers. In keeping with their teaching role, they may also assign readings to assist students in better understanding their clients or improving certain skills. Practicum experience is designed to help students learn specific social work skills and knowledge in accordance with their learning contracts. Field instructors also strive to help students integrate the content from core courses with what students are learning in the field.

From an agency's perspective, students require supervision (sometimes very close supervision), which takes away from the field instructor's own productivity—unless the students' contributions offset the investment of time. Field instructors will be relieved when you can help, but until you demonstrate that you can handle certain tasks, expect your supervisor to keep a careful watch over you. Gradually, as you demonstrate your competence and your field instructor becomes more comfortable with your skills, supervision will become more relaxed. Students who require too much supervision and those who cannot be trusted with even the smallest of assignments may be asked to leave.

Most often, field instructors will be cautious not to give students any assignments that would exceed their level of expertise. The initial tasks may be fairly elementary. Agency supervisors will gauge students' performance on these tasks before giving them more advanced or demanding assignments. If your work is sloppy and careless, there will be little reason to give you more responsibility or more complex assignments. Similarly, if you take too long or fail to complete your assignments, you will not be perceived as a resource or an asset to the agency, but as a liability.

In our experience, the amount of time allotted for supervisory conferences changes as the semester progresses. Generally, supervisors spend more time with students at the beginning of the placement than when students are past the first several weeks of orientation. Field instructors want to get students off to a good start and want to be sure that students understand agency policy and procedures. Once students are involved and doing well, supervisors may not be so deliberate or constant in monitoring how they are doing.

Set a specific time each week with your field instructor to ensure that supervision occurs.

Because students seem to do better when supervision is consistent and predictable, we recommend that you set a specific time each week with your field instructor to ensure that supervision occurs. If this detail was overlooked in your learning contract, do not let several weeks go by without at least one hour of supervision. Do not settle for five minutes here and ten minutes there. The quality of supervision provided on the run is not the same as when supervisor and student have time to think about what has been learned and what still needs to be learned.

HOW DO I MAKE SUPERVISION WORK FOR ME?

Getting the most out of supervision requires that you know what supervision is, what the dynamics of the supervisory relationship are, and what specific actions facilitate effective supervision.

Supervisors oversee the work of others. Supervisors administer and coordinate work; they provide consultation to help their supervisees perform more effectively and efficiently. Supervisors explain important agency policies and procedures, provide on-the-job training, assess performance, and make suggestions for improvement. In addition, supervisors participate in the hiring and firing of employees, mediate problems between their subordinates and the agency, and sometimes fill in for employees who are sick or absent. They are repositories of knowledge about the agency and the clientele. Above all else, supervisors are responsible for ensuring that clients are provided quality services.

Interesting dynamics are generated in the process of supervision. From the subordinate's perspective, some supervisors are not good teachers. They may not know how to correct gently or how to make a suggestion without it sounding like criticism. Unfortunately, these supervisors can hurt feelings without intending to do so. A former student once reported that her supervisor thought that she "had to be critical" or the student would not think she had a knowledgeable field instructor.

From the supervisor's perspective, some individuals clearly resent having a boss who tells them what to do. Supervisors have a difficult time overseeing individuals who are irritated at the very thought of having to account for their activities and who may find passive-aggressive ways to sabotage a supervisory relationship (e.g., showing up late for supervision or "forgetting" about a supervisory conference and scheduling a client at the same time).

Some nontraditional social work students have had managerial experience in other careers before deciding to become social workers. It may be difficult in such situations to accept the fact that, although they may be peers in age or in other life experiences, the student–field instructor relationship is not a peer or reciprocal relationship.

The time that you spend with your agency supervisor should be an opportunity for you to grow professionally, by availing yourself of the supervisor's practice experience and knowledge. If you are feeling overwhelmed or confused, supervisors can help you rank your tasks so that the most important ones are completed first. If you do not know how to do your assigned jobs, your supervisor can provide direction as to what to do, how to do it, and when to do it.

A good supervisor should help to reduce your anxiety and increase your sense of competence and self-worth by listening to you and demonstrating concern when you encounter difficulties. He or she should be a successful problem solver who follows through with commitments. Hopefully, your supervisor will tell you when you are doing something right, as well as explain when you are doing something unacceptable.

You can get the most out of your supervisory conferences by planning for them. Before a scheduled conference, write down a list of questions you have, problems you want to discuss, or observations you want to make. Be prepared to inform your agency supervisor what assignments you have accomplished and which assignments are nearing completion. Be able to account for how you have spent your time. If you are not being given enough to do, ask for new assignments or additional responsibilities.

Get the most out of your supervisory conferences by planning for them.

If you have a client who is making no progress or who is a difficult case, take advantage of the time with your agency supervisor to discuss possible solutions. There may be other ways to view the problem or alternative treatment strategies or resources—or the situation may be too complex for a student to handle. We all learn from our mistakes. Do not be afraid to be completely honest with your agency supervisor. For instance, assume that you unthinkingly used a poor choice of words that caused Mrs. Jones to storm off in anger. You feel that it is your fault and that the client may never return to the agency. By sharing this with your supervisor, you may learn that Mrs. Jones is irascible and in the past has stomped off in anger on the average of once a month or so. Instead of being worried (and maybe feeling guilty) about offending Mrs. Jones, sharing this information may help you to learn more about Mrs. Jones's personality and level of functioning.

Supervision can help you develop professionally—but only if you want to learn from it. Ask questions about things you want to know. Ask for articles or books that would help you to understand the cases you are handling. Be active in learning from your supervisor. Don't be shy in asking for help if you are having difficulty. Reflect on the feedback you have been given.

HOW WILL MY FACULTY FIELD LIAISON EVALUATE ME?

We cannot inform you of exactly what your faculty field liaison will personally expect of you. However, you can get some idea of these expectations from the syllabus and from the instructor's presentation at the first class meeting (or at the time you received your syllabus or field manual). This is the time to ask questions if you want to know more about how you will be evaluated.

On the basis of our own experiences supervising students in the field and our contacts with other faculty field liaisons, we can talk generally about what faculty field liaisons expect of students. To understand this perspective, you must keep in mind that although faculty field liaisons are concerned with what you are learning and your performance in the agency, they are at the disadvantage of not seeing very much (if any) of your work in the agency. Because they have the responsibility of assigning a grade to your efforts, they need feedback from your agency supervisor and evidence of your learning that they can collect from assignments. Some faculty field liaisons allow written assign-ments to carry more weight than evaluations from agency supervisors. These faculty field liaisons typically expect that all assignments will be completed on time, that any field logs or process recordings will be kept current, and that you show up for scheduled appointments to discuss the placement. If your grade is more dependent on written assignments than on agency input, then you may earn a lower grade than you think you deserve, even if you are doing superior work in the agency.

Grading schemes are often somewhat subjective. One faculty field liaison may let the course grade be largely determined by the agency supervisor's rec-ommendation; a second may weigh written assignments or case presentations more heavily; a third may penalize you for missing seminars or classes; and a fourth may pass everyone as long as no problems occurred in the agency. Your course syllabus should state specifically how your grade will be determined. Many programs use a pass/fail method that reduces the pressure and focus on a particular grade.

You can avoid failing or unsatisfactory grades, as a rule, by following the syllabus and using common sense. Beyond this, conventional wisdom would tell you to avoid asking for exceptions to existing policy or rules. The follow-ing true illustrations are provided to help you understand what faculty field liaisons *do not* want in their students.

> Nancy decided about halfway through the semester that she did not like her practicum supervisor. Without telling anyone, she went into the agency on a Sunday morning and cleaned out her desk. When she didn't show on Monday or Tuesday, the supervisor called the faculty field liai-son to see if Nancy was ill.

A more responsible student would have informed the faculty field liaison of perceived problems in the agency and would have allowed the faculty field liai-son time to investigate and work out a new field instructor, new responsibilities, or a new practicum.

> Susan missed the first three meetings of her required weekly practicum seminar. It was necessary, she said, because she needed to work and as a result had to schedule practicum clients at the same time as the seminar. She could not understand why her faculty field liaison was unhappy with her lack of attendance. "After all," she said, "the agency staff are pleased with me."

> Rob managed to delight agency staff with his good humor and ability to work with children, but somehow he never found time to write his logs or document the number of hours he spent in the agency. His paperwork for his faculty field liaison was late by several weeks on each occasion that it was due.

It is easy to see how some students will distinguish themselves as being conscientious "Excellent" students and others will fall short of that mark when faced with situations such as these. Neither agencies nor faculty field liaisons expect you to have supernatural abilities in order to succeed. Usually, success comes about through attention to details, such as completing assign-ments on time, conforming to the expectations of the syllabus, showing up when expected in the agency, displaying common courtesy, showing improvement in social work skills, and abiding by the code of ethics.

BOX 4.1 Wilson's List of 20 Professional/Personal Characteristics

Professional Responsibility

Poise and Self-Control

Assertiveness

Personal Appearance as Related to Agency Standards

Effectiveness in Planning and Arranging Work Responsibilities

Ability to Assume Responsibility for Own Learning

Ability to Work within the Purpose, Structure, and Constraints of the Agency and to Make Suggestions for Change in a Responsible Manner

Ability to Identify and Use Community Resources

Interviewing Skills, Including the Ability to Recognize and Interpret the Meaning of Nonverbal Communication

Written Communication Skills, Including the Ability to Record with Clarity and Promptness

Ability to Assess Situations Both Within and Outside the Client System and Determine Priorities

Ability to Develop and Maintain Professional Relationships with Consumers from Various Cultural, Ethnic, and Racial Backgrounds

Relationship with Coworkers (Other Students in the Agency as well as Agency Staff)

Relationship with Staff of Other Agencies

Demonstration of the Acceptance and Use of Basic Social Work Values, Ethics, and Principles

Effectiveness in Providing Services to Individuals and Families

Effectiveness in Providing Services to Small Groups

Effectiveness in Providing Services at the Community Level

Use of Supervision

Development of a Professional Self-Awareness, Including the Need for Continued Professional Growth

Some practicum instructors use an evaluation form devised by Wilson (1981). She lists 20 professional/personal characteristics on which a student can be evaluated using behavioral expectations. (See Box 4.1.) Consider, for example, the characteristic she calls "Professional Responsibility." Students can be measured on this behavior along a continuum. A student functioning at the "Excellent" level is "consistently responsible about all aspects of work and makes excellent use of time." A "Likely to Fail" student "appears bored with his or her work and puts self-interests first and has a pattern of tardiness and/or absenteeism."

Your faculty field liaison may use this or some other scheme to evaluate your performance in the agency. Urbanowski and Dwyer (1988), for instance, have conceptualized criteria for field practice performance that vary slightly depending on whether the student is a graduate or undergraduate, and if undergraduate, first or second semester. A sampling of these items is as follows:

First Semester Undergraduate

Functioning within the agency and community. The student begins to understand the structural components of the agency and has developed a good roster of social agency resources that would be helpful to clients.

Second Semester Undergraduate

Functioning within the agency and community. The student has comfort with the more commonly used policies and procedures and has the ability to interpret them clearly to clients and the community. The student organizes assignments so that maximum services are provided for all clients. The student shows concern about obvious community problems.

First Semester Graduate

Functioning within the agency and community. The student knows the structure and function of the agency and understands the administrative hierarchy and the process of decision making at the local agency level.

The student can make connections between the agency goals, policies, and procedures, and the services offered to clients. The student implements these services in accordance with the needs of the client and is aware of the inherent inequities in the overall social service system for special groups.

Second Semester Graduate

Functioning within the agency and community. The student assumes responsibility for continual learning about the agency and for creatively using the resources within it. The student has a solid knowledge of the operations of surrounding social systems and knows how to use these systems for the welfare of clients. The student is sensitive to the violation of clients' rights and explores action to remedy such situations.

Most programs develop their own forms to evaluate students in practicum. Field education directors may also borrow examples from other schools and revise them to their own liking. Although evaluation forms may vary in length and complexity, the great majority of them tap many of the same common dimensions.

HOW DO I JUGGLE ALL MY ROLES SIMULTANEOUSLY?

During the course of a semester, many students experience anxiety from having to juggle too many roles and demands simultaneously. Studies and family responsibilities may conflict with work obligations, often causing a no-win situation. Whatever obligations they choose to meet, these pressured students may feel stress or guilt from omitting other, equally important obligations.

What can you do to reduce the problems caused by role conflicts? A good starting place is to consider your priorities. For example, if you are a parent, you will probably decide that the needs of your children have to come first. Taking care of sick children, preparing their meals, and finding time for them are more important than getting all As. Likewise, you may have to let some household chores slide temporarily and give up certain community involvements so that you have adequate time to study. "Something is going to have to give," one married undergraduate said, "I just can't do everything that I used to."

People who are well organized find it easier to juggle the additional roles of being a student and a practicum intern. You can assess your own level of organization. You may be disorganized if you

- Have frequent feelings of being behind
- Procrastinate so long on an assignment that it becomes an emergency or a panic situation
- Miss a deadline
- Misplace necessities such as car keys or glasses
- Forget scheduled appointments or meetings
- Take more than ten minutes to unearth a particular letter, bill, or agency report from your files
- Are surprised at the end of most days by how little you have been able to accomplish

If you identify with two or more of these items, then you may need help in developing organizational skills. Three items are usually essential for better organization: a day-by-day calendar, a pocket-sized notebook, and a daily to-do list. Use the calendar to record all appointments, deadlines, and crucial events. In your notebook, jot down errands and tasks you need to do as they occur to you. Think about your long- and short-term goals. Write the things that must be done in order for you to accomplish your goals on your to-do list and on your calendar. The to-do list should be compiled every day and should contain no more than ten specific items. Prioritize the items so that the most important are completed first.

Here are a few other suggestions for getting the most out of the time available to you: Dedicate a few minutes each day to planning. When you think about tomorrow, prepare to do the most difficult tasks first and at a time when you will be free from interruptions and can concentrate most effectively. Recently, a student attending a social work convention asked the director of a large agency how he was able to supervise more than 80 employees. He replied that he came into the office at 6:30 every morning because he was able to get more paperwork and planning done between then and 8:30 than throughout the rest of the entire day. He purposefully looked for a quiet time in the agency and then put it to his best use.

Limit the number of outside activities that drain away your time while you are a student intern. Carefully consider requests being made of you. If you almost always say yes to additional projects or responsibilities outside the practicum, try imposing a temporary moratorium. If it is difficult to refuse new requests, then always try to say that you will think about the request and have an answer tomorrow. If you decide that it is not in your best interest to help, call and explain. Keep your response simple and to the point. Inform the other person that you would like to help but simply do not have the time.

Try to avoid insignificant activities that clutter your life and distract you—for example, watching soap operas or game shows on television while preparing for classes the next day.

Break large tasks into smaller segments. This will make the job seem much more manageable and will help you avoid procrastination. For instance, if you have a 20-page term paper to write, plan to go to the library on Sunday to gather your resources. Create the outline for your paper on Monday. On Tuesday, write the introduction to the paper, and continue in this way to divide up the major task.

One final thought about juggling many roles: This situation can be viewed negatively or positively. On one hand, it could be seen as an "impossible" situation destined to create difficulties. On the other hand, it could be seen as an opportunity to develop better organizational skills while engaged in learning how to be a social worker. Having many commitments can actually work to your advantage by structuring your time. One graduate student explained:

> When I have time available for studying, I don't waste a minute! I never put things off any more because I can't predict when one of my children might get sick or when my boss might ask me to work extra hours. Being a mother and an employee has actually helped me to prioritize my activities and to get the most out of the hours in my day.

Professional Identity

Critical Thinking Question: What improvements can you make to be more effective in your internship?

DO I NEED TO WORRY ABOUT MY PERSONAL SAFETY IN THE FIELD PRACTICUM?

Although social work is not as hazardous as coal mining, commercial fishing, or police work, the practice of social work is not entirely without risk. For example, removing a child when the parents are not cooperative can be a potentially harmful situation. Because of this, the police department is often contacted to assist when difficulty is expected. Restraining violent adolescents or adults and breaking up fights in residential group homes are two other examples where social workers could place themselves at risk.

Social work students are well advised to think about their personal safety at all times. You want to maintain a constant sense of "situational awareness," in other words, knowing what is in front of you, behind you, and beside you. You want to be prepared should something go wrong. Research (Knight, 1999; Rey, 1996) provides evidence that social work students *very much* need to be alert to the possibility that they or their property may be attacked or threatened. Be especially concerned and prepared to move to safety whenever a client becomes agitated or issues verbal warnings like, "Now you are really making me mad." While you shouldn't worry that every client is out to get you, it is good practice to always be prepared, should something go wrong; don't be naive and unprepared. Risk scans and risk assessments help social workers become more knowledgeable about the likelihood of potentially threatening situations.

WHAT IS A RISK OF HARM SCAN?

Social workers have a duty to assess the risk of harm for potential violence with every client they engage. Walker (1994) and his colleagues developed a "general risk of harm scan." The following are their cautions and risk scan rubric.

Even the most apparently harmless individuals can, under certain circumstances, become violent toward themselves or others. As social workers we cannot be expected to foresee all specific violent acts, but we are expected to gather information relative to an individual's risk for harm.

In first interviews, social workers should ask direct questions about three domains of risk: (1) self-harm, (2) harm to others, and (3) harm to self caused by others.

The following are *examples* of questions that might be asked when scanning for risk:

Self-harm
▶ Have you considered harming yourself? If so, how would you do this?
▶ Have you ever given thought to suicide? Are you thinking of it now?

Harm to others
▶ Have you injured others in the past? What happened?
▶ Have you found yourself thinking about harming others? In what ways?
▶ Do you lose your temper easily? What happens?

Harm to self inflicted by others
▶ Do you ever find yourself fearing injury or harm from someone? Why?
▶ Is anyone threatening to harm you?
▶ Have you ever been seriously injured by someone? How so?
▶ Do you feel unsafe in your home? In what way?

If the individual answers affirmatively to questions in one or more of the domains, the social worker should conduct a risk assessment. If the individual answers negatively to all domains, the risk scan should suffice. However, the social worker should always remain vigilant for the appearance of risk factors and may want to repeat the scan from time to time.

WHAT ARE RISK ASSESSMENTS?

Walker and his collaborators (1994) also developed risk assessments for domestic violence, addiction, and mental health. Here they offer advice and a rubric for assessing potential domestic violence perpetrators.

Risk assessments delve deeper into clients' backgrounds to try and understand their propensity for violence. Social workers study contextual, life history, dispositional, and clinical factors. For example, in the area of domestic violence, contextual factors could include a client's belief that his or her partner is involved with another person.

Perpetrators have a higher risk status for violence when they:

▶ believe their partner is involved with another person, have guns readily available, experience significant economic hardship or perceive injury to their self-esteem (contextual factors). Lethality is at its zenith when the recipient of violence leaves the perpetrator through separation, divorce, or to live with someone else (the most significant contextual factor);

▶ have lengthy histories of violence and aggression; have childhood experience of physical, sexual, and emotional abuse; or are a witness to domestic violence in childhood (life history factors);

▶ have an angry hostile disposition, a significant marker for harm to self and others, (dispositional factors) include being very controlling, not attached to others, being suspicious and jealous; and

▶ use substances, (do not have to be dependent or abusing a substance of choice), have a brain injury, experience mood variations, exhibit personality disorders (*clinical features*).

Some risk mitigating factors for the perpetrator:

▶ Desire to avoid negative consequences such as arrest, protective order, or incarceration

▶ Willingness to participate in any treatment program that might be indicated

▶ Empathy for others

▶ Belief that violence to others is wrong

Engage, Assess, Intervene, Evaluate

Critical Thinking Question: How can you help a client experiencing severe stress to address the problem?

HOW DO I MANAGE ANGRY AND HOSTILE CLIENTS?

Despite much education and training, social workers sometimes find themselves confronted with angry and potentially dangerous clients. Although it is not pleasant to think about, an irate client may verbally abuse you, curse and shout, threaten you with harm, or even assault. Do not be naive and think that because you want to help others, clients will always be polite, compliant, and appreciative. They will not. Some clients have poor impulse control and lack anger management skills. Involuntary clients may resent being involved with a social service agency. Others will be impaired by alcohol or drug use. The best protection you can have is to anticipate what *might* or could happen in any situation—and plan accordingly.

First, try your best to stay calm and composed. Remind yourself that the client's anger may be natural and understandable given the situation. The client may have strong feelings of injustice. The system may have been too impersonal, bureaucratic, or inflexible. Because you represent the system to the client, he or she may be taking advantage of finding a sympathetic ear to unload anger and frustrations that have been building over time.

Second, Hepworth, Rooney, Rooney, Strom-Gottfried, and Larsen (2006) suggest that it is extremely important to address a client's anger and complaints. As much as possible, try to be empathic and understanding. Allow these clients to talk and explain why they are so angry. Speak in a soft voice and move slowly. Encourage the client to sit; If he or she does not, you should remain standing. Do not position yourself in a corner or behind furniture where it would be difficult to escape if necessary.

Third, do not reflect back anger you may feel. This will help you better influence the client's behavior positively. More than likely, the client will watch how you react, so you need to be aware of how your actions could be interpreted. If the client is agitated, use the same techniques you would use for a nervous client; for instance, ask if you can get the client a cup of coffee or something to drink. Trust your intuition. If you sense that you are in danger of being hurt, get out of the situation as quickly and coolly as possible. Say that you need a drink of water, or that you have to check on something—then leave the room and seek help.

Do not take risks that will jeopardize your personal safety.

Above all else, do not take risks that will jeopardize your personal safety. If your intuition tells you that a situation is dangerous, do not plow headstrong into it because you don't want to be embarrassed that you couldn't handle it. Always seek help when you sense that your safety or that of others is in danger. Discuss with your field instructor and other staff members your apprehensions and ways to handle difficult situations. Such conversations may allay your fears and give you suggestions for ensuring your safety.

WHAT OTHER PRECAUTIONS CAN I TAKE?

The best protection is to anticipate what *might* or could happen in any situation where there is potential for violence—and plan accordingly.

Additionally, we suggest following:

a. Learn the agency's established procedures for dealing with violent situations. For example, one agency has workers call the front desk and ask for "the blue folder" when they feel threatened and want another person to come to their office. Workers request "the red folder" when they want everyone to come to their office and they also want the police called.

b. If no safety procedures exist, talk with your field instructor about developing guidelines.

c. Find out whom you should contact when you need emergency help. Have important phone numbers (e.g., security) in a prominent place beside the phone.

  d. Take advantage of the informal communication system within the agency to learn which clients are known to be violent and the best approach for handling them.

  e. Be aware of conditions in the agency, such as long waiting periods, that might be conducive to frustration and anger. Do what you can to improve these conditions.

  f. Make sure the office furniture is arranged so that it is easy to escape if an assault is imminent; avoid having the client sit between you and the door.

  g. Be aware that jewelry such as large, dangling earrings and necklaces, and other items of clothing (scarves and ties) can be easily grabbed and used to choke or pull you.

Finally, the importance of maintaining a constant sense of "situational awareness" and planning ahead cannot be emphasized enough. Preparation and prevention is the best protection.

WHAT SHOULD I KEEP IN MIND WHEN MAKING A HOME VISIT?

Social workers make home visits for many reasons. Whether student interns are observing, visiting a client with another staff person, or conducting their own home visit, they should be clear about the purpose of the visit. The purpose determines how the home visit is arranged, what content is covered during the interview, and what things are to be observed.

Many home visits are conducted to *investigate possible cases of abuse or neglect.* After a complaint is issued, social workers go out as quickly as possible. Because they want to see exactly what is happening in the home, in as natural a setting as possible, they may not call ahead. Ideally on an initial investigation, two social workers (or one social worker and a police officer if the situation seems volatile) would visit. When going into unknown situations, an inherent element of danger exists and two persons together provide greater safety. Additionally, two workers can gather more information than a single social worker. They can divide their effort so that, for example, one speaks to a parent while the other talks to the children. This arrangement allows for less manipulation by the client. Going into a different room or part of the house also allows greater opportunity to observe ventilation, heating, sanitation, and safety hazards within the home.

Clients being visited are often frightened and intimidated and will perceive you as an authority figure. Clients may be angry about allegations made against them. Although you can be empathic about their feelings, you are required to explain your job clearly. Try not to be threatening, as you need to lay the groundwork for potential future social work intervention.

Here are additional suggestions for safety when visiting a home: Know where you are going; have a map handy; keep your car full of gas and in good repair; lock your car doors; have a cell phone with you; and let someone at your agency know that you are leaving and when you expect to return. Furthermore, upon arrival at the home, park in a visible place, not on a side street; be aware of your surroundings and act like you know what you are doing; have everything organized and carry as little as possible into the home; never have both arms full. Examine the house or apartment from the outside; do not go inside if you feel in any way that it is a potentially dangerous situation. Trust your intuition. Once inside, know where the exits are; do not go into the kitchen where many things lie that could hurt you; stand if the client stands. If at any time you feel threatened, leave immediately. Always have an excuse in mind, "Oops, I forgot about a dental appointment! I'll have to be in touch later." Do not feel guilty; protect yourself.

If the *purpose of the home visit is to offer assistance,* then it is almost always best to call ahead and ask clients when you may visit. This enables more efficient use of your time—you will be less likely to find no one at home. Giving notice also conveys an attitude of respect for the client's privacy and recognition that the client's time is important and should not be inconveniently interrupted. Many people do not enjoy it when others just show up on their doorstep—particularly people they do not know well. Another advantage of informing these clients ahead of time is that they can gather any necessary papers or documents.

As you enter a home, engage in small talk for a few minutes until you and the client have a chance to relax. You can thank the client for his or her directions, mention something you saw as you drove or walked to the client's house, or comment on objects you see in the home—photographs of family members, homemade articles, collections that might indicate hobbies, or books or magazines being read.

One of the main advantages of making a home visit is that you can gain a much better understanding of how an individual or a family functions on a daily basis. In a short amount of time you can observe interactions among family members, assess the family's resources, and begin to understand what a day in the life of your client is like.

Almost all students are nervous the first time they make a home visit. With experience, they will feel more and more at ease. One child protection worker recounted his first home visit as follows:

> I felt like a child playing a grown-up's game. How was I going to pull this one off? I remember being so nervous. I walked into the client's home, pulled out a notebook with a long list of questions, and in a very stiff manner began my interrogation. I scarcely lifted my head up to hear the answers. Now, several years later, when I run into my former client we always laugh about that first meeting. She, too, remembers being extremely nervous, so much so that she never realized how uncomfortable I was!

Plan on taking 45–60 minutes at the house. If you know you will want to return, ask when you can come back. Whether you take someone with you on a subsequent visit depends on how the first visit went.

HOW DO I KNOW IF I'M STRESSED OUT?

Despite good organizational skills, planning, and wise use of available time, most students occasionally experience high stress. Individuals react uniquely to stress, but here are some common symptoms:

- Inability to sleep
- Irritability
- Feeling pressured or "smothered"

To avoid stress, prioritze
your tasks and plan.

▶ Headaches and stomachaches
▶ Weight loss or gain
▶ Being tearful or more emotional
▶ Being unable to concentrate or focus on a task

HOW CAN I EFFECTIVELY MANAGE
THE STRESS IN MY LIFE?

Stress is not all bad. It can motivate you to get things done. However, too much stress can immobilize you. When you sense you are approaching the limits of your ability to handle the stresses in your life, think about how you relax. What helps you deal with stress? Here are some common ways to reduce daily stress:

▶ Prioritize—new demands may have to wait
▶ Exercise (even walking)

> ♦ Do something enjoyable (go to a movie, start a novel, garden, or engage in a favorite hobby)
> ♦ Talk with a close friend
> ♦ Play a musical instrument or listen to music
> ♦ Take a short nap
> ♦ Do deep-breathing or relaxation exercises
> ♦ Examine any recurrent thoughts for irrational, perfectionistic beliefs
> ♦ Make a plan
> ♦ Enlist some help
> ♦ Try to find some humor in your situation
> ♦ Reframe and look for the positives

If you are feeling highly stressed, bring the subject up in your seminar and see if other students are feeling the same way. You may be surprised to learn that others are feeling just as stressed as you are. This group can serve in some ways as a support group for you. Also, it may assist you by suggesting resources or providing information that could help with a problematic client or situation. If, however, you have followed just about all of the suggestions provided here and you still have such a high level of stress that it is presenting problems for you, then it is time to seek a competent professional for assistance. Your field instructor or faculty field liaison may suggest that you contact your university counseling center, or he or she may suggest professionals in the community.

Research Based Practice

Critical Thinking Question:
What research-based information on making risk assessments informs your practice?

THE STUDENT INTERN'S "BILL OF RIGHTS"

Sometimes when you are new to a situation it is hard to know whether your experiences are unique or similar to the experiences of others. Being a student intern differs from being a student in the classroom, and the newness of the internship experience and the responsibilities given to you may be almost overwhelming at times. If you are feeling this way, you may not be getting enough supervision from your field instructor. To give you some basis for reality checking, Munson (1987) has drafted a set of rights to which practicum students are entitled:

1. The right to a field instructor who supervises them consistently at regularly designated times.
2. The right to a sufficient number and variety of cases to ensure learning.
3. The right to growth-oriented, as well as technical and theoretical, learning that is stable in its expectations.
4. The right to clear criteria for performance evaluation.
5. The right to a field instructor who is adequately trained and skilled in supervision. (pp. 105–106)

If you feel that your "rights" are being overlooked or violated, discuss this matter with your faculty field liaison. On many occasions, faculty intervention can help to clarify responsibilities and smooth things out. And when necessary, it is the faculty field liaison's role to advocate for a student and to ensure that the student is not being mistreated, being given poor supervision, or ignored. Do not be afraid to consult with your faculty field liaison when your intuition or best judgment tells you that things are not right with your supervision or treatment in the agency. In the event that your faculty field liaison is the problem, discuss your difficulties with your academic adviser, the field education director, or academic head of your social work program.

MYTHS I CAN DO WITHOUT

One of the refreshing aspects of working with students is their idealism. There's something quite wonderful about the energy and enthusiasm that students bring, their interest in trying to make the world a better place. However, the "School of Hard Knocks" sometimes forces students to adjust erroneous assumptions after a painful lesson. We've listed some myths that we've discarded over our careers. You might want to do a little self-examination to see if you, too, might be stereotyping or over-idealizing—it just might save you some disappointment and grief.

Nine statements that are *not* realistic:

- All social workers love their jobs
- All social workers are conscientious, ethical, trustworthy individuals
- Social workers always do what is in the client's best interest
- Organizations are always concerned about waste, inefficiency, or inept, marginally productive employees
- Clients will always like you
- Clients will keep most, if not all, of their appointments
- Every problem can be solved
- The primary responsibility for solving clients' problems rests only in your hands
- Every client wants to get better

This is not to say that social work is a career filled with unprincipled professionals or that clients won't astound you with their courage as they battle to change their lives and improve conditions for their children and loved ones. However, don't fall into the snare of romanticizing clients or expecting all social workers to be paragons of virtue. If you are lucky, you will find one or more mentors, solid, competent social workers, who will, by their example and instruction, help you form reasonable and sensible expectations about those with whom you will be working.

SUMMARY

Whether you are a new employee or a new student just beginning in an unfamiliar agency, you will likely have questions about the expectations others will have of you. This chapter examined the new role of being a student in a professional setting and answered questions related to making use of supervision, being evaluated, and handling the stress of juggling multiple roles.

Role of a Student in an Agency

1. Students play vital and unique roles in social service settings. What tasks/activities have you been assigned to date? Check those listed here, and add to the list under the category "other." I'm expected to:

_____ read policies and procedures manual(s)

_____ carry a caseload

_____ research problem areas relative to particular cases, for example, Alzheimer's disease

_____ help with client assessments

_____ attend case conferences

_____ attend staff meetings

_____ accompany staff on home visits

_____ observe group sessions

_____ observe family therapy sessions

_____ attend particular types of sessions, for example, termination with a client

_____ assist with a research project

_____ assist with an evaluation project

_____ update the agency resource directory

_____ visit some of the agency's community resources

_____ attend task force meetings

_____ attend coalition meetings

_____ participate in community planning meetings

_____ help conduct a needs assessment

_____ participate in special community projects, for example, a fund-raising activity

_____ interview agency staff

_____ complete agency paperwork

_____ other

_____

_____

_____

_____

2. List the tasks volunteers complete at your agency.

a. _____

b. _____

c. _____

d. _____

e. _____

3. How do volunteer tasks differ from those engaged in by students? What do volunteers do that students do not do? What do students do that volunteers do not do?

Volunteers: _____

_____

_____

_____

Students: _____

_____

_____

_____

4. What tasks or activities are students *not* allowed to do in their first internship at the agency?

_____

_____

_____

Supervision Sessions

Supervisors oversee the work of others and provide consultation to help others perform their work responsibilities more effectively and efficiently. Ideally, you will have one-hour weekly supervisory meetings.

Each supervisory meeting will cover routine topics as well as particular subjects relevant to your current week's work. Check which topics were covered in your last supervisory session, and then describe issues you brought up and issues brought up by your supervisor.

1. Indicate the topics covered in your last supervisory session:

_____ agency policy(ies)

_____ tasks completed

_____ agency procedures

_____ problem-solving methods

_____ my strengths

_____ an area(s) I need to work on

_____ my supervisor's area(s) of expertise

_____ skill demonstration(s) by my supervisor

_____ an ethical dilemma

_____ a mistake I made

_____ books/articles I need to read

2. Questions I asked of my supervisor:

_____

_____

_____

3. Issues brought up by my supervisor:

_____

_____

_____

Preparation for the Next Supervision Session

1. Topics I'd like to be covered in my next supervisory session:

   a. _____

   b. _____

   c. _____

2. Questions I will ask in my next supervisory session:

   a. _____

   b. _____

   c. _____

3. Tasks well done and/or strengths that I will discuss in my next supervisory session:

   a. _____

   b. _____

   c. _____

4. Problems I will address in my next supervisory session:

   a. _____

   b. _____

   c. _____

5. Things I'd still like to learn:

   a. _____

   b. _____

   c. _____

Field Liaison Evaluation Criteria

1. Check the components that your faculty field liaison will use to determine the grade you will earn in your field course. To the right of these, indicate what percentage of your grade will depend on that variable. (Note: If the course syllabus is unclear as to expectations for your grade, ask your professor what the criteria will be.)

   a. _____ written assignments   _____ percentage

   _____ field logs   _____ percentage

   _____ process recordings   _____ percentage

   _____ other   _____ percentage

   b. _____ agency supervisor's evaluation   _____ percentage

   c. _____ seminar participation   _____ percentage

   d. _____ case presentation(s)   _____ percentage

   e. _____ other syllabus expectations   _____ percentage

   _____

   _____

2. Check the criteria your agency supervisor, faculty field liaison, and/or you will use to determine how effective you have been in your agency setting this semester.

   _____ attendance

   _____ completion of a learning contract

   _____ professional appearance

   _____ use of supervision

   _____ ability to engage in self-directed learning

   _____ effectiveness in planning work responsibilities

   _____ ability to work within the constraints of the agency setting

   _____ ability to identify community resources

   _____ ability to use community resources

   _____ problem-solving skills

   _____ performance in social work roles (e.g., advocate, case manager, counselor)

   _____ ability to empathize

   _____ interviewing skills

   _____ ability to interpret the meaning of nonverbal communication

   _____ written communication skills

   _____ professional relationship skills with coworkers

   _____ professional relationship skills with clients

_____ acceptance and use of basic social work values

_____ awareness of personal values

_____ respect for client self-determination

_____ ability to maintain client confidentiality

_____ demonstration of respect for all clients and coworkers

_____ other _____

Managing Stress

Almost all field students experience stress at some point in an academic semester.

1. How do you know when you are stressed? Describe symptoms you have when you experience stress.

   _____

   _____

   _____

2. List at least three things you can do when you feel stressed.

   a. _____

   b. _____

   c. _____

3. Write a self-care plan to keep balance and prevent stress. What are some preventive things you can do each day or week?

   _____

   _____

   _____

Succeed with PEARSON mysocialworklab

Log onto **www.mysocialworklab.com** to access a wealth of case studies, videos, and assessment. (*If you did not receive an access code to* **MySocialWorkLab** *with this text and wish to purchase access online, please visit* www.mysocialworklab.com.)

1. **Read the MySocialWorkLibrary case study: "Dan."**
   In this case Dan is abandoned by both his abusive biological father and a mother who would withhold food from him for as long as two days as a child and punish him physically and emotionally. Given that social workers intervene to help their clients resolve problems, which gender do you think might work best with Dan on this issue and why?

2. **Watch the Core Competency video: "Intervention."**
   The client, Ms. Davis, seems to have established a good working relationship with the social worker. But what if she had been a difficult, noncompliant, argumentative client? How would you manage such a client?

PRACTICE TEST
The following questions will test your knowledge of the content found within this chapter.

1. What would be the best course of action if you experience role conflicts from having too many competing roles?
   a. Clean out my desk and start again next term.
   b. Consider my priorities.
   c. Give myself additional time to complete responsibilities.
   d. Skip meetings and appointments when necessary.

2. If a fellow student is overly stressed, you might expect all of these symptoms *except*
   a. Being tearful or more emotional
   b. Heightened sense of concentration
   c. Irritability
   d. Weight loss or gain

3. What does research show about social workers' need to have "situational awareness?"
   a. Supervisors always take care of this for you.
   b. Electronic calendars and organizers are a great help.
   c. Social work students need to be alert to threats or attacks.
   d. Students who know self-defense are more likely to get hurt.

4. When on a home visit, it is a good practice to
   a. Immediately state the possible charges or complaint
   b. Immediately inform the client that he or she might be arrested
   c. Put the client at ease by describing your student status
   d. Engage in small talk for a few minutes

Short Answer Question:

Maria has been assigned a home visit where the partner of the client has previously been arrested for domestic violence. She's a little worried about going alone. How should she handle this situation?

ASSESS YOUR COMPETENCE
Use the scale below to rate your current level of achievement on the following concepts or skills associated with each competency practice behavior presented in the chapter:

1	2	3
I can accurately describe the concept or skill.	I can consistently identify the concept or skill when observing and analyzing practice activities.	I can competently implement the concept or skill in my own practice.

_____ Although I may have many roles, I know how to manage them.

_____ Use my knowledge to help a client reduce the stress in his or her life.

_____ Obtain information needed to conduct risk assessments with clients.

Answers

Key: 1) b, 2) b, 3) c, 4) d

5

Contexts in Which
Social Workers Operate

Core Competencies in This Chapter (Check marks indicate which competencies are covered in depth)									
☐	Professional Identity	✓	Ethical Practice	☐	Critical Thinking	☐	Diversity in Practice	✓	Human Rights & Justice
☐	Research-Based Practice	☐	Human Behavior	☐	Policy Practice	✓	Practice Contexts	☐	Engage, Assess, Intervene, Evaluate

OVERVIEW

Every professional faces boundary issues from time to time. Boundaries are limitations on our activities. Like fences, they are there to protect and maintain. They may be laws regarding proper conduct, local agency policy, or even ethical mandates. Within some settings, certain procedures or practices may have developed over the years. Occasionally, we run into boundaries that we don't like. Because boundaries are not always apparent, we may not even know that there is a boundary issue until a supervisor, an instructor, or a peer points out a problem. This chapter will familiarize the student with boundaries that arise when working in an agency and provide guidance on how to behave as a professional.

WHAT ARE THE DIFFERENCES AMONG VOLUNTEER, STUDENT, AND EMPLOYEE ROLES?

Every day, each of us assumes many roles. For instance, our behavior may reflect our status as a son or daughter, mother or father, student, employee, or volunteer. Social service agencies differ in how they view student interns, and their understanding of the internship role will determine what students will be given to do, the amount of supervision they will receive, and how their performance will be evaluated. Your own educational experience will be enriched by a clear understanding of the differences among the volunteer, student, and employee roles.

Depending on the agency, the differences between a volunteer and a student intern may be barely perceptible. For instance, both volunteer counselors and student interns at a rape crisis center may have to complete 40 hours of training and orientation before they have any client contact. In other settings, such as a hospital, volunteers have very different responsibilities from those of student interns.

Although students and volunteers might at times be given similar tasks, students have the additional responsibility of learning why a task was done, why it was done the way it was, and how that task relates to the larger picture of planned intervention. Being a student involves thinking, analyzing, and reflecting, as well as doing. Students are expected to see the connection between assessment, planning, and intervention. They should feel that they may ask questions and ask for reference material in areas where they have little knowledge, and should be given the opportunity to observe and practice new skills.

Volunteers tend to be given mundane chores (e.g., addressing envelopes or answering telephone calls) because they are seen as just "helping out." Such volunteer assignments generally do not require close supervision. Although you as a student may be given some of the same responsibilities as volunteers, these should make up only a small portion of your time in the practicum. If you find that the bulk of your practicum time is filled with tedious chores that do not allow you to grow intellectually as a social worker, your agency may view you more as a volunteer than as a student.

As an intern, you ought to be working with clients, families, and groups directly (unless you are in certain administrative or research placements).

You should have questions about what you are doing. Similarly, your field instructor should be interested in how you are doing and should want to know about the progress of your cases. Your direct, private supervision should be no less than one or two hours a week and should include suggestions from the field instructor regarding other approaches, strategies, and theories, perhaps including information about how the field instructor handled a similar situation (more on how to make the best use of supervision in Chapter 4).

Unlike volunteers, who may work as much or little as pleases them, students must spend a specified number of practicum hours in their assigned agencies. Both volunteers and students need their supervisors to agree to their proposed schedules before starting in the agency. Sometimes days and hours are negotiated—one day might be more convenient than another. This contrasts rather markedly with the employee who is told the days and exact hours to work. Employees may be given little choice in tasks or responsibilities to perform. Agencies expect more from employees than from students or volunteers in productivity and knowledge about their jobs. But then, of course, employees are generally rewarded financially for their trials and tribulations.

In some situations, clients accept volunteers more easily than they do students. One undergraduate volunteering in a mental hospital explained:

> The patients were more accepting of me when I was a volunteer because they believed I came to the hospital not because I had to, but because I cared and wanted to be with them. They saw students as being interested in them as subjects for research rather than as individual human beings.

Students placed in residential facilities may find that residents resent students who come into their lives and then leave abruptly at the end of the academic term.

Unlike employees and students, volunteers are seldom evaluated. Generally speaking, there are never enough volunteers in agencies, and even inept volunteers are often tolerated. Volunteers may be informed that their services

Ethical Practice

Critical Thinking Question: Why is it considered a moral duty of social workers to provide evidence-based practice?

Where Boundaries Are Likely to Be Found	
At the **agency** level	Is it a public or private agency? To whom is the agency accountable? How are services funded? What is its history, philosophy, and mission? How is it structurally organized? How important is it to keep good records?
At the **program** level	Are certain programs selective—choosing their participants from the larger client pool? Does participation in one program preclude participation in others?
At the **client** level	Who is eligible to be a client? What are the expectations of proper client behavior? How do clients typically interact with staff? What kind of demands can clients make on staff? When are clients referred?
At the **staff** level	Do some staff have more clout or more privileges than others? What informal rules exist regarding staff behavior toward clients? What is considered unethical behavior? Who supervises whom? How important is it to be accountable for one's time?

are no longer needed if they are unreliable (e.g., they do not show up on the days expected or do not accomplish assigned tasks). Students, on the other hand, are usually formally evaluated at the midpoint and toward the end of their academic terms. Social work students' experience in the practicum is guided (and to some degree regulated) by their learning contracts, which specify educational goals and objectives. Faculty field liaisons ensure that meaningful learning is occurring and help troubleshoot any problems that develop.

Students sometimes feel that they are being treated as free labor. For instance, one student complained bitterly when she was asked (in a residential setting) to help with some of the housekeeping chores. However, all of the paid staff were expected to perform certain menial chores to keep the facility clean and neat. The student was not being asked to do anything that staff members themselves did not do. However, students should be concerned when most assignments seem to be unrelated to professional responsibilities. If you think that you are being unjustly treated because you are a student, then you have a legitimate complaint that you should share with your field instructor. On the other hand, if you are being assigned an unpleasant chore or responsibility that other staff members also perform or take turns doing, you probably have little reason to complain.

Case Example

Jim shows up for the first day of his practicum and discovers that the agency is closed to clients. The whole agency is in a retreat because of a recent reorganization. He finds his field instructor, who invites him to accompany her to a series of staff meetings. At times the discussion becomes heated. Junior staff members disagree with their supervisors. Jim does not think that this is proper and by noon is beginning to wonder if he has made a mistake in selecting this agency. By 3:00 P.M., however, things seem to have smoothed out, and a genuine sense of camaraderie is evident. In fact, staff members have decided to come into the agency on Saturday, on their own time, to have a clean-up, fix-up day. Because their maintenance and improvement budget has been severely cut over the past three years, they intend to paint several offices on their own and to wash windows both inside and out.

Questions

1. Should Jim also volunteer to work on Saturday?
2. What would be the advantages of getting to know the staff members on an informal basis?
3. What if Jim already had plans to go out of town?
4. Should he feel that it is beneath his dignity to wash windows or paint?

WHAT DO I NEED TO KNOW ABOUT INTERDISCIPLINARY TEAM MEETINGS?

Many students will have the opportunity to participate on interdisciplinary teams often found in hospitals, nursing homes, schools, rehabilitation centers, and prisons. As a rule, the student's role initially will be that of observer until the student has a case to present or is asked to become more involved by the field instructor or other team members. This will usually happen after the student has had occasion to work with or observe clients being discussed by the team.

*Team members share
a common purpose
when they pool their
knowledge, ideas, and
plans.*

The persons who make up interdisciplinary teams have their particular expertise and responsibilities. Team members share a common purpose as they meet to pool knowledge, ideas, and plans for intervention. Interdisciplinary teams offer a framework within which specialists can work together to provide services for the whole client.

Students need to understand the overall purpose of a particular team, who makes up the team, how membership is decided, and its agreed goals. The goals determine how often the team members will meet and how they will reach and implement decisions. It is also helpful to know the backgrounds of the individual team members and their philosophies, roles, and attitudes. The pooling of members' unique perspectives allows for consideration of the problem from many different angles. These points of view justify each person's inclusion on the team.

If you are expected to be an active team member rather than an observer, do not be intimidated. You may have information not acquired by other professionals or a better relationship with the client that has allowed new information to sift out. Especially if you have had an opportunity to see the client in a different capacity (e.g., with other clients or family members), your insights will be valued.

When you are not speaking, listen carefully to what each person is saying. Come prepared and be familiar with the cases that are to be discussed. Facilitate communication, provide information useful for problem solving, and see that arrangements are made for any needed coordination of services. Note that agencies usually schedule a particular day a week certain days a month for their staff meetings. You will usually be expected to arrange your schedule so that you can attend these meetings.

CAN A FRIEND SUPERVISE ME?

Occasionally a student will discover that a friend has obtained a position in an agency and would be willing to provide supervision. As a rule, students should avoid seeking placements where friends, neighbors, family members, or others who might be less than objective would be the supervisor. Asking someone with whom you have a close relationship to supervise you likely would not be approved by your faculty field liaison and could get you into trouble if discovered later. For you to optimize your learning and grow professionally, it is necessary that your agency supervisor's objectivity not be impaired.

SHOULD I CONTRACT WITH CLIENTS?

We believe that students are generally well advised to contract with their clients. Before we share some ideas about developing effective contracts with clients, however, we want to briefly discuss the concept of contract and its importance in social work practice.

The *Social Work Dictionary* (third edition) defines a *contract* as a "written, oral, or implied agreement between the client and the social worker as to the goals, methods, timetables, and mutual obligations to be fulfilled during the intervention process." A contract ensures accountability for all parties in performing the tasks essential for the agreed goals. Contracts are not always written; however, more and more social service agencies are moving in that direction.

The importance of a contract with a client follows from basic social work values, particularly the client's right to self-determination. Social work is not something done to clients; it is conducted with their cooperative efforts. Clients are expected to identify and rate the priority of their needs. Unless incapacitated, they are in the best position to determine what will be helpful to them (i.e., what courses of action to pursue) and when their needs have been met. Goals cannot be chosen for clients; they result from discussion, clarification, and other social work processes. During the course of intervention, a contract helps both social worker and client stay focused on the purpose of their work together. In addition to stating the agreed goals, the contract specifies the activities or interventions to be used, their frequency, any fees, and other agreements.

The essentials for developing contracts—discussed in Chapter 3—were derived from the SPIRO model (Pfeiffer & Jones, 1972)—which suggests (1) that *specific* goals be written, (2) that these goals be *performance* oriented, (3) that the *involvement* (roles) of the respective parties be stated, (4) that goals be *realistic* (feasible), and (5) that the results of your efforts be *observable* (measurable).

Contracting entails much more than we can tell you in this brief section. (If you need more information on the topic, you are encouraged to consult Hepworth, Rooney, & Larsen, 2002; or Sheafor, Horejsi, & Horejsi, 2000.)

WHAT DO I NEED TO KNOW ABOUT AGENCY RECORDING?

Recording is an essential part of social work practice. The profession has always emphasized recording for two important reasons. First, it is assumed that there is an essential connection between good recording and the effectiveness of service. Second, recording is required in all types of practice in varied fields and settings. Its importance has been aptly explained by Siporin (1975): "The recording registers significant facts, evidence, judgments, and decisions about the people, problems and situations involved; it defines the reality of the helping situation and experience; presents the quantity and quality of service; and describes and explains the course of helping action" (p. 332).

Recording in social work may take many forms, from process recording—which involves a detailed narrative of all that happened during a client contact—to summary recording and the use of face sheets (intake or admission forms), agency documents, and reports of various kinds. Kagle (1984) has succinctly identified multiple ways that social service records can be used: to assess client and community needs; document services received and the continuity of care; communicate with others providing services to the client; supervise, consult, and educate students and workers; share information with the client; evaluate the process, quality, and impact of service; make administrative decisions; and do research.

Field instructors will orient their student interns to the recording requirements of their agencies and will help students learn how to fill out the various forms according to the breadth and depth of specificity required. Record keeping can also be a valuable tool in students' own professional growth. Although it would be impossible to prepare students for every type of form that they will encounter on entering a practicum, we can share some general guidelines to help with agency recording.

First of all, keep in mind that the agency record is an official document. It is a permanent register that, while usually confidential, can be subpoenaed as legal evidence. This official record often includes highly personal anecdotes from clients' lives. Kagle (1984) observes, "The client's obligation to share personal information is predicated upon a reciprocal obligation on the part of the social worker and the organization—the obligation not to reveal this information except in specified, socially valued circumstances" (p. 116). This ethical duty is also a legal responsibility. Because of the sensitive nature of this material, confidentiality cannot be stressed enough.

Hepworth, Rooney, and Larsen (2002) provide several general guidelines for maximizing the confidentiality of agency records:

1. Record no more detail than is essential to the function of the agency.
2. Describe clients' problems in professional and general terms. Do not incorporate details of intimate matters except where necessary (e.g., a child's description of sexual abuse).
3. Do not include verbatim or process recordings in case files.
4. Do not remove case files from the agency except under extraordinary circumstances and then only with authorization.
5. Do not leave case files open on the desk or out in the open where they might be read by other clients or unauthorized personnel.
6. Keep case records in locked files. Use security features to protect data stored on your computer.

If you are in doubt about the level of detail to include, discuss this matter with your field instructor. In some agencies, staff members may keep personal notes that are not a part of the official files. Your field instructor or faculty field liaison may even require you to keep a journal of your practicum experiences. Many agencies, however, discourage personal notebooks because of the risk that highly sensitive material as well as agency files could be misplaced, lost, or not safeguarded. Also, be advised that if you keep personal notes, these could be subpoenaed should your client be involved with or involve your agency in a legal suit. Therefore, if you want to keep a notebook, discuss this matter with your field instructor.

If you are permitted to keep personal notes, you may want to enter in them significant pieces of information about your clients and your impressions, analyses, or hunches. Because such notes could contain ideas or insights that are speculative and inappropriate for the official record, do not allow anyone else access to them, and do not keep them longer than absolutely necessary. Also, be sure not to use clients' full names, addresses, or other information that could personally identify them should you lose or misplace your personal notes.

There is much more to recording and, more specifically, to writing up a summary statement of an interview or assessment. *Summary records* are abstracts of a client's problem, the services provided to the client, and the client's progress. Agency policy specifies the form and content of such records. Because summary records may be subject to review by a number of people, it is usually good practice to include in them only that which is required and verifiable.

Many agencies rely on the problem-oriented record as a conceptual framework for cataloging essential information. Typically, staff members report both objective and subjective information as well as an assessment and treatment plan for the client. If your agency uses a problem-oriented approach, it is reasonable to expect that this process will be amply explained. However, if you need more explanation of this type of record keeping, please refer to Appendix A. Because of its special educational value, we will discuss process recording separately.

HOW DO I REFER A CLIENT TO ANOTHER AGENCY OR PROFESSIONAL?

As professionals, social workers' commitment to clients demands that we make the best possible match between their needs and the resources most likely to help. A *referral* is the linking of a client with an agency, program, or individual professional who can provide a needed service. A referral to an outside resource may be made at the time of intake, at any time during the ongoing work with a client or, often, while terminating service with a client.

Many reasons necessitate making a referral. You might identify, for instance, the need for a diagnostic service or consultation to assist with the intervention you will be providing to the client. On other occasions, the referral may demand a collaborative working relationship in which the referring agency coordinates services and retains primary responsibility for the case.

Here are some of the most common reasons for making a referral outside of an agency:

1. Lack of staff with necessary skills.
2. Lack of sufficient staff.
3. Clients have problems beyond the usual function of the agency.
4. Presumed superiority of the quality of some other agency's resources.
5. Presumed quantity of services available in another agency.
6. Another agency or program has been given responsibility for certain problems.

Referring clients to other resources requires careful work. Weissman (1976) has reported that within a group of individuals referred to an agency for service, 32 percent had no contact with the agency and another 20 percent had no involvement with the agency after the initial contact. Thus, in more than 50 percent of the cases, the purpose of the referral (linking a client with needed resources) had not been served.

The referral process involves several types of interventions and consists of three stages: advising and preparing clients for referral, referring and aiding clients in linkage with needed services, and following up on the referrals.

Generally, when you have identified a need that cannot be met at your agency, you should make a referral to an outside resource. Your first task in this stage is to advise the client of this and to make sure that the client agrees. The decision to seek additional help should emerge from your joint deliberation. It may be necessary for you to present information to help the client realize the necessity of the referral. Do not underestimate the resourcefulness of clients. Explore with them resources within their own natural support system (e.g., family, friends, neighbors) as well as other formal community agency resources.

While deciding together what resource would be the best match for the clients' needs, respect the clients' right to self-determination. Encourage clients to express their feelings about seeking additional help elsewhere as well as their feelings about the specific agency or professional being considered. Deal with any doubts, fears, or misconceptions about the resource being discussed. If brochures or pamphlets are available, share these and other information, but be careful not to make promises about what this agency or professional will do.

If the nature of the referral means that a client will have no further dealings with you, and if you sense that the client is feeling a sense of loss or ambivalence about terminating work with you, acknowledge that the time the two of you have spent together has been meaningful. Take pains to prevent the client from feeling that he or she is being rejected or betrayed. Do not sabotage the referral by giving covert messages that no one will be as caring as you are.

In the second stage of the referral process—referring and aiding clients in making the linkage—you will need to estimate the client's ability to make the necessary connections. "Some clients can be given full rein to make a contact and complete the procedures on their own. Some clients need to be carefully rehearsed and escorted" (Siporin, 1975, p. 314).

When possible, use a multipronged approach. For instance, you may have the client schedule the necessary appointment from the phone in your office so that you can be there to assist. You may follow this by making a written request or report, getting the client's permission to share pertinent agency files, or helping the client complete an application form.

Weissman (1976) suggests the use of the following connection techniques:

1. Write out the necessary facts: the name and address of the resource, how to get an appointment, how to reach the resource, and what the client may expect upon arriving there.

2. Provide the client with the name of a specific contact person at the resource.

3. Provide the client with a brief written statement addressed to the resource, describing in precise terms the nature of the problem and the services desired by the client. Involve the client in composing the statement.

4. In case the client is apprehensive or diffident about going to the resource alone, arrange for a family member or friend to accompany the client. You may choose to accompany him or her yourself. (p. 52)

The third stage of the referral process consists of following up with the client. There are several ways to go about this. You might ask the client to call you after the initial contact. Or, with the client's permission, you may call the client at a date after the scheduled first contact with the referred resource. Another approach is to plan a session with the client before and immediately after the scheduled appointment with the resource.

Your field instructor may need to assist you when making referrals that require a consultation or a collaborative arrangement. At times, your student status may work to a disadvantage because your authority is not equal to that of other professionals with higher status.

Case Example

An adolescent who has been having a difficult time with his parents is one of your clients. He is a bright 16-year-old who is attractive and personable. You like him a lot and suspect that he is more open with you than he was with his previous social worker. He is rather moody, however, and seems to be very depressed on occasion. Today, he seems more depressed than you have ever seen him. You suspect that he is planning either to run away from home or possibly to commit suicide. When you try to probe, he becomes uncooperative. You ask him to sign a contract agreeing not to commit suicide. He refuses, saying that it is unnecessary. At the end of the appointment, he gets up and says, "Maybe I'll see you next week."

Questions

1. Should you inform the adolescent's parents that he is potentially suicidal?
2. Should you arrange an inpatient hospitalization?
3. Is it necessary to involve your agency supervisor?

WHAT IS MANAGED CARE?

Managed care is a collective term for several approaches to controlling costs and improving quality of care. Although some of these approaches have a long history, others are new. Several trends in the American health care system created the need for managed care. These included (1) unnecessary and inappropriate utilization of services; (2) unlimited access to high-tech equipment and expensive procedures; (3) a lack of incentives for controlling costs; (4) an overemphasis on ongoing treatment of diseases and disorders with no attention to prevention; and (5) an excessive focus on insight, awareness, and exploratory factors, rather than goal-focused symptom reduction (Browning & Browning, 1996). Many different organizations are involved in managed care, including Health Maintenance Organizations (HMOs), Preferred Provider Organizations (PPOs), and Employee Assistance Programs (EAPs).

HMOs are closed-group systems in which patients receive care *only* from providers employed by the HMO, usually at its facilities. The HMO is paid by the insurer on a per capita basis, and it provides prepaid comprehensive care (as spelled out in the contract). A primary physician determines which services will benefit the patient and thus also functions as a gatekeeper.

PPOs are less restrictive on who provides services. Instead of employing practitioners and maintaining their own facilities, PPOs contract with local providers who serve the insured clients in their own offices. Practitioners join the network as "preferred providers." This means they must agree to reduce their fees to negotiated contract levels and limit the length of services in a cost-effective manner as determined by the PPO's case managers.

EAPs use case managers to assess the problems of employees, provide minimal intervention, and refer them to independent providers. "EAP Managed Care is handled by trained clinicians and is one of the gentler forms of external control" (Browning & Browning, 1996, p. 6). However, there is often an understanding that short-term cost-effective services will be rewarded with future referrals.

Concepts underlying managed care are Utilization Review (UR) and case management. UR requires a detailed written justification for treatment, a comprehensive treatment plan, and planned discharge goals. These are scrutinized for medical necessity and appropriateness. Specific treatment procedures and number of sessions are authorized, and additional services must be justified. The insurance company or managed care organization (MCO) representative who does the case/utilization review is often called a *case manager*. Case management as a concept is still evolving; however, the common tasks of a case manager include assessing need; identifying, planning for, and linking to services; advocating for the client/patient; coordinating services; and monitoring the process and progress of case management (Dhooper, 1997). Thus organizational strategies used in managed care fall along two dimensions: one involving the establishment of policies and procedures that regulate benefits, payments, and providers, and the other employing "gatekeepers" to review and authorize services at various points (Wagner, 2001).

Although managed care started in the field of health care and extended to mental health, it is being increasingly used in social services. In general, managed care is to be found wherever third-party payers are involved. It has become the "new 'scientific' paradigm for business to counteract allegedly 'profligate' doctors and 'bleeding-heart' social workers" (Davidson, Davidson, & Keigher, 1999, p. 163). Social workers need skills to ensure that managed care stays committed to both its purposes—cost control and quality of care, and ensuring that the former does not eclipse the latter.

HOW DOES MANAGED CARE AFFECT SOCIAL WORK PRACTICE?

Managed care can affect social workers in various ways. Social workers are employed by MCOs; they review care plans and decide what services to authorize. Others work for state or local governments and are involved in purchasing insurance plans for such groups as recipients of Medicaid and government employees. Social workers are also employed by hospitals, mental health centers, and social work agencies and deal with MCOs in the interest of their programs and clients. Still others are in private practice and must negotiate with MCOs on behalf of their clients.

Social workers in MCOs may encounter boundary issues with allegiance to employers and commitment to professional values.

Social workers working for MCOs may encounter boundary problems in finding a balance between allegiance to their employers and commitment to their professional values; that is, they may feel torn between ensuring profits for the company and providing needed services to clients. They must function as true case/care managers rather than mere case reviewers. Similarly, those working for a state government must seek deals that provide for the best needed services while saving the government money.

Social workers employed in health and human services in managerial positions are challenged to meet clients' needs and maintain the agency's fiscal solvency. They must struggle to make the most fair and equitable allocation of scarce resources and provide services that may not be reimbursed by MCOs. Those working as service providers must also do more with less, informing their clients of the limits of services and advocating with MCOs for more resources.

Social workers in private practice also have to respond simultaneously to the needs of their clients, the demands of MCOs, the dictates of their profession, and the need to financially survive in business. They often find themselves in competition with other social workers for referrals and reimbursement and join large group practices to be attractive to insurers. They must negotiate with MCO's case managers for the number of counseling sessions that will be reimbursed.

Another great impact of managed care is in the area of confidentiality in the professional–client relationship, a basic tenet of social work practice. There has been a virtual demise of the client's right to confidentiality in the managed care environment because of the need to share information and obtain approval for services. "With the use of managed care information systems that include telephone reviews, voice mail, faxes, cellular telephones, and highly unregulated computerized databases, there are few guarantees, if any, that sensitive information is stored securely" (Davidson & Davidson, 1996, p. 209), which gives rise to the possibility of ethical and legal dilemmas for social workers.

WHAT SPECIALIZED KNOWLEDGE AND SKILLS ARE IMPORTANT IN A MANAGED CARE ENVIRONMENT?

Managed care requires that all parties understand the boundaries (e.g., policies and procedures) within which it operates. Accordingly, students need to make sure that clients qualify for services and that documents are in order, and they must understand the perspective of managed care organizations. Listed here are some specific things to think about in order to prepare for working in a managed care environment.

1. *Knowledge of the managed care organization.* Understand the MCO's (1) mission and goals, (2) means used to achieve those goals, and (3) measurements used to monitor progress toward those goals. This will help when negotiating a more adequate response to client needs with the MCO.

2. *Knowledge of the changes in managed care organizations.* Managed care is an evolving system that responds to societal demands and legal requirements. (Congress is debating a Patients' Bill of Rights.)

3. *Knowledge of the accreditation standards for managed care organizations.* Several accreditation initiatives are under way, including the National Committee on Quality Assurance (NCQA). More and more purchasers of managed care services are requiring NCQA certification. NASW is represented in this organization (Davidson, Davidson, & Keigher, 1999).

4. *Knowledge of client/patient rights under managed care.* Every contract with a MCO spells out the extent, conditions, limits of benefits, and procedures for appeals or grievances. Clients/patients have the right to (1) be treated with dignity, (2) clear information about their benefits, (3) an explanation of their condition and treatment, and (4) an updated list of service providers and any subsequent changes (Managed Mental Health Care, 1996).

5. *Knowledge of managed care in relation to special needs and at-risk populations.* Managed care has the potential to become the strategy for providing comprehensive and cost-effective services even to groups that have complex needs and multiple chronic problems, such as the elderly, disabled, and mentally ill.

6. *Skills for comprehensive assessment and flexible interventions.* "Common to all managed care mental health service delivery models are biopsychosocial assessments, brief interventions, and use of standardized treatment to attain functional outcomes" (Philp & Berkman, 2001, p. 40). In the *bio* part, the practitioner inquires about any physical problems that may be affecting the client's functioning. The *psychological* part of the assessment focuses primarily on symptoms described in the *Diagnostic and Statistical Manual* (*DSM-IV*) and how those impact the client's life. The *social* part reviews social influences in a person's life, including relationships with significant others that may be causing or contributing to the problem. The social worker must also be able to intervene so that there is maximal positive impact in a short time.

7. *Skills for appropriate documentation.* Managed care is a data-driven system that requires "acceptable treatment protocols, standardized assessments that link clinical and fiscal data, comprehensive service records, and reports specific to individual consumers" (Greene & Sullivan, 2001, p. 179). Providers must be able to collect and document the appropriate data.

8. *Skills for case-level advocacy.* The major difficulty most clients have in a managed care system is the limitation placed on services. The social worker must use his or her clinical as well as social advocacy skills at times to obtain services for clients. Education, persuasion, negotiation, and bargaining are some of the strategies for case-level advocacy.

9. *Skills for brokering.* When the client's insurance company/MCO refuses to pay for needed services, the social worker is obligated to look for other resources to fill the gap and link the client to those resources. These skills involve knowing, discovering, and mobilizing resources relevant to the client's needs. These resources are generally classified into three groups: (1) formal health and human services, (2) various self-help groups, and (3) the client's own natural support system.

10. *Skills for social action for social justice.* When a service system denies access to care needed by groups of people, it becomes an issue that requires social action aimed at changing the policy. Knowing how the political system works is extremely important for this. Strategies include (1) building coalitions and partnerships with like-minded, knowledgeable, and committed individuals and groups; (2) educating and involving others; (3) keeping in touch with and providing relevant information to policy makers; (4) becoming a trusted source of reliable information on the issue for the media; (5) testifying before appropriate committees and commissions; and (6) seeking influential legislators to sponsor the desired legislation.

SHOULD I SHARE PERSONAL INFORMATION WITH CLIENTS?

In an effort to understand and relate to you, clients may ask personal questions such as, "Are you married?" "Do you have children?" "How old are you?" "How much do they pay you to do this?" If the student can share the information without feeling an invasion of privacy, then it is okay to answer such questions. Answer, if you can, in a brief and straightforward manner without comment about the meaning of the question. Such questions may arise out of simple social curiosity. Sometimes, however, it is preferable to be a little vague in answering. In response to a question about his or her age, a student might reply, "I'm thirtyish."

Clients may ask about your experience because of a genuine interest in the helper's qualifications. Some clients may be reassured to know that you have completed courses in child development or that you will be completing your degree in May. Do not overexplain or become defensive. The client has a right to decide whether to continue with you or to ask for someone else. If you feel that the client is troubled by your lack of experience, ask, "Are you afraid that I won't be able to help you?" or "Does this bother you?" Most clients will be so appreciative of someone assigned to help them that your qualifications will not be a major issue.

If you feel that a client's questions are a little too intrusive, you can deflect them by stating, "We really need to stay with the issue at hand." Generally, this will help clients refocus on what they have come to the agency to obtain or accomplish.

Even though you may see no harm in answering a question about where you live, never give out your address or home phone number to clients without the knowledge of the field instructor. More than one student has been surprised when infatuated or disturbed clients have made unwanted and unanticipated visits to their apartments or homes. Also, nuisance phone calls are always a possibility when you give out your home phone number. Clients who may be suicidal or who may need to reach you in another emergency can call the agency's after-hours number, or you can direct them to call a 24-hour crisis counseling center until you can be reached again at the agency. (In extreme situations, the 24-hour crisis counseling center could be given your home phone number so that they could inform you when a client is having problems. You could return the client's call without the client learning your home phone number.)

Similarly, it is not advisable to correspond with active or former clients without your agency supervisor's knowledge, even if the clients are incarcerated and in another state. Although you may wish to correspond with a favorite client or an inmate out of concern or friendship, these situations can get misinterpreted and out of hand. Someone sitting in a jail cell all day with little to occupy his or her time may build elaborate fantasies and begin to see you in a way you had not intended.

There are social work practitioners who believe that self-disclosure can be a powerful therapeutic intervention. In the words of Goldstein (1997), "the thoughtful and sometimes spontaneous use of self-disclosure can be a form of emphatic attunement and responsiveness that is essential for the successful engagement and treatment of certain individuals" (p. 42). For instance, it might be helpful to a client struggling with an addiction to know that you have been in recovery for three years for a drug or alcohol problem. However, revealing personal information requires skill in discerning the needs of the client, the likely meaning of self-disclosure for the client, and the timing and wording of the disclosure (Deal, 1999). Answers to questions such as the following will help you determine whether and how much to disclose. Would your disclosure help clients to talk more honestly and specifically about themselves? Would your disclosure help them put their problems into a new perspective or consider new alternatives for action? (Corey & Corey, 1998, p. 73). If not, then there is little to be gained by disclosing.

Examine your own motivations for self-disclosure. You do become more vulnerable when you share your experiences, feelings, thoughts, and reactions. Talk to your supervisor about self-disclosure and how he or she feels about this issue in particular case situations. It is better to be cautious than to be a blabbermouth with clients. Sharing too much about your current personal problems and frustrations can be both inappropriate and wrong. It could be the kind of thing that might result in your being asked to leave the agency.

HOW DO I WORK WITH DIFFICULT OFFICE STAFF AND SUPERVISORS?

Unfortunately, sometimes host agencies have employees (and they may be office assistants or even your field instructor) who are, to say it politely, difficult individuals. They may be argumentative or uncooperative, or they may ignore or simply not find the time to respond to your requests (i.e., photocopying, obtaining supplies, or scheduling a conference room). The worst thing you can do in a situation like this is to become angry and raise your voice or try to retaliate by doing something hurtful. The better strategy is to find a way around the obstacle in your path—there are several ways to do this.

But first, before you label another person "difficult," you should examine your own behavior. Were you considerate of the other person's feelings? Did you drop a lot of work onto the assistant's desk when he or she was trying to meet a deadline? Did you demand or imply that your needs were more important than others'? Did you somehow suggest that the other person was incompetent or not very smart? Were you impatient?

Oftentimes when office assistants complain about those who give them work to do, their major issue is that they aren't treated with respect.

If after your self-examination you don't feel that you were at fault and if the problem continues, then it is probably worth talking to your field instructor—particularly if the assistant or other worker is doing something that is keeping you from doing your own work on a timely basis. Be prepared, however, for the possibility that some long-time employees have been difficult for so long that others in the office have given up trying to change the behavior of the problematic employee. It may be easier to do your own photocopying rather than trying to get the office manager to supervise more closely the assistant who won't do your work—this is a decision you may need to make.

If the difficult person in the agency is your field instructor, you need to be attentive to the little things that irritate him or her. If the issue is that you have been late in arriving at the agency, set your alarm clock 15 minutes earlier each day. If the complaint is that your work doesn't look professional, take extra pains to proofread and spell-check your documents before giving them to the field instructor. Remember, your role is to learn and it may very well be that the field instructor is trying to make a point—to teach you to attend to something that you have been careless about.

If you do your self-examination and find that you have been doing your level best and that you and your field instructor still can't seem to get along, it is time to talk to your faculty field liaison about possibly moving out of that practicum the following term. Most often, you will not be allowed to leave in the middle of a term unless the field instructor or others in the agency have done something especially egregious—so don't get your hopes up. Also, be very careful to whom you complain. Even a fellow student or coworker that you think might be discreet could let it slip in conversation with other employees that you feel that your field instructor is a jerk. If that word gets back to your field instructor, he or she may not give you good ratings at evaluation time. Further you might "cook your own goose" in terms of not being able to return to the agency at a later time for employment. In brief, don't say anything negative about anyone in the agency unless it is to a person with sufficient clout to address the problem. Even then, be sure that you are not at fault.

WHAT IS EVIDENCE-BASED PRACTICE?

Evidence-based practice (EBP) is the use of interventions that are the best possible professional response to the problem or situation of a client/client system. This becomes possible by incorporating research regarding the most effective interventions into one's professional work. EBP originated in medicine. In the 1980s, a group in the Department of Clinical Epidemiology and Biostatistics at McMasters University in Canada began creating a systematic approach to critically appraising and using research that physicians could build into their clinical decision making. This group's efforts resulted in 25 articles published in the *Journal of the American Medical Association* between 1993 and 2000, which taught clinicians the basics of EBP. Those articles have been compiled into two books, *User's Guides: Manual for Evidence-Based Clinical Care* (Guyatt & Rennie, 2002a) and *User's Guides: Essentials of Evidence-Based Clinical Practice* (Guyatt & Rennie, 2002b). With the passage of time, the concepts of EBP have become common language in the helping professions including social work.

EBP helps to answer important practice-related questions such as which interventions are beneficial, are likely to be beneficial, or have an unknown effectiveness (and therefore could be ineffective or harmful).

EBP provides important information about beneficial, likely to be beneficial, and unknown interventions.

The essential idea of EBP is to rely upon the best available scientific evidence of effective interventions, provide the client information about the efficacy of those interventions, and allow the client to make the final decision (Thyer, 2003). According to McNeece and Thyer (2004), " 'Best research evidence' means clinically relevant research from basic and applied scientific investigations, especially drawing from intervention research evaluating the outcome of social work services, and from studies on the reliability and validity of assessment measures, . . ." (p. 9). There has been a common assumption that evidence should be research evidence from the quantitative tradition. Evidence from systematic reviews and meta-analyses is highly valued because it is less likely to provide misleading information about the effect of an intervention (Sackett, Rosenberg, Gray, Haynes, & Richardson, 1996).

Typically, the practitioner hopes to find a systematic review that provides useful information about the effectiveness of the intervention in question. When there is not a systematic review available, the best evidence is usually obtained from a study that was a randomized control trial. If studies of that nature are not found, then well-designed studies without randomization can be accepted as evidence. Lower levels of evidence include well-designed cohort or case-control studies, multiple time series, and then, at the lowest level, expert opinion, clinical experience, and descriptive studies.

Pollio (2002) is of the opinion that systematically collected information from a variety of sources, such as focus groups, narratives, case studies, and even personal experiences, can be the evidence that informs practice. However, the social worker must be a critical assessor of all knowledge. In the words of Raines (2004), "Truth in human services may not be absolute, but it ought to be 'good enough' to help our clients" (p. 72). Hence, evidence in EBP should be knowledge derived from sources that have been tested and found to be credible (Higgs & Jones, 2000).

A good place to start looking for information on effective interventions is the Campbell and Cochran Collaborations. A list of systematic reviews available on the electronic Campbell Library can be found at: http://www.campbellcollaboration.org/review_list/index.php. You can search for interventions on the Cochran Collaboration Web site at http://www.cochrane.org/.

Steps in EBP:

1. Convert information needed for practice decisions into answerable questions.
2. Search for the best evidence with which to answer the questions.
3. Critically appraise the information in terms of its impact, validity, reliability, and applicability.
4. Consider the evidence given one's expertise, client values, and preferences; integrate the information to make a practice decision.
5. Evaluate the practice decision. (Gambrill, 2008)

WHY IS EVIDENCE-BASED PRACTICE ESSENTIAL FOR SOCIAL WORKERS?

EBP is not a passing fad. It is already informing practice in the helping professions. There are several reasons why social work is adopting it.

1. Throughout the history of social work, we have sought a place alongside the established professions. We have come a long way but the need to enhance our public credibility is stronger than ever. EBP will substantially help in this regard.

2. EBP will force social work professional organizations, educational institutions, and individual practitioners to accelerate the work on creating, testing, communicating, and utilizing knowledge, which makes our interventions the best possible response to micro and macro social problems. It will also help us move away from an authority-based practice.

3. Several sections of the NASW Code of Ethics (National Association of Social Workers, 1999) point to the moral duty of social work professionals to provide clients their best practice efforts. The content and message of those sections are illustrated in the following excerpts from the Code.

1.01 The social worker's primary responsibility is to promote the well-being of clients.

1.02 Social workers respect and promote the right of clients to self-determination and assist clients in their efforts to identify and clarify their goals.

1.04 (a) Social workers should provide services and represent themselves as competent only within the boundaries of their education, training, license, certification, consultation received, supervised experience, or other relevant professional experience.

4.01 (a) Social workers should accept responsibility or employment only on the basis of existing competence or the intention to acquire the necessary competence.

(b) Social workers should strive to become and remain proficient in professional practice and the performance of professional functions. Social workers should critically examine and keep current with emerging knowledge relevant to social work. Social workers should routinely review the professional literature and participate in continuing education relevant to social work practice and social work ethics.

(c) Social workers should base practice on recognized knowledge, including empirically based knowledge, relevant to social work and social work ethics.

5.01 (b) Social workers should uphold and advance the values, ethics, knowledge, and mission of the profession.

(d) Social workers should contribute to the knowledge base of social work and share with colleagues their knowledge related to practice, research and ethics.

5.02 (a) Social workers should monitor and evaluate policies, the implementation of programs, and practice interventions.

4.01 (c) Social workers should critically examine and keep current with emerging knowledge relevant to social work and fully use evaluation and research evidence in their professional practice.

Hence, it is clear that engaging in EBP is an ethical obligation of social workers.

4. We live in an age of accountability. Societal expectations of helping professions have changed markedly in recent times. Social work is no exception. Sources of funds for human services are requiring service agencies to show that their programs and activities are effective. Professional programs and practices are being transformed by managed care and its influence toward time-limited and rational models of care (Pollio, 2002). Social workers as professionals are accountable to our clients, societal institutions that sanction our practice, professional and service organizations under whose auspices we function, our colleagues, and ourselves. We must show that our activities are in the client's best interest—that they are ethical, goal-directed, effective, and efficient (Rosen, 2003).

Thus, accountability is an obligation of our profession—we must clearly reveal our functions and methods and assure our clients and communities that we are not only competent but also utilizing interventions based on the best information available. "Social work needs to showcase what it routinely does well by developing evidence of best practice on which to base learning and positive growth by making this visible both within the profession and to the public" (Ferguson, 2003, p. 1008).

Human Rights & Justice

Critical Thinking Question: How does the Health Insurance Portability and Accountability Act of 1996 (HIPAA) protect human rights?

HOW DO I PREPARE FOR EVIDENCE-BASED PRACTICE IN MY OWN WORK?

Because you are new to social work, it may be easier for you to appreciate, learn, and master EBP than for those who have relied primarily on wisdom arising from their own practice. You will find the following suggestions helpful in learning how to incorporate EBP into your work with clients.

1. Make conscious efforts to become a *life-long learner.* That will ensure that you stay abreast of the latest professional knowledge, approaches, and technologies.

2. Browse the table of contents of professional journals in your field, and regularly read articles reporting research on interventions. Skim the Campbell and Cochrane Collaboration Web sites frequently for new studies. Form a group in your agency to discuss interesting findings, or consult with a colleague for another perspective on the article.

3. Become a reflective worker. A reflective worker critically appraises everything happening on the professional front and does not take anything on faith alone. He or she does not adopt an approach or methodology because it feels good or because that is the way it is "usually" done. Employ a twofold strategy: Develop the habit of reflecting on the "what," "why," and "how" of the work you are doing, and find the time for reflection through appropriate time management.

4. Accept responsibility for contributing to the knowledge base of the social work profession (i.e., make presentations and write manuscripts reporting the results of your interventions).

5. Most importantly, *master the process of EBP.* Ask yourself such questions as: "What has been shown to *help . . .*?" "What treatment *works best*?" "What group therapies *improve*?" "What community-based interventions *reduce*?" (McNeece & Thyer, 2004). The questions can also be more specific as in: "What psychosocial intervention reduces *the risk of teenage pregnancy*?" "What individual therapies are the most successful in getting clients to stop *abusing crack cocaine*?" "How can schools reduce *student absenteeism*?" Or, "What treatments are effective in improving *prenatal care adherence*?" (p. 13).

6. Track down and investigate the best available evidence. Crisp (2004) has suggested that the following questions be considered in selecting the evidence to use in professional practice.

   a. Why am I using this evidence?

   b. Am I using this evidence because it is readily available or because I believe it to be credible?

   c. Is the basis of the evidence methodologically sound?

   d. Am I using this evidence without considering how appropriate it is for the context because it comes from a well-respected resource?

   e. To what extent do personal factors impinge on my evaluation of this evidence?

   f. Will others be convinced by this evidence?

   g. Is it possible that there is more appropriate evidence? If so, do I have the resources (including time) to search for other evidence?

   h. Are there reasons why this evidence cannot be applied?

   i. Is it possible that this evidence has been superseded? (pp. 81–82).

7. Appraise the evidence. Obviously, the context in which the intervention was applied needs to be a close fit to the population and agency in which you are considering adopting the intervention. Further, you should make an assessment regarding the strength of the research methodology, the reliability of the instrument, and the soundness of the findings. Gray (2001) suggests that practitioners should filter any evidence through their own expertise and experience. That will help in determining if the evidence-based approach is adoptable or needs to be modified.

8. Evaluate progress. Questions such as "Is the new approach working?" and "Is the new program effective?" have to be answered through systematic evaluation of the effectiveness of the intervention. Monitoring and evaluating the progress of a case or a program is a must and the last vital step in the EBP process.

HIPAA protects patients' privacy in health care settings.

In summary, weave the essentials of EBP into your professional practice by:

- Treating every intervention as "an explicit, systematic, and rational problem-solving process" (Rosen, 2003, p. 201).
- Locating and employing the strongest research-supported interventions.
- Engaging in an "ongoing recursive evaluation of outcome attainment, further adjusting the intervention based on evaluative feedback" (Rosen, 2003, p. 202); and share your experience of what has worked with the professional community.

WHAT IS HIPAA?

HIPAA is the Health Insurance Portability and Accountability Act of 1996 (Public Law 104–191), also known as the Kassebaum-Kennedy Act named after its sponsors, former Senator Nancy Kassebaum (R-KS) and the late Senator Edward Kennedy (D-MA). This Act has had a dramatic effect upon all those who work in health care. Before we describe the changes it has brought about and the essential provisions of this law, a brief description of the antecedents of its passage will indicate its importance and set the stage for further discussion.

During the Clinton presidency, an effort for a comprehensive reform of the U.S. healthcare system failed. That failure, however, highlighted the problems of the system and the need for change. HIPAA was Congress's response to two of the system's major problems.

Problem 1: People were losing their health insurance if they left or lost their job. Insurance companies also would refuse to insure or refuse coverage for preexisting health conditions. It was difficult for families to have continuity of health care during job changes or unemployment of the breadwinner even if they could pay for the continued coverage of health insurance.

Problem 2: It was becoming increasingly difficult to preserve the privacy of medical information because of such changes as the (1) provision of medical care where many persons need access to patients' records, (2) requirements for reporting cases of child and elder abuse, (3) government's monitoring of care paid for with public funds, (4) demands by private insurance and managed care companies for patient records before authorizing payment, (5) computerization of medical record keeping, and (6) development of the Internet (Appelbaum, 2002). These changes were making obsolete the old rules regarding the disclosure of medical information.

The "portability" part of HIPAA addresses *Problem 1* by providing rights and protections for participants and beneficiaries in group health plans. It (1) provides protection for coverage for group health plans that limit exclusions for preexisting conditions, (2) prohibits discrimination against employees and their dependents based on their health status, (3) allows for a special opportunity to enroll in a new plan to individuals in certain circumstances, and (4) gives the right to purchase and continue individual coverage if group health plan coverage has been lost in certain situations.

The "accountability" part of HIPAA deals with *Problem 2.* Its response is quite complex but has the potential for revolutionizing patient information. It has generated extreme reactions from health care providers. Some believe that HIPAA will encourage the development of a national health information system (Coffey et al., 1997); it is also seen as helping to move health care into the electronic age, decreasing the increased risk of exposing individual health information, improving efficiency by cutting down on administrative cost and paperwork, reducing fraud and abuse, and facilitating access to medical information (Brendel & Bryan, 2004). Others have reacted to the enactment of HIPAA with a "virtual collective groan" (Flores, 2005). They hold that the law has added to the financial burden of health care organizations and has created new problems.

The major provisions of HIPAA and the rules, regulations, and standards created under its requirements that affect the policies and protocols of health and mental health organizations and practices of health care and mental health care providers are outlined next. Major sources of this information are Olinde and McCard (2005) and U.S. Department of Health and Human Services (2003).

The *Standards for Privacy of Individually Identifiable Health Information* called the *Privacy Rule* established, for the first time, national standards for the protection of health information. The Privacy Rule addresses (1) the use and disclosure of individuals' health information (called *Protected Health Information*) by organizations subject to the Privacy Rule (*covered entities*) and (2) individuals' rights to understand and control how that information is used. The Office of Civil Rights within the Department of Health and Human Services is responsible for enforcing the Privacy Rule. The Privacy Rule is described as providing a "federal floor" of safeguards for confidentiality of medical information.

The *covered entities* regulated by the Privacy Rule are essentially all health care providers (including hospitals and business associates working for physicians, dentists, and others who electronically transmit health information where patients can be individually identified) and those working with health plans (i.e., health, dental, vision, and prescription drug insurers, health maintenance organizations, Medicaid, Medicare, and Medicare supplement insurers, long-term care insurers, and others).

Practice Contexts

Critical Thinking Question: If you have volunteered in an agency years ago and later become a social work intern there, what might influence the relevant services you provide?

Protected Health Information (PHI) under the Privacy Rule refers to information that identifies the individual and individually identifiable health information that is transmitted or maintained by health care providers (and others fitting the description of covered entities). This includes name, address, birth date, Social Security number, demographic data, and information that relate to the individual's past, present, or future physical or mental health or condition, provision of health care, or past, present, or future payment for provision of health care.

Excluded from protected health information are (1) employment records maintained by the covered entity in its capacity as an employer, (2) education records covered by the Family Educational Right and Privacy Act, and (3) records of students held by postsecondary educational institutions used exclusively for health care treatment.

Under HIPAA, disclosure of PHI by a covered entity is allowed only as (1) required by the Privacy Rule, (2) permitted by the Privacy Rule, and (3) authorized by the individual who is the subject of the information.

1. *Required Disclosures.* A covered entity must disclose protected health information in only two situations: (1) to individuals (or their personal representatives) when they request access to or an accounting of disclosures of their PHI and (2) to the Department of Health and Human Services when conducting an investigation.

2. *Permitted Disclosures.* A covered entity is permitted to disclose PHI without the individual's authorization for treatment, coordination and management of services, payment, and health care operations (i.e., quality assessment and improvement activities, medical reviews, audits and compliance-related legal services, specified insurance functions).

3. *Disclosure Authorized by the Individual.* An individual may authorize the release of his or her PHI, *but* the authorization must contain the following elements to be valid under HIPAA.

   a. *Core elements:*

      i. a description of the information to be used or disclosed

      ii. the name and other specific identification of the person/s authorized to make the disclosure

      iii. the name and other specific identification of the person/s to whom the covered entity may make the disclosure

      iv. a description of the purpose of the requested use or disclosure

      v. an expiration date that relates to the purpose of the use or disclosure

      vi. signature of the individual and date

   b. *Required statements* adequate to place the individual on notice of:

      i. the individual's right to revoke the authorization

      ii. the ability or inability to condition treatment, payment, enrollment, or eligibility for benefits on the authorization

      iii. the potential for the disclosed information to re-disclosure by the recipient

   c. *Plain language:* The authorization must be written in plain language.

   d. *Copy to the individual:* The covered entity must provide the individual with a copy of the signed authorization.

To learn about other HIPAA requirements, refer to: www.HIPAA.org.

There are serious civil and criminal penalties for violating HIPAA. Civil penalties are $100 for each violation up to $25,000 per calendar year. Criminal penalties are as follows: A person who knowingly obtains or discloses individually identifiable information faces a fine of $50,000 and up to one-year imprisonment. The penalties increase to $100,000 and five years in jail if the wrongful conduct involves false pretenses, and to $250,000 in fines and up to ten years in jail if the wrongful conduct involves the intent to sell, transfer, or use individually identifiable information for commercial advantage, personal gain, or malicious harm. It is, however, noteworthy that HIPAA does not allow for private actions by patients (Feld, 2005). They must complain to the Office of Civil Rights and cannot go to a court of law in cases of the violation of their rights.

HOW DOES HIPAA AFFECT SOCIAL WORK AND SOCIAL WORKERS?

HIPAA is the first comprehensive federal protection for the privacy of personal health information. It imposes a uniform set of privacy protections on public and private health care entities and attempts to standardize health-related records. Interestingly, a goal of HIPAA is to assign one unique identifier (a code) to each patient to be used by all covered entities throughout the country, "a code that would allow each person's medical contacts to be aggregated from birth to death" (Appelbaum, 2002, p. 1813). This aspect of the law is on hold due to the complexity of implementation, but the HIPAA mandate remains. The effects of HIPAA are already far-reaching in the world of health and mental health care and before long, indirectly, HIPAA will start affecting other human services as well. It is already happening in school systems. School social workers already are involved in informing parents of their right to informed consent about their children's records and their right to review the records and request that information they consider educationally irrelevant be expunged from those records (National Association of Social Workers, 2003). It is likely that standards like those of HIPAA will be regulating social services organizations and programs in the future.

The largest proportion of social workers are working in health care organizations such as hospitals, outpatient clinics and programs, home health aid agencies, hospices, and mental health settings such as psychiatric hospitals and community mental health centers. Over 60 percent of all providers of mental health services in the United States are social workers. All these workers are involved in the compliance of HIPAA regulations and standards. There are also a large number of social workers in independent practice who provide services to clients; they are also health care providers and are "covered entities" under HIPAA. Any practicum placement or job in a health or mental health setting will require you to be familiar with HIPAA policies and procedures.

Several aspects of the law are particularly important to social workers. HIPAA gives patients broad access to their records. A patient can review his or her record, have copies of the record, request that the incomplete and incorrect information in the record be changed, and ask for a list of entities to whom the record has been disclosed. However, access to the record can be denied if

HIPAA gives patients broad access to their records.

there is a reasonable likelihood that (1) the release of information would endanger the physical safety of the patient or another person; (2) the release of information in the record about another person would cause substantial harm to that person; or (3) in the case of a request by an agent of the patient, the release would cause substantial harm to the patient or another person. Similarly, a patient's request for amendment of his or her record can be denied but the involved correspondence between the CE and patient must become a part of the record.

However, HIPAA gives *psychotherapy notes* special protection in recognition that "the information contained in psychotherapy notes is likely to be qualitatively different from that found elsewhere in the medical record" (Appelbaum, 2002, p. 1815). Psychotherapy notes cannot be released without the explicit authorization of the patient. These notes document the contents of conversations between the patient and therapist during an individual, group, or family counseling session and are separated from the patient's record. These notes can be released to patients. However, "it is wise for clinicians to have a policy regarding release of psychotherapy notes, thereby providing grounds for asserting that such releases are not arbitrary and that all patient requests are being dealt with equally" (Brendel & Bryan, 2004, p. 180). You should make sure that your psychotherapy notes meet the HIPAA requirements and keep them separate from the medical records. Always get the client's consent to discuss his or her case and treatment with other clinicians unless it is a clear emergency as defined here. Make sure that minor clients understand your obligations to their parents and guardians.

HIPAA provides many exceptions to the traditional consent requirement for release of some or all of protected health information as follows:

1. In situations posing a serious threat to public health or safety
2. In cases of suspected child abuse and neglect
3. In response to a request for discovery or a subpoena attorney on the assurance that the attorney has made reasonable efforts to notify the patient of the request
4. In response to a request from a law enforcement officer for the purposes of "identifying or locating a suspect, fugitive, material witness or missing person"
5. In response to the need for national security-related information by national security agencies and secret service
6. In situations where other entities are assisting the holder of PHI in raising funds
7. For purposes of marketing services delivered by the facility that originally treated the patient
8. In situations where an Institutional Review Board waives the requirement for authorization for research use

Brendel and Bryan (2004) recommend that you discuss your agency's privacy-related policies and practices with every client at the very outset of your involvement. "This discussion might include how e-mails, phone messages, answering machines, and note taking are managed in your practice" (p. 182).

Yes, HIPAA does require that social workers be very attentive to documentation and the sharing of patient data. The good news is that patients have a great deal of control of their information. The downside is that more paperwork is required that oftentimes seems unnecessary to all parties. However, there is no indication that the HIPAA requirements will be drastically reduced or changed in the near future, so it is best to become familiar with them if you are planning on an educational experience or job in the healthcare arenas.

SUMMARY

This chapter has examined different roles and contexts that the student may need to know about while in an internship. Primary focus was given to managed care, HIPAA regulations in health care settings, and evidence-based practice.

Professional Boundaries

Agency supervisors have different expectations for students than they do for volunteers and for employees. Briefly contrast the roles of volunteers, students, and employees along the following dimensions:

1. Salary

   _____   _____   _____
   Volunteer   Student   Employee

2. Number of Hours Worked per Week

   _____   _____   _____
   Volunteer   Student   Employee

3. Days of the Week and Hours of the Day Work Is Done

   _____   _____   _____
   Volunteer   Student   Employee

4. Evaluation of Performance

   _____   _____   _____
   Volunteer   Student   Employee

5. Motivation for Working in the Agency

   _____   _____   _____
   Volunteer   Student   Employee

6. Incentives for Doing Exceptional Work

   _____   _____   _____
   Volunteer   Student   Employee

7. Having to Deal with Clients' Problems after Hours

   _____   _____   _____
   Volunteer   Student   Employee

Recording

1. Locate an agency providing similar services to the one where you are placed as an intern. Visit that agency and ask to learn how it records information about the services it provides to clients. If possible, collect a copy of the forms it uses for recording. Compare its method of recording information about provided services with your agency. In your opinion, which agency provides the best way to record information about services provided? Why?

   _____

   _____

   _____

   _____

   _____

   _____

   _____

   _____

   _____

2. Record a role play between two of your classmates. Ask each student to critique your recording for accuracy and for objectivity. (Provide your recording on a separate sheet.)

3. Write four advantages and disadvantages for writing while a client is speaking.

   Advantages

   1. _____

   2. _____

   3. _____

   4. _____

   Disadvantages

   1. _____

   2. _____

   3. _____

   4. _____

      a. List several ways you might lessen the effects of the disadvantages.

      _____

      _____

      _____

b. Do the advantages outweigh the disadvantages? How do you feel when someone is writing when you are talking?

_____

_____

_____

_____

4. What types of recording does your agency employ?

_____ process recording

_____ progress notes

_____ summary recording

_____ biopsychosocial histories

_____ periodic summaries

_____ checklist

_____ other (describe)

_____

_____

_____

Managed Care

Find an article that specifically addresses managed care and the types of service that most interest you. Identify the article (author, year, title, journal), and summarize its major points.

_____

_____

_____

_____

_____

_____

_____

_____

_____

_____

_____

_____

_____

_____

_____

_____

_____

_____

Self-Disclosure

1. Talk to your agency supervisor about self-disclosure and how much or how little personal information should be revealed. What is the agency policy on self-disclosure?

_____

_____

_____

_____

_____

_____

2. What are some facts about yourself that the agency would allow you to share with clients in order to build rapport?

_____

_____

_____

_____

_____

_____

3. What types of things should students not self-disclose in your agency?

_____

_____

_____

_____

_____

_____

Log onto **www.mysocialworklab.com** to access a wealth of case studies, videos, and assessment. (*If you did not receive an access code to **MySocialWorkLab** with this text and wish to purchase access online, please visit* www.mysocialworklab.com.)

1. **Read the case study "Mikki's Story."** This case describes various theoretical approaches to the problem of domestic violence. Given the worker's successes and failures in the case, how might you approach the case, and what might you do differently?

2. **Watch the Core Competency video: "Applying Critical Thinking."** We learn that the husband's drinking may be a large contributor to violence in the home. What other factors do you think might be involved that haven't yet been discussed in this video?

PRACTICE TEST The following questions will test your knowledge of the content found within this chapter.

1. Numerous factors determine the boundaries found at the agency, program, client, and staff levels. Which one of the following was not discussed as a boundary issue affecting your role as a student?
   a. Agency's expectations of its professional and support staff
   b. Agency's protocol for client services
   c. Agency's protocol for client records
   d. Student's learning contract

2. A contract with a client reflects the essentials of social work philosophy and intervention process. Which topic was not mentioned in the discussion about contracts?
   a. A contract emphasizes client's right to self-determination.
   b. A contract emphasizes the worker–client joint assessment and decision-making.
   c. A contract emphasizes that the social worker and the client stay focused.
   d. A contract provides a baseline for periodic reviews of progress.

3. Which one of the following is the most undesirable approach to dealing with a difficult office staff?
   a. Examining your behavior toward the "difficult" person
   b. Discussing the problem with your field instructor
   c. Branding the person as "difficult"
   d. Becoming angry and retaliating in a hurtful way

4. Which of the following methods is the least helpful in preparing you for evidence-based practice?
   a. Keeping current with the latest professional knowledge, approaches, and technologies
   b. Talking to your mentors about their favorite intervention approaches
   c. Tracking down the evidence of the best available effective interventions
   d. Appraising the evidence and determining the applicability of the intervention to the case and situation in hand

Short Answer Question:
Bob is in an agency that has been around for 80 years or more and is known for having a very traditional way of working with clients. Bob wants to discuss the importance of responding to recent changes in the client population and the need to use research evidence to inform practice in the agency. Should he discuss this with his field instructor or simply learn what they have to teach him without trying to bring about change?

ASSESS YOUR COMPETENCE Use the scale below to rate your current level of achievement on the following concepts or skills associated with each competency practice behavior presented in the chapter:

1	2	3
I can accurately describe the concept or skill.	I can consistently identify the concept or skill when observing and analyzing practice activities.	I can competently implement the concept or skill in my own practice.

_____ apply the NASW Code of Ethics and understand why research evidence should be used to inform practice.

_____ familiar with the Health Insurance Portability and Accountability Act of 1996 (HIPAA) and understand how it protects human rights.

_____ appreciate that changes in service delivery and practice can occur as populations change over time when there are emerging societal trends.

6

Client Systems: The Recipients of Service

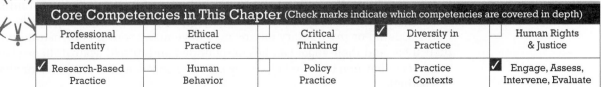

Core Competencies in This Chapter (Check marks indicate which competencies are covered in depth)				
☐ Professional Identity	☐ Ethical Practice	☐ Critical Thinking	☑ Diversity in Practice	☐ Human Rights & Justice
☑ Research-Based Practice	☐ Human Behavior	☐ Policy Practice	☐ Practice Contexts	☑ Engage, Assess, Intervene, Evaluate

OVERVIEW

Many social work students have never been required to ask for professional assistance or exposed to persons remarkably poor or different from their own families of origin. Questions arise about how to best communicate and work with individuals, families, and communities that are unfamiliar. This chapter helps students in understanding and working with new client systems.

WHO ARE CLIENTS?

If there were no problems, crises, difficulties, or requests for help in the world, then social workers would have no clients. Of primary concern to us is the client system, that is, the person or persons to whom our services are provided. Client systems may be individuals, families, small groups, organizations, or communities. Ideally, you will have opportunities to work with client systems of various sizes in your practicum experiences.

WHAT IS IT LIKE TO BE A CLIENT?

Have you ever had a flat tire on a country road and then discovered that your spare was gone or that you had no jack? What would it be like to be in a strange city and accidentally lock your car keys inside your car? Would you be comfortable stopping a complete stranger and asking for assistance? People who are accustomed to having such things as savings accounts, family members and friends willing to help, and a good credit rating sometimes find it difficult to imagine not having any of these resources.

In an effort to help new students to become more empathic with the problems of the homeless, one seminary took students to a nearby city and gave them just enough money to make one phone call in case of an emergency. The students were instructed to learn about the city's social services by being homeless for 48 hours. Imagine how you would feel in such a situation. If it were an unfamiliar city and you were without a car or money, what emotions would you have? Would you know where to go? Would you feel overwhelmed? Bewildered? Lost? Fearful?

We can assume that most clients are experiencing significant problems and stress when they come into our public service agencies. They want help with their problems and relief from the stress that they are experiencing. Many clients have never had to ask for assistance from anyone before, and they may not know what kinds of help are available or whether they might qualify.

Other clients have made use of agency services before and may know the rules and procedures better than you do. They may be impatient, demanding, or even rude. Their frustration may come from having to deal with impersonal bureaucrats, completing long application forms, or living on the barest minimum of economic assistance in a decaying and dangerous neighborhood. Court-ordered or involuntary clients may have many sources of frustration in their lives, and their anger can be compounded and turned against themselves or others if they don't ask for help. They may also appear anxious, self-destructive, or apathetic.

We all react differently to stress, and clients are much like us, but often without our resources. Some clients may view themselves as failures because of their problems. They may feel ashamed or bewildered—as when a tragic and unexpected situation has occurred. Take, for example, the woman who has just learned that her child has been sexually abused by her live-in partner. Imagine the range of emotions that the mother must feel—anger at the perpetrator, grief over the violation of the child and possible loss of an adult relationship, and guilt from not having been able to prevent the abuse. To these feelings we can add confusion over the best course of action (e.g., prosecution) and fear that the child has been permanently damaged or scarred.

When enough stress is heaped on some clients, they may break down and psychologically surrender. Many clients express a sense of being over-whelmed. They may become depressed, isolate themselves, and require help with problem-solving strategies. Certain clients will try to ignore or deny their problems and muddle through. Occasionally there are self-referred or volun-tary clients who, after hesitating for months or years, enter therapy with a great sense of urgency. For them, nothing can be done fast enough; they may pres-sure you to see them two or more times a week. In contrast, clients who are involuntary (because they have been mandated to seek help by a judge or offi-cer of the court) may be hostile and uncooperative.

As a social work student in a practicum, you must accept each client as a unique human being who has immeasurable worth and dignity. You must understand the client's unique set of problems as the client experiences them. This entails being nonjudgmental and accepting of individual differences. Even if the client's problems are of his or her own making, you must realize that the client has needs that are not being met, and you must implement a plan to make the client more healthy or whole.

You must accept each client as a unique individual who has immeasurable worth and dignity.

Occasionally, clients' problems will be so complex and convoluted that you will feel overwhelmed and inadequate. Even "simple" cases given to a stu-dent may later be found to be much more complicated than the presenting problem indicated. At any time that you feel inundated and unsure how to proceed, you should discuss this with your agency supervisor.

WHAT DO CLIENTS EXPECT FROM ME?

One of the joys (and sometimes one of the frustrations) of social work is that the profession exposes practitioners to many different types of people. Social work clients may be well educated and sophisticated or have little education and be ill-informed about what happens during the helping process. For instance, one client was overheard telling a friend that nothing happened dur-ing the 50-minute counseling session; she added, "All we did was talk."

Some clients are so limited in their ability to articulate family or individ-ual dysfunctioning that they express their problems in terms of having "bad nerves." In their minds, complex problems can be solved with a prescription. As a result, they may request or even expect the social worker to provide phys-ical relief of these symptoms by helping them to obtain a prescription for med-ication. Even if they do not expect pills, clients may anticipate rapid relief from the difficulties that brought them to the agency.

Clients completely unfamiliar with the process of counseling may be con-fused or may misunderstand the purpose of the social worker's questions. It is necessary to inform them that social workers help clients by talking with them to discover more about their problems and strengths. However, the social worker cannot merely tell clients that intervention will consist mostly of talking; he or she may need to elaborate or provide concrete examples. Consumers of social work interventions may expect the social worker to do most of the talking and to *tell* them what to do or how to change their lives. They may not understand that social workers do not give this kind of advice.

Clients with a little more sophistication may expect that social workers will conduct the intervention by talking, but they may have unrealistic expectations—hoping that all the problems in their household will be resolved within three or four weeks. Because a social worker helped a friend, neighbor, or relative with a specific problem in a brief period of time, some clients may envision a "cure" in the same amount of time—not realizing the difficulty in making comparisons with others.

Using your knowledge of human nature, you can anticipate all of the following:

1. Clients want to be treated as individuals and helped with their problems. Although not all clients expect immediate improvement in their life situations, most do not have the patience to wait months for the first signs of progress. Communicate some sense of hope that things will improve, but avoid making any promises that all of their problems will be resolved. Similarly, it is unwise to give specific dates by which clients can expect improvement.

2. Clients do not want to be inconvenienced. Usually, they want the initial interview to be scheduled without delay. They want the social worker to meet with them at convenient times, and they resent being kept waiting. Furthermore, they want the intervention to be as inexpensive as possible.

3. Clients may be unaccustomed to talking about personal problems. They may have never told any other person about their feelings, hopes or dreams, sexual difficulties, or the mental illness within their families. During the helping process, you should encourage the client to learn that not only such topics can be discussed without embarrassment or crudity but also that expressing painful feelings in a therapeutic environment brings about progress.

4. Clients expect you to be the authority—to guide the conversations, to ask the questions, and to act as if you are in charge. If you are too indecisive, then clients will perceive a lack of competence. Clients expect you to have better information about how to solve their problems than they have. They may also expect you to have specialized knowledge that you do not have. Often it is appropriate to tell the client that you do not have certain information. On other occasions, you may feel more comfortable telling the client that you will attempt to find the necessary information and will have it available at your next session. Do not allow clients to force you into the role of advice giver. Clients must make their own choices.

5. Clients expect to be able to tell their problems to a sympathetic professional who will be sincere in trying to help them while protecting their confidentiality. Listen attentively to each client. Do not stereotype clients or make hurried judgments. Treat every client as you would want to be treated.

Case Example

The intake secretary motions for you to come over to her desk one afternoon. In a hushed voice she tells you to expect a client tomorrow who is going to be "angry, demanding, and obnoxious." Although you know that clients are not always going to be pleasant and enjoyable to work with, several times that afternoon your mind goes back to what the secretary said. In preparation, you pull Mrs. Havolec's case record and read it. She has been a client on at least four occasions—always presenting a different problem and always terminating on her own against professional advice. Usually she stops coming to the agency when it appears she may be on the verge of making some significant progress. She is a chronic client, and there are ample notes attesting to her being grouchy and quick tempered. Your reading of her record also uncovers that she seems to be the most ill-humored with the receptionist and that she becomes more agreeable and congenial when she interacts with persons of greater authority and status. You wonder whether you should bend the agency's policy and not inform Mrs. Havolec tomorrow that you are a student.

Questions

1. In the interest of getting along better with the client, would it be okay to wait a couple of sessions or so to inform Mrs. Havolec that you are a student?
2. What would you do if Mrs. Havolec demanded (after spending 15 minutes with you) to be transferred to another worker?
3. Would you feel comfortable asking her to give you a fair chance—to wait at least another 45 minutes or so before deciding she had to have another worker?

SHOULD I INFORM CLIENTS THAT I AM A STUDENT?

Miller and Rodwell (1997) reported that in a survey of social service agencies, where BSW and MSW students were placed for field instruction, 51 percent of the administrators and field supervisors indicated that students were instructed to identify themselves as students. Additionally, another 20 percent of the respondents said that instructions varied by individual field instructors, and 18 percent said that students were told to use their own judgment.

The authors of this text take the position that students have the ethical responsibility not to mislead clients and therefore ought to disclose their student status. Arguments for informing clients include these: Disclosure allows the student to be fully authentic in the relationship, and it will prevent problems later on during termination. Furthermore, it might be hard to keep this information from clients (e.g., clients may call when students are not in the agency, and the receptionist might reply that they are unavailable but will be back from school by noon). Also, concealing one's student status might cause problems for the agency if a serious problem occurred (e.g., the client commits suicide) and the surviving family was looking for grounds to go to court.

Students have an ethical responsibility to clients and should disclose their student status.

In at least one state, Massachusetts, the chapter of the National Association of Social Workers (NASW) has recommended that social work students identify themselves as trainees, interns, or students either verbally or by using name tags and designate their status in the signing of any notes in official records.

Historically, many agencies haven't required students to identify themselves for several reasons: (1) Students receive close supervision, (2) students typically have small caseloads allowing them to give more attention to each case, and (3) agencies did not want to create unnecessary problems for students or for themselves. Frequently agencies feel that students bring interest, enthusiasm, and commitment to their clients that results in a sense that clients get no worse service, and sometimes even better service, from student interns than they get from regular staff members.

In one agency that comes to mind, clients who cannot afford private counseling are told that they may receive help from a student immediately or wait six to ten weeks for a "free slot" to open up. Many clients choose students. However, clients who are not comfortable with students should be afforded other options.

Certainly, students should not be defensive or feel obligated to make self-deprecating remarks because they are students. Every professional has to start as a student. Hepworth and Larsen (1990) suggest that instead of saying "I will see you for eight sessions because that is all of the available time before school ends," one should say, "I will see you for eight sessions because that is sufficient time" (p. 599). The latter provides for a more positive working relationship and takes the emphasis off being a student.

Because we believe that clients should be informed about the qualifications of those providing services to them, we believe that generally students should identify themselves as such sometime during the first session unless the client is in crisis or makes a one-time or brief telephone contact.

HOW DO I KNOW IF I AM HELPING MY CLIENTS?

Two clients provide interesting illustrations for knowing when a client has been helped.

> The first client, a young woman, was brought to the community mental health clinic because of an inability to leave her home without fainting. The student soon discovered that the onset of the client's problem coincided with an incident when she had been brutalized by her former husband. He had kidnapped her from a parking lot and taken her to a remote spot, where he had tied her up and beaten her.
>
> The social work intervention consisted of empowering this woman by brainstorming and role playing the courses of action open to her in any situation in which she might again encounter her ex-husband. (She could carry a police whistle, carry a can of mace, drive with her car doors locked, etc.) After about six weeks, the client skipped her final session. A short time later it was learned that she was successfully employed in a department store. It was obvious that this client had been helped.
>
> Another client had multiple problems and was resistant to solving them. She was obese and had low self-esteem. Her intelligence was slightly below normal. She had an alcoholic and unemployed husband and was herself unemployed and abusing drugs. The student displayed the same enthusiasm with this client as he had with the other client. He attempted to find her strengths and build on them.
>
> The client's happy moments seemed to be largely associated with a period of time when a local motel employed her as a motel maid.

She enjoyed the camaraderie of working with the other women and having a paying job. She felt sure that the motel people would hire her back again. However, by the end of the semester, absolutely no progress had been made. She was no closer to going back and asking for her old job than she had been the day she walked into the agency. She still had all sorts of domestic and personal problems. At the end of the summer, the student felt like a complete failure as he transferred the case to another social worker. This client obviously had not been helped at all.

The point of these two stories is that frequently there are clear, visible indicators that clients have improved (e.g., they quit drinking, secure employment, avoid getting into trouble with the law). Other times, it is practically impossible to detect any real growth or movement on the client's part. How is a student to evaluate the planned intervention?

Although the second of these two clients was more difficult and would have been a challenge for even an experienced social worker, the student would have had a greater probability of helping this client if clear objectives had been developed in the contract phase. Clients are often vague and have complaints such as "I want to feel better about myself" or "I want to stop being so nervous." Sometimes they do not know exactly what is wrong except that they are feeling unhappy or blue. It is very hard to know when you have helped a client if the treatment goal is as ambiguous as to "help the client to feel better about self."

The key to knowing when you have helped a client is to identify a specific problem or behavior with which you can monitor improvement. If a client says "I don't like myself," you need to ask, "How can I help?" or "What are you doing when you begin thinking that you don't like yourself?" Such probing will usually lead to a specific behavior or situation that is troubling the client. For instance, the client who initially indicated that he did not like himself may be terribly shy and reluctant to begin dating. If the client would like himself better by becoming more confident to begin dating, then focus the intervention on this. The criterion for success can be the client's securing that first date. Or, if the client does not know anyone interested in dating him, the target behavior may be having the client approach four different persons and ask for a date within a 30-day period.

Another client who says that he does not like himself may actually be expressing a desire to lose weight. You need to clarify this. If in fact the client is seriously overweight and believes he will like himself better if he can lose 65 pounds (and this seems to be his major concern), then the target behavior becomes the loss of weight.

Behaviors that can be monitored and reduced include angry outbursts, physical punishment of children, tardiness or absences from work, or instances of saying yes when the client really wanted to say no. Because psychometric scales exist for measuring certain attitudes or attitudinal traits, scales can be administered at the beginning and toward the end of intervention to see if clients have made gains in self-esteem or assertiveness or if they are less depressed or anxious. (A number of instruments for monitoring improvement in clients are contained in Corcoran & Fischer's *Measures for Clinical Practice,* 1994.)

The systematic monitoring of a client's progress is a research method known as single-subject or single-system design. It is beyond the scope of this book to explain these techniques in detail; however, you can refer to Royse (1999) or Royse, Thyer, Padgett, and Logan (2001) for more detailed instruction.

Research Based Practice

Critical Thinking Question: How might a single subject research design be used with clients at your practicum agency?

However, the process essentially involves deciding on the target behavior to monitor, obtaining a baseline (an understanding of the frequency or stability of the behavior prior to intervention), beginning the intervention, and then recording or graphing any changes in the behavior (Figure 6.1).

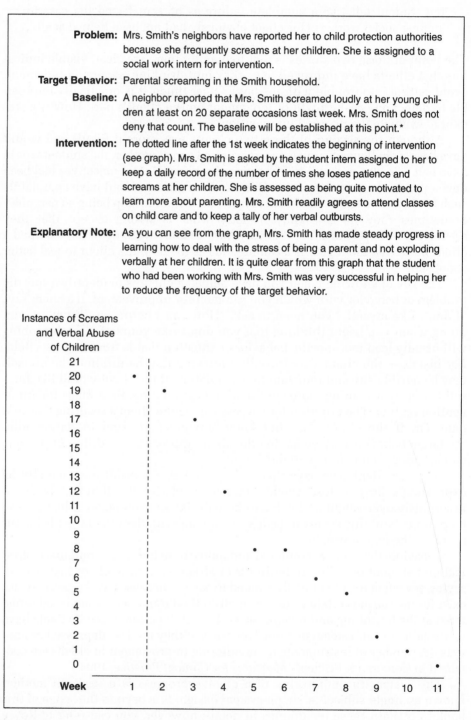

Problem: Mrs. Smith's neighbors have reported her to child protection authorities because she frequently screams at her children. She is assigned to a social work intern for intervention.

Target Behavior: Parental screaming in the Smith household.

Baseline: A neighbor reported that Mrs. Smith screamed loudly at her young children at least on 20 separate occasions last week. Mrs. Smith does not deny that count. The baseline will be established at this point.*

Intervention: The dotted line after the 1st week indicates the beginning of intervention (see graph). Mrs. Smith is asked by the student intern assigned to her to keep a daily record of the number of times she loses patience and screams at her children. She is assessed as being quite motivated to learn more about parenting. Mrs. Smith readily agrees to attend classes on child care and to keep a tally of her verbal outbursts.

Explanatory Note: As you can see from the graph, Mrs. Smith has made steady progress in learning how to deal with the stress of being a parent and not exploding verbally at her children. It is quite clear from this graph that the student who had been working with Mrs. Smith was very successful in helping her to reduce the frequency of the target behavior.

Figure 6.1
Single-Subject Design for Intervention with Mrs. Smith

WHAT DO I DO WHEN A CLIENT WON'T TALK?

Many clients feel reluctant to speak with social workers: They may be shy, rebellious, or confused. You can begin by welcoming the client to your office, suggesting where they can sit and asking if they would like something to drink. Try beginning conversations by asking questions that begin with the word "what"; they are easier to answer because they do not require analytical thinking as do "why" or "how" questions. "What" questions provoke defensiveness with far less frequency and often encourage clients to describe a course of events.

Next, tell the client what you have already been told. Very often they will want to correct what you have heard, add to the information, or make comments about the account. Use their name frequently to show a unique interest and compliment quiet clients when they do talk (e.g., say, "I'm glad you told me that.") Avoid writing and stress confidentiality. Use empathy, "It is hard to talk to someone you have never met."

Many clients will open up with thoughts and feelings when the social worker provides an activity to do (e.g., with teens playing cards or a board game may distract them and they will begin to talk). Also, asking "What have you done today?" is a fairly easy question and keeps the focus in the present that often reduces tension. Change the interview focus; find what interests them—hobbies, leisure activities, movies, music, and so on.

Clients who have been ordered to receive agency services may not feel cooperative. Professionals may have threatened them with going back to jail, with the loss of a job, or with losing custody of their children. Because of racism, poverty, and other societal factors, clients may resent your being a part of the system that has restricted or regulated their activities. Mandated clients may know about others who have committed the same offense and yet received a lighter sentence from the court.

If the client remains sullen and will not talk with you, then let silence prevail. Do not threaten clients but let them clearly know your role and the consequences of their not communicating the required facts. For example, in a school setting you could tell a student that he or she will have another chance to talk later in the day. To build trust, be sure to follow up.

If everything you try does not work, explain that the client can sit the whole 50 minutes without talking—not talking is a legitimate choice available to every client. However, you hope this will not be the client's decision. If the client chooses not to talk, then you can put the time to good use by completing paperwork at your desk. Finally, give clients the agenda for next week so they can have ample time to think about it. Be patient. Some clients find it hard to trust and to make new relationships.

WHAT DO I DO WHEN THE CLIENT WHO WON'T TALK IS A CHILD?

The unfamiliarity of the office setting may frighten children. Reassure the child that the two of you just need to talk for a little while. If the child is particularly fearful, acknowledge that children sometimes are a little scared at first, but that they soon forget that when they find how easy it is to talk to you. If after this explanation the child still will not answer any questions, do not show any frustration or anger—instead say, "That's okay. Let's do something different." Any agency that regularly has children as clients should have some toys available.

It may take multiple attempts to help some clients.

Show the toys to the child and say, "I wonder what you'd like to play with?" Gabel, Oster, and Pfeffer (1988) suggest that at this point the child may involve you in the play and then begin talking. Sometimes you can encourage conversation by parallel play or by making occasional remarks. If this does not work, they advise making something interesting from modeling clay or from paper and crayons. Ask for comments about what you are doing. Realize that with this type of child, the relationship will be built gradually, possibly requiring several sessions before the child feels comfortable enough to talk. If after your best efforts the child still does not communicate, try bringing in one or more family members to be with the child. Anxiety may be lessened when the child observes how other family members can converse with you without adverse results.

HOW DO I DEAL WITH NONCOMPLIANT CLIENTS?

Noncompliance is very frustrating, particularly when the client seems to be relating well to you, owns up to the problem, agrees with the plan to do something about the problem, but fails to keep appointments or does not complete expected tasks. Although the reasons for noncompliance are not always clear, these clients tend to be labeled "resistant" and "unmotivated," and workers may give up on these clients too easily.

Richardson, Simons-Morton, and Annegers (1993) have used values expectancy theory to suggest that when the costs of treatment outweigh the expected benefits, people choose noncompliance. The "costs" of compliance need to be viewed much more broadly than expenditures of finances or time. For instance, there are the costs of changing habits and altering lifestyle, the cost of acknowledging and dealing with a disease or health risk, and the cost of submitting to outside authority and losing control of one's life.

You may find the following suggestions helpful in dealing with noncompliant clients:

▶ Try to understand what it will "cost" to change from the client's perspective. Examine the disadvantages and obstacles as well as the benefits to change. Being "sick" can be more gratifying than being well. What is lost when one becomes "well"?

▶ Recognize that noncompliant behavior may be the client's way of dealing with overwhelming circumstances, an attempt to reestablish personal dignity and control, getting attention, or even a need to express rage or hurt.

▶ View noncompliant behavior as taking place within a context where motives are competing or in conflict. Clients may be experiencing problems but still be stuck in denying their severity or their larger ramifications. Examine your problem-solving strategy. Does it ask too much of the client?

▶ Encourage clients and reinforce the efforts they make toward compliance. Watson (1994) found that an inexpensive follow-up procedure, a second encouraging phone call, increased the compliance of clients who were initially noncompliant with referral recommendations of employee assistance counselors.

▶ Convey the expectation that clients assume responsibility and become compliant. You may have to help clients achieve an optimal balance between discomfort and hope. This can be done not only by encouraging clients to recognize the extent of their dissatisfaction with the problem and the hurt and anxiety it causes, but by also building on the hope that the problem *can* be solved with effort.

Engage, Assess, Intervene, Evaluate

Critical Thinking Question: How might you handle a client who is uncooperative with agreed upon plans?

Clients can be noncompliant in many ways—one of the most common is for them to continue to drink or do drugs when they are supposed to be abstaining. Many agencies have policies that require clients to be sober in order to receive services. If you smell alcohol on a client's breath or have good reason to suspect that he or she is continuing to abuse drugs, then you may have no choice but to temporarily or permanently suspend services. But before you confront a client about this type of noncompliance, be clear about your agency's policies and how your supervisor would want you to inform the client.

WHAT OPPORTUNITIES DO SOCIAL WORKERS HAVE FOR WORKING WITH DIVERSE CLIENTS?

Many beginning social work students are very excited about working with people from a variety of backgrounds; however, they also may wonder if they will be able to succeed with clients from wide-ranging circumstances. Clients may vary with regard to religious beliefs, skin color, age, sexual preference, lifestyle, native language or country of origin, socioeconomic class, and hundreds of ways that are not easily anticipated.

A former student of one of the authors had lived with her missionary parents in Africa for most of her growing up years. She had two children, had suffered abuse from her father and husband, and had entered college at the age of 30. The professor wondered what they might have in common. The student seemed to read the professor's mind when she gave this advice:

> Remember, people everywhere experience the same emotions: they feel loved, abandoned, scared, joyful, and helpful. If you can communicate on a feeling level, you will have the competence to relate to anyone in the world. We human beings all share the same emotions. We experience them at different times and with various levels of intensity, but we all can relate on a feeling level.

This advice has proven immensely helpful, whether working with a war veteran, an abused child, an adult struggling with mental health issues, or a recent refugee to our country.

Sociologists, anthropologists, and social workers remind us of commonalities in worldviews and experiences in minority cultures. These may include the following:

1. the meaning of family for its members with family's needs, prestige, stability, and welfare superseding the individual's aspirations, comfort, health, and well-being;
2. extended family ties creating a large network of kinship;
3. place of religion in the lives of people affecting their attitudes and everyday life practices;
4. experiences that have included various forms of prejudice, economic discrimination, political disenfranchisement, and physical violence;
5. poverty and lower economic status;
6. different levels of acculturation; and
7. culture-related disorders (Dhooper & Moore, 2001).

Case Example

Walking to class one day, a social work student you barely know informs you that he could never work with gay or lesbian clients. He says that he would get rid of them as quickly as possible if he were ever assigned this type of client. You are too stunned to reply. You sense that this student is terribly homophobic. You wonder whether this student has ever read the NASW Code of Ethics.

Questions

1. Does the student have a good understanding of social work values?
2. What would you say to the student?
3. Would the situation have been any different if the student had said that he could not work with African Americans?
4. What if he had said that he could not work with alcoholics or child molesters?

WHAT ARE THE MOST IMPORTANT PRACTICE PRINCIPLES FOR WORKING WITH CLIENTS WHO ARE DIFFERENT FROM ME?

Maslow (1970) has helped us understand that in addition to food, water, oxygen, clothing, and safety, we all have needs to belong and love, to achieve and be competent, and to fulfill our unique potential. We need others to value or appreciate us and to think that we are important. These things are essential, no matter what our skin color, gender, or native language. We always relate to other human beings when we think about the things that we have in common. Although we may differ on what constitutes the "good life," most of us want to be safe and secure, to have enough food, to have our loved ones around us, to have access to medical care and entertainment, and to have outlets for work or creative expression. *Recognize universal human needs.*

Sometimes, however, it is possible to "universalize" too much. Not everyone will like the same foods as you, nor agree with your notion of the best presidential candidate or the best religion, nor express his or her sexuality in the same way as you. We all have common human needs, but as human beings we sometimes seem driven to differentiate ourselves from others. Some of these differences are cultural, acquired in the process of living and growing up, and learned unconsciously. Clients' unique needs are the result of the interplay of individual personality and cultural factors. *Do not over-universalize the commonality of human needs.*

To work effectively with clients, social workers must recognize, understand, and accommodate both their universal and unique needs. Ignorance of a client's culture has to be overcome consciously. Students can learn about the unique characteristics of others by reading, observing, listening, and being sensitive to the fact that not everyone will have the same preferences and values. *Realize that clients are simultaneously similar to others and unique.*

Until you understand them better, you may find that clients from different cultures or backgrounds are not as open with you as they may be with other staff. Because of language difficulty or other factors that make you feel uncomfortable around them, they may sense that you do not accept them. If a client from another culture is resistant, ask yourself if you are viewing the client in a stereotypical manner or judging narrowly from your own cultural perspective. If the answer is yes, you will probably want to talk with more-experienced staff members or your field instructor about techniques to try with this client. Do not rely blindly on standard counseling techniques with clients from other cultures without questioning whether these or other techniques are more appropriate. At a minimum, do some reading on a particular client's culture. *Consciously avoid taking a stereotypical view of people.*

When working with people who have different values, it is probably inevitable that some clash will occur. Such incidents present opportunities for students to examine their own values. When working with clients, remember that professional values take precedence over personal values. Social workers do not have the right to impose their religious or moral values on others. Ethical practice entails making the welfare of the client the primary obligation and providing nondiscriminatory service. Every client is entitled to fairness, equal access to services, respect, impartiality, confidentiality, empathy, and a nonjudgmental attitude. Students who allow biases and prejudices against other persons to interfere with the quality of care provided to clients violate professional ethics. *Remember that the client's welfare is your foremost concern.*

Here is a list of effective practice intervention strategies for assessing culturally diverse clients.

- Consider all clients as individuals first, as members of minority status next, and as members of a specific ethnic group last. This will prevent overgeneralization.
- Never assume that a person's ethnic identity tells you anything about his or her cultural values and patterns of behavior. There can be vast within-culture differences.

- Treat all "facts" about cultural values and traits as hypotheses to be tested anew with each client.
- Identify and build on the strengths in the client's cultural orientation.
- Be aware of your attitude about cultural pluralism.
- Engage the client in the process of learning what cultural content— beliefs, values, and experiences—is relevant for your work together.

    Note: All minority groups in this society live in at least two cultures—their own and the majority culture. The difficulty of surviving in a bicultural environment may be more important than their cultural background. Not all aspects of a client's cultural history, values, and lifestyle are relevant to social work. Only the client can identify which aspects are important.

These additional practice principles come from Dillard (1983):

- Be aware that the nonverbal component constitutes more of the communication than its verbal component.
- Recognize that eye contact can be a problem for many ethnic groups.
- Use self-disclosure judiciously.
- Summarize from time to time.
- Use confrontation carefully with certain racial groups.
- Remember that openness, authenticity, and genuineness are respected in all cultures.

WHAT DO I NEED TO KNOW TO WORK WITH PEOPLE WITH DISABILITIES?[1]

Regardless of the agency setting, social workers find themselves interacting with clients who have disabilities. In fact, there are approximately 46 million people with disabilities in the United States. According to the Americans with Disabilities Act (ADA), these individuals must meet one of the following criteria:

- have a physical or mental impairment that substantially limits one or more life activities;
- have a record of such an impairment;
- be generally regarded as having an impairment.

When a client with a disability requests a specific disability-related service from an agency, it may not be clear whether the service is one that must be provided under the guidelines of the ADA. Generally speaking, if clients without disabilities are eligible for a particular service, then clients with disabilities can expect the same level of service. Most institutions have an "ADA" compliance officer who should be contacted for questions regarding the law as well as to clarify the services expected to be available to all clients—including those with disabilities. Because accommodations required under the ADA are made on an individual basis, it is important to individualize the services needed. Agency personnel, the ADA compliance officer, and the client with the disability should be included in deciding on accommodations.

---

[1]This response is written by Dr. Marlene Huff.

The agency may provide services beyond those required by the ADA, but it is important to understand the differences between services mandated by this law and those provided voluntarily. On occasion, a client with a disability will request an accommodation that could cause an undue burden on the institution. In these cases, the spirit of the ADA encourages all involved parties to agree to a compromise as the most appropriate way to reasonably accommodate the individual, given the resources of the agency.

Social work professionals also need to be aware of facility accessibility requirements. The agency personnel responsible for facility accessibility can assist in determining whether the facility meets state and/or federal architectural standards.

A person's disability may not, however, be the reason that he or she is seeking social work services. All clients have multiple roles. They may be grandfathers or grandmothers, mothers or fathers, sons or daughters, employees, or students *who happen to have a disability*. In other words, the disability probably will not be the characteristic that the clients use to define themselves.

Dealing with clients who have disabilities can be an enjoyable experience if certain basic rules of "disability etiquette" are followed. First, treat every client with a disability as a unique individual. People with disabilities have often been stereotyped when, in fact, they are exactly like all other clients.

Second, be sure to communicate in "person first" language. That is, if you must indicate that someone has a disability, say, "Chad cannot climb steps." Don't say, "Poor disabled Chad can't climb steps." Similarly, Nancy might prefer to be known as someone living with or challenged by paraplegia as opposed to being labeled a paraplegic.

Third, always communicate directly with the person who has the disability. Refrain from addressing your questions to the personal assistant or sign language interpreter unless you can't get your questions answered any other way.

Labels to Avoid	People First Language
The handicapped or disabled	Clients with disabilities
The mentally retarded or "he's retarded"	Clients with mental retardation
She's a Down's; she's a mongoloid	She has Down's syndrome
Birth defect	Congenital disability
Epileptic	A person with epilepsy
Wheelchair bound or confined to a wheelchair	Uses a wheelchair
Developmentally delayed	She has a developmental delay
He's crippled; lame	He has an orthopedic disability
She's a dwarf; midget	She has short stature
Mute	Nonverbal
Is learning disabled or LD	Has a learning disability
Afflicted with, suffers from, a victim of	Person who has . . .
She's emotionally disturbed; she's crazy	She has an emotional disability
Quadriplegic, paraplegic	He has quadriplegia, paraplegia

Special Considerations for Interacting with Clients with Low/No Vision

▶ Identify yourself by name. Don't assume that you will be recognized by the sound of your voice.

▶ Maintain eye contact even if the person with vision difficulties does not look back at you. There should be no change in the tone of your voice.

▶ All animals used for assistance are "working" animals. Do not feed or distract the animals unless the owner gives permission.

Special Considerations for Clients Who Have Problems Hearing

▶ Speak clearly and directly. Do not exaggerate or shout.

▶ Do not cover your mouth as the person may depend on reading your lips to understand the conversation.

▶ Be visual. Use your hands and body to make gestures and expressions that help communicate your verbal message.

▶ When appropriate, arrange for a sign language interpreter to maximize communication with those who primarily use sign language.

▶ If you are not communicating as effectively as you would like, communicate the message in writing.

Communication is also impeded at times by the discomfort felt when one has had little interaction with people who have disabilities; feelings of awkwardness and uncertainess are not unusual. Interacting can be more comfortable if you remember that:

▶ You don't need to avoid words such as walking, running, standing, or seeing. People with disabilities use these terms just the same as persons without disabilities.

▶ When it appears that an individual might need assistance, ask if you can help.

▶ It is not necessary to pretend that there is no disability. Ignoring a disability can be disrespectful.

▶ If an individual's speech is difficult to understand, don't hesitate to ask the person to repeat the sentence.

Remember that persons with disabilities are entitled to the same level of confidentiality as clients without disabilities. Be sure that your office space is physically accessible, or arrange to meet the person at another location. Once you are made aware that a client has a disability and will require accommodations in order to access agency services, make sure that there will be no obstacles preventing that person from receiving the services requested.

Diversity in Practice

Critical Thinking Question: How might utilizing your self-awareness allow you to work more successfully with diverse populations?

HOW DO I WORK WITH LESBIAN, GAY, BISEXUAL, AND TRANSGENDERED PEOPLE?[2]

Working effectively with members of any stigmatized group can pose a number of challenges for social workers. We must work to overcome cultural and unconscious barriers that might interfere with our ability to treat all clients with respect, dignity, and unconditional positive regard. As social workers we are ethically compelled to work diligently for social justice for all marginalized and disenfranchised groups. Unfortunately, when it comes to working with lesbian, gay, bisexual, and transgendered (LGBT) people, social workers may often fail to meet these professional responsibilities. In fact, past research indicates that social workers and social work students often demonstrate high levels of homophobia (Black, Oles, & Moore, 1996; Wisniewski & Toomey, 1987). This finding is particularly troubling when coupled with the reality that social workers see more clients than other mental health professionals. The need to address homophobia in the profession is more than a matter of

---

[2]This response is written by Dr. Melanie Otis.

professional integrity, however. This mandate is also clearly delineated in the Council on Social Work Education's (CSWE) Educational Accreditation Policy Statements and the National Association of Social Workers' (NASW) Code of Ethics.

Overcoming homophobia and heterosexism requires conscious effort. To increase knowledge and understanding about LGBT people, students need to explore the growing number of books, journal articles, videotapes, organizational materials, Internet resources, and other materials that can provide important information for professional growth and development. It is notable, however, that research consistently suggests that the most significant factor related to lower levels of homophobia is whether one knows a LGBT person (D'Augelli, 1989; Lance, 1992). Although such relationships cannot be manufactured, an increasing number of LGBT organizations and individuals participate in community education and activities aimed at bridging the gap between LGBT and non-LGBT individuals. Field experience, volunteer activities, and other community involvement may provide such opportunities.

The most important piece of information a social work professional needs to work effectively with LGBT people is deceptively simple: It is a realization that they, too, are people. LGBT people are sons, daughters, brothers, sisters, parents, coworkers, and neighbors. Their daily lives are challenged by many of the same things that impact non-LGBT clients. Unfortunately, this simple perspective is often difficult for many to achieve. Socialization, personal convictions, religious beliefs, and lack of alternatives to persistent negative stereotypes lead many to feel that LGBT people are not deserving the same rights and protections as afforded by non-LGBT people.

It is also important to understand the unique experience of LGBT people in a society where homophobic views are often expressed openly and without apology. Even though it is socially unacceptable to use derogatory terms to describe people of color, anti-gay/lesbian jokes are often made without fear of sanction.

Although some strides have been made, LGBT people remain at risk for discrimination in all areas of life, including employment, child custody, and housing. In the absence of pervasive civil rights protection, such discrimination is often legal, leaving individuals with no recourse. Furthermore, the stigma attached to being non-heterosexual leads many to remain closeted and fearful of discrimination and victimization. Such fears may impact an individual's willingness to

---

Tips for Social Workers

1. Create an inclusive environment in your social work practice.
2. Work to educate yourself and then continue to ask questions—and listen.
3. Do not attribute all LGBT client concerns to the individual's sexual orientation.
4. Do not ignore the relevance of homophobia and heterosexism in the lives of LGBT clients. Concerns over discrimination and victimization are legitimate.
5. Pay attention to your use of language and the assumptions that are built into that language (e.g., marital status).
6. Be familiar with available resources—and cognizant of gaps in community resources.
7. Become an advocate—confront homophobia in your agency, community, and profession.

The Facts of Life for LGBT Youth

- LGBT youth are two to six times more likely to commit suicide than their peers;
- Twenty to 40 percent of homeless youth in urban areas are reported to be LGBT;
- Sixty-nine percent of LGBT youth report experiencing some form of harassment or violence in school;
- Forty-two percent of LGBT youth do not feel safe in their schools because of their sexual orientation;
- Ninety-seven percent of students in public high schools report regularly hearing homophobic remarks from peers; and
- Fifty-three percent of students report hearing homophobic comments made by school staff.

These facts are from multiple studies. A good source of information on homosexuality and bisexuality with practice guidelines and references can be found at http://www.apa.org/pi/lgbc/guidelines.html. You might also consult www.pflag.org for additional resources and advocacy.

disclose important information concerning his or her personal life and social support network when seeking services from social workers. For many LGBT people rejected by their families of origin, their partners and LGBT friends in the LGBT community have become their most significant source of social support (Weston, 1997). Traditional heterosexist views on family preclude an awareness of this significant, and unfortunately common, aspect of many LGBT people's lives. Effective social work practice, however, requires an awareness of both the common threads in human experience and the unique experiences and needs of LGBT people.

WHAT IS IT LIKE TO WORK WITH SMALL GROUPS OF CLIENTS?

Many agency supervisors give students opportunities to observe, to participate in, and sometimes, to lead groups. Groups may be categorized in several ways; perhaps the most common scheme divides them into either task- or treatment-oriented groups (Kirst-Ashman & Hull, 1993).

Task groups exist to achieve specific goals and objectives. These goals determine how the group operates, which roles members play, and how the social worker functions within the group. Task groups include boards of directors, task forces, committees and commissions, legislative bodies, social action groups, agency staff, and multidisciplinary teams. Treatment groups include growth, therapy, educational, socialization, and support groups.

Many times field instructors can help you begin to understand the various roles, for example, educator, facilitator, evaluator, listener, negotiator, and energizer, that social workers assume within groups. They can also help you build on or develop skills in motivating, helping all group members participate, checking overly aggressive members, developing win–win outcomes, stimulating the discussion process, recognizing and resolving conflict, encouraging team building, and structuring group meetings.

Many students enjoy working with groups because they can cultivate their leadership skills while helping others develop new problem-solving strategies. At the same time, going into a group of unknown individuals can be scary. Unless you have been given the role of leader or facilitator, it is probably best that you not come on too strong in the first meeting or two with a group; rather, listen and observe the natural group processes.

WILL I BE WORKING WITH FAMILIES?

Yes, often the family is the focus of social work services because problems faced by an individual are generally influenced by dynamics within that person's family.

A family group has many characteristics of a small group but is also distinct for at least three reasons. One is that it is intergenerational, extending over long periods of time and with strong emotional bonds. Second, a family is a well-established system in which each member plays an important role. Third, family problems belong to the whole family, not just to particular members (Johnson, 1995).

Social work students need to develop an understanding of the wide variety of forms that families take in our society. They must acquire skills in assessing a family and its situation and then creatively devise, with the family, strategies for solving its problems. Volumes have been written on effective family therapy, and it is well beyond the scope of this book to cover that. Students may, however, find Zastrow's (1995) summary of the theoretical frameworks of Virginia Satir, Salvador Minuchin, Jay Haley, and Ivan Boszormenyi-Nagi a good place to start learning more about various strategies for working with families.

Students must develop an understanding of the wide variety of families in our society.

WHAT ARE THE COMMON CHARACTERISTICS OF MINORITY FAMILIES?

Whether minority families have their roots in Africa, the Caribbean Islands, Mexico, the various countries of Central and South America, Asia, the islands of the Pacific, or the Great Southwest, there are striking commonalities[3] in their cultures, experiences, and worldviews, such as:

Meaning of the Family: Family has a special meaning and place in the lives of people in minority groups. That meaning includes persons from outside the nuclear group. Minority families give more importance to the family and family obligations. They socialize their members to consider the family's needs, prestige, stability and welfare as of more importance than their own aspirations, comfort, health, and well-being. Significant value is placed on family cohesion and loyalty.

Extended Family Ties: Great importance is placed on an effort invested in maintaining a wide network of kinship. The form of the extended family may vary, but it is generally multigenerational. It may include grand parents, uncles and aunts, and cousins from both sides of the family as well as family friends and other fictive kin. This is true of the African American, Latino, Native American, and Asian American families.

Experience as Americans: Minority families often share a history of being victims of racism and oppression. The hostility from the larger community expresses itself in the form of prejudice, economic discrimination, political disenfranchisement, physical violence, immigration exclusion, social segregation, and denial of equality.

Poverty and Lower Economic Status: Large proportions of these families live below the poverty line. Even those who succeed in attaining middle-class status hit the glass ceiling and experience a lack of upward mobility. Their limited success often generates jealousy and resentment in others, which find expression in discrimination, harassment, intimidation, vandalism, and violence.

Level of Acculturation: Most of these families share a commonality in terms of the varying levels of acculturation (adaptation to the host culture) of their members as individuals and as members of minority groups. This is true of the Native Americans who have always lived here as well as the most recent newcomers from Asia, Africa, and Latin America.

---

[3]Most of this information is taken from Dhooper and Moore (2001).

Place of Religion: Religion plays a significant role in the lives of these families and their communities. It affects their attitudes and practices in all dimensions of life. Religious faith and religious institutions represented by priests, pastors, and indigenous healers influence their definition of problems and approaches to dealing with them.

Culture-Related Disorders and Culturally Conditioned Expression: There are culture-related disorders among groups that these families belong to. For example, Dana (1998) has included spirit intrusion, soul loss, root work, ghost sickness, and taboo breaking as culture-bound disorders among American Indians. Many Asian Americans attribute mental illness to natural and spiritual causes. They tend to experience stress psychosomatically as owning and expressing emotional problems is discouraged.

HOW SHOULD THESE COMMONALITIES INFORM MY INTERVENTION WITH MINORITY FAMILIES?

1. Explore these family characteristics as a part of your psychosocial assessment because these can be a source of strength or strain in individual cases.

2. Expect the possibility of a clash between the family's roles, rules and expectations, *and* the ideas of individualism, independence and assertiveness that its members, particularly children, espouse. However, most families deeply care about their members and would do everything possible for their well-being. Use models of family intervention that focuses on family structure.

3. Consider the extended family as a possible source of tangible and intangible help for the family. This is particularly important because many minority families view human services as insensitive and unresponsive to their needs. The patterns of extended family integration vary as do the types of support extended families provide (Sarkisian, Gerena, & Gerstel, 2006).

4. Use empowerment-oriented approaches with these families because most of them are economically poor and are suffering from a general sense of powerlessness. Family therapists are increasingly dealing with issues of social justice as these affect the lives of their clients (Beitin & Allen, 2005).

5. Acknowledge that a family's low level of acculturation and/or differential acculturation among its members can create or contribute to its problems and exacerbate their special needs. Be sensitive to the family's peculiar situation.

6. Whereas religious faith can foster belief in fate, it can also be a source of strength for facing the demands of life. View religion as a plus and religious institutions and personnel as a resource.

7. Since most of these families do not believe in psychiatric dynamics and psychological explanations of behavioral difficulties, look for a structured, concrete, tangible, problem-focused, goal-directed, and result-oriented approach in working with them.

WHAT IS MACRO PRACTICE?[4]

Macro social work practice involves working with individuals through larger systems such as organizations, communities, and institutions to address social problems and promote social change. These macrolevel systems are also referred to as "arenas for change" where social work practitioners apply various methods of intervention in an effort to improve interactions between individuals and their social and physical environment.

Like social workers engaged in direct practice with individuals, social workers practicing at the macrolevel must also be knowledgeable in the use of the problem-solving process to bring about planned change in organizations, communities, and societal institutions. This involves being able to recognize and assess problems, develop alternative strategies, select and implement a specific plan for change, and evaluate results. A macro practice approach to social problem solving also emphasizes the identification of organizational and local community assets to enhance the capacity of individuals to effectively bring about change. Such a grassroots approach is used to empower residents and other community members to identify social problems within their local neighborhoods and to develop and implement change strategies to improve those conditions. One example of this is the formation of neighborhood associations or block clubs.

Macrolevel practice also requires that social workers be skilled in a variety of intervention roles to enhance societal well-being. Brueggemann (2002) groups these intervention methods into three primary arenas of change: formal and informal organizations, neighborhoods and communities, and social institutions.

Macro practice within the organizational arena is concerned with the ability of a social service agency to function effectively in the distribution of resources to those in need. Planning, coordinating, and evaluating the delivery of services, along with the overall performance of the agency, determine whether the mission of the organization is being carried forth. Social workers in this arena might take on the role of administrator, overseeing the daily functioning of the organization and working with staff, consumers, and community stakeholders to monitor the quality and effectiveness of the services provided. It is important for macrolevel social workers to have an understanding of the power structures and cultural climate those define how an organization functions. This knowledge will assist in the design of interventions that are responsive to the needs of consumers and staff.

Organizing individuals within a community to gain access to resources and services in order to improve quality of life is another form of macro practice. In this case, the community arena of macro practice encompasses both geographically defined communities (e.g., neighborhoods) and communities of interest. A community of interest refers to a group of individuals that share some common feature (e.g., race, religion, lifestyle), interest (e.g., cooking and gardening), or ideology (e.g., environmental protection). The intervention role of community organization focuses on mobilizing community members in an effort to develop a collective power base capable of addressing social problems and formulating local solutions. Community organizing draws upon indigenous leadership to empower community members through consensus building to identify and solve their own problems. Social workers in this

Macro social work is about bringing change within organizations, communities, and societal institutions.

---

[4]This response is written by Dr. Robin Ersing.

arena facilitate the process of building community capacity and improved networks for collaboration with other groups.

Finally, macro practice at the societal level involves addressing social injustices by bringing about changes in policies within institutions that contribute to racial, gender, and economic inequality. In this arena, social workers are instrumental as activists, organizing social movements to champion the rights of the oppressed and marginalized groups. Social workers play an important role by encouraging individuals to register to vote and to lobby their elected representatives. They also are instrumental in preparing policy briefs to educate and inform legislators and other decision makers on the social and economic inequalities that impact children, adults, and communities. Macro social work practice in this arena often involves conflict and confrontation aimed at bringing about a shift in power and resources to eliminate disparities among segments of the population.

SUMMARY

Many social work students have never been required to ask for professional assistance or exposed to persons remarkably poor or different from their own families of origin. Questions often arise about how to best communicate and work with individuals, families, and communities that are unfamiliar. This chapter has provided information to assist students in understanding and working with new client systems.

Confidentiality

1. What are your agency's policies about clients' confidentiality?

_____

_____

_____

_____

_____

2. What would you do if a client told you something and asked you not to tell anyone, not even to your supervisor?

_____

_____

_____

_____

_____

3. When is it acceptable to break a client's confidentiality?

_____

_____

_____

_____

_____

Recipients of Service

1. All social workers have preferences for the types of clients with whom they like to work.

   a. What are some of your preferences?

   _____

   _____

   _____

   _____

   b. What types of problems do you find most interesting or rewarding when you are assisting clients?

   _____

   _____

   _____

   _____

2. Social workers face many challenges as they work with people to solve problems.

   a. What age group would you find most difficult to work with (e.g., preschool children, teenagers)? What could you do to overcome your hesitancy to work with this group?

   _____

   _____

   _____

   _____

   b. Setting aside the client's age, what types of problems would you find most difficult to work with? What could you do to overcome your hesitancy to work with this group?

   _____

   _____

   _____

   _____

Student Safety

1. What are your agency's procedures for dealing with hostile clients?

_____

_____

_____

_____

_____

2. What emergency numbers should you place besides your office phone?

_____   _____

_____   _____

_____   _____

3. What precautions has your field liaison suggested with regard to home visits?

_____

_____

_____

_____

_____

4. Are there any safety concerns you feel should be discussed with your supervisor? If so, what are they?

_____

_____

_____

_____

_____

_____

Practice and Research

1. Select one of your clients and draw up a single-subject design on another sheet. Describe here the behavior you and the client want to measure over time. Is it one that is easy to observe, measure, or count?

_____

_____

_____

2. What are your intervention goals? Will the single-subject design be useful in informing you and the client about whether the intervention has been helpful?

_____

_____

_____

3. Ask if a program evaluation has been conducted recently for any of the agency's programs—look particularly for any connected with your internship. Read the evaluation. What recommendations did the evaluators make?

_____

_____

_____

4. Knowing what you do about the program, what recommendations would you make for the program now that you are somewhat familiar with it? Are there any suggestions for changes or improvement that you would like to discuss with your supervisor?

_____

_____

_____

_____

_____

Working with Others Different from Ourselves

1. People all over the world experience the same emotions—happiness, sadness, guilt, jealousy, and so on. Describe a feeling elicited by a client with which you could easily identify.

   _____

   _____

   _____

2. Make a conscious effort to have a conversation with someone of a different ethnic background or someone who lives a different kind of lifestyle. Or, attend a meeting of Al-Anon Family Group. Listen for anything that you might have in common. Then, identify some of the ways you might be dissimilar.

   Similar: _____

   _____

   _____

   Dissimilar: _____

   _____

   _____

3. Who is the person at your agency or university responsible for Americans with Disabilities Act (ADA) compliance? Interview that person and list at least three things you learned from him or her about accessibility, service eligibility, and making reasonable accommodations.

   _____

   _____

   _____

4. Read a journal article about human sexuality or sexual orientation. What information in the article helps you better understand persons whose sexual orientation differs from your own? What questions about sexuality does the article leave unanswered? Give the citation of the article that you read (author, year, title, journal, etc.).

   _____

   _____

   _____

   _____

   _____

   _____

Working with Groups, Families, and Communities

1. What experiences have you had leading small groups?

   _____

   _____

   _____

2. What skills do you feel you need to develop in order to effectively lead groups?

   _____

   _____

   _____

3. Describe a group you have participated in where everyone felt appreciated and respected. How did the leader(s) make that happen?

   _____

   _____

   _____

   _____

   _____

   _____

4. Describe the neighborhood within which your social service setting is located. How is it like and different from the neighborhood in which you grew up?

   Like: _____

   _____

   _____

   Unlike: _____

   _____

   _____

Succeed with PEARSON **mysocialworklab**

Log onto **www.mysocialworklab.com** to access a wealth of case studies, videos, and assessment. (*If you did not receive an access code to* **MySocialWorkLab** *with this text and wish to purchase access online, please visit* www.mysocialworklab.com.)

1. **Watch the Core Competency video: "Building Self-Awareness."** The social worker in this video spends quite a bit of time learning about the meaning of the client's name and the part of Uganda from which he came. How will acquiring this knowledge help the social worker to recognize value differences and "build a bridge of connection?"

2. **Watch the Core Competency video: "Engaging the Client to Share Their Experiences."** Focusing on the action or behavior of the social worker, Hugo Kamya, what did he do that engaged the client and encouraged him to talk?

PRACTICE TEST The following questions will test your knowledge of the content found within this chapter.

1. What should social workers take into consideration when working with a client who has a disability?
   a. ADA mandates provision of all services.
   b. Ignore the disability.
   c. Feel comfortable saying, *seeing, walking, running*.
   d. Find out all their disability limitations.

2. Which tip was not discussed relative to assessing and intervening with culturally diverse clients?
   a. Consider all clients as individuals first.
   b. Build on the strengths found in the cultural orientation.
   c. Assume that an ethnic identity tells you everything important.
   d. Treat each "fact" about cultural values as a hypothesis to be tested with each client.

3. The text offers all but which of the following tips in working with lesbian, gay, bisexual, and transgendered people?
   a. Confront homophobia in your community.
   b. Pay attention to your use of language.
   c. Attribute almost all LGBT client concerns to their sexual orientation.
   d. Be familiar with available resources.

4. A client you have just met will not speak. How would you help the client talk?
   a. Ask questions that begin with "what."
   b. Be firm about consequences of not talking.
   c. Show your disapproval by doing paperwork.
   d. Try discussing the weather.

Short Answer Question:

John grew up in a rural community where there was a lot of stereotyping of minorities and persons who weren't strictly heterosexual. He is now an intern in a large inner-city agency where persons of color are a large part of the caseload and the agency has a special outreach effort for the HIV/AIDS population. How can John be sure that he is respecting the diversity found among his clients and not letting the cultural values from his childhood affect his current assessments and intervention planning?

ASSESS YOUR COMPETENCE Use the scale below to rate your current level of achievement on the following concepts or skills associated with each competency practice behavior presented in the chapter:

1	2	3
I can accurately describe the concept or skill.	I can consistently identify the concept or skill when observing and analyzing practice activities.	I can competently implement the concept or skill in my own practice.

_____ apply single-subject research designs with clients at practicum agency.

_____ use interpersonal skills with noncompliant clients to keep the focus on agreed-upon outcomes.

_____ utilize self-awareness and am able to control the influence of my personal values and biases when working with diverse groups.

Answers

Key: 1) c, 2) c, 3) c, 4) a

7

Acquiring Needed Skills

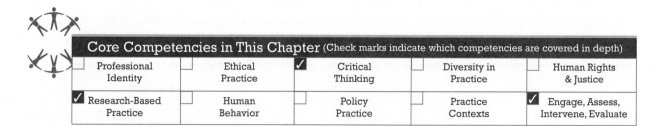

Core Competencies in This Chapter (Check marks indicate which competencies are covered in depth)				
☐ Professional Identity	☐ Ethical Practice	✔ Critical Thinking	☐ Diversity in Practice	☐ Human Rights & Justice
✔ Research-Based Practice	☐ Human Behavior	☐ Policy Practice	☐ Practice Contexts	✔ Engage, Assess, Intervene, Evaluate

OVERVIEW

This chapter is designed to help students feel less nervous about beginning to work with their clients by providing a brief refresher on topics usually covered in students' practice courses.

DO MOST STUDENT INTERNS FEEL NERVOUS AND INADEQUATE?

Yes, probably a majority of students beginning a new practicum can expect to experience some nervousness—which does not indicate that students are not suited for social work, only that they want to do well and are aware that they still have much to learn. Changes in routines and new experiences involve an element of risk, which is always a little scary. Consciously or unconsciously, student interns may think, "What if I don't do well in this placement?" "What if my agency supervisor expects too much?" "What if I can't help my clients?" or "Should I have taken additional classes before registering for the practicum?" In a study we conducted (Rompf, Royse, & Dhooper, 1993), about four of every ten students going into a practicum expressed self-doubts or felt deficient in the skills needed to perform well in their agencies. Students going into their first practicum were more anxious than students who had previously been in a practicum.

Logistical concerns can also be a source of anxiety. Questions may surface such as, "What if traffic is terrible and I am late the first day?" or "Where will I go for lunch?" These concerns can usually be managed by thinking ahead. To plan for the length of time it takes to travel, students can, for instance, drive to the agency a time or two before the practicum starts. They can look for a parking lot near the agency or call the agency supervisor beforehand and ask where to park. And students can always pack a lunch for the first day until they discover where others in the office eat.

You should realize that it is okay to feel anxious—it is a common experience—and that making specific plans often helps to reduce the anxiety. In a book we recommend for students, Corey and Corey (1989) share some of their initial experiences in starting out:

> In one of my earlier internships I was placed in a college counseling center. I remember how petrified I was when one day a student came in and asked for an appointment, and my supervisor asked me to attend to this client . . . . Some of the thoughts that I remember running through my head as I was walking to my office with this client were, "I'm not ready for this. What am I going to do? What if he doesn't talk? What if I don't know how to help him? I wish I could get out of this!" (p. 11)

Such anxieties and concerns are normal and all right for students to experience, because as social workers they will often have to support clients when they make changes in their lives. It is good for students to recall their own feelings when encountering change and new situations.

WHAT SKILLS MIGHT I BE EXPECTED TO DEVELOP?

The diversity of human problems and their manifestation at different levels—individual, group, neighborhood, community, institutional, and societal—create the breadth of social work as a profession. Accordingly, different methods, approaches, and strategies have been conceived so that intervention can be applied in various situations and contexts.

The basic problem-solving method taught in practice courses is applicable across all situations and provides the basis for deciding how to intervene. Similarly, there are skills common to all levels of human organization. These include listening, observing, relationship building, interviewing, assessing, contracting, mediating, advocating, planning, and evaluating.

We expect that most students entering a practicum for the first time will be practicing micro-level skills. Although some students may go into macro-level placements without ever developing the skills required for working with individual clients, we think that this is rare. Most students start by learning how to work with clients one-on-one. The balance of this chapter will focus on the skills that are needed and problems that may arise in such settings.

HOW DO I START INTERVIEWING A CLIENT?

According to Kadushin (1972), social workers spend more time interviewing than in any other activity. It is the most frequently employed social work skill. In view of its importance, it is natural for student interns to feel somewhat uneasy whenever they begin to think about the responsibility of interviewing that first client. So relax a bit if you feel uneasy—most students (and probably clients, too) face the first interview with some apprehension.

It may help to realize that the physical environment gives you some measure of control during the interview. Freedom from distraction, privacy, and open space between participants in a room with comfortable furniture and adequate ventilation and light will make it easier for the client and for you. Check the interviewing room ahead of time (if the room is different from your office) to ensure that the temperature setting is right and that there will be enough chairs (e.g., if a family is expected). Sit in the room; get accustomed to it. Think of the questions you will need to ask. If you do not feel at ease there (e.g., insufficient privacy), then try to arrange for another office before the client arrives.

In a quiet office it is easier to feel relaxed and to listen thoughtfully and give the client your full attention. Consider the arrangement of the furniture and whether it is better to sit behind the desk or away from it. Sitting behind a desk emphasizes the authority of the social worker and lends more formality to the meeting. Sitting away from the desk may help to create rapport a little more quickly.

An interview can be conceptualized as a three-stage process: (1) the opening, or beginning, stage; (2) the middle, or working-together, stage; and (3) the ending, or termination, stage. Each has a different focus and different tasks to be accomplished. Let us look at each of these stages in more depth.

The beginning stage starts when the interviewer greets the client, does whatever will make the client comfortable, and defines the purpose of the interview. Think of interviewing as a purposeful conversation. There is a specific reason that you will be talking with the client. After introducing yourself, therefore, it is often a good idea to ensure that the client is clear on the purpose of the interview. Always give the client an opportunity to discuss any special needs. In the initial interview, the intent is generally to learn about the client, the problem he or she faces, the efforts that have been made to solve the problem; to identify untapped resources that may exist; and to find out what the client's expectations are of the worker and the agency.

It is safe to assume that the client has questions about the helping process (e.g., how the helping will occur, how long it will take, what it will cost). Imagine yourself as a client in a strange agency seeking help for a comparable problem. What questions would come to your mind? Answering these questions, and pointing out that the agency exists for clients with this type of problem, will assist in breaking the ice. Asking for help from strangers is not always easy, and in this phase it is important to help clients feel that they are in the right place and have made the correct decision.

As both of you begin to feel more comfortable, encourage the client to verbalize his or her feelings about the problem situation. An age-old social work maxim, "Begin where the client is," suggests that you attempt to understand the problem from the client's perspective. Avoid going into the interview with a preconceived idea about what the client is like or is apt to say. Do not form opinions too early or become guilty of stereotyping the client and hearing only what you have decided he or she will be saying.

Even while introducing yourself and describing the agency's policies, programs, and resources, convey an interest and a willingness to understand the client's point of view. Each of your communications should reflect an interest in the client. For instance, gently probe, inquire, guide, and suggest. Do not cross-examine, make accusations or demands, or dominate. Both verbal and nonverbal messages should express an interest in the client.

The character of the case and the personal characteristics of the client will influence the interviewing process. With some types of problems, you will need to proceed more slowly than with others. The middle stage of the interview process is purpose-specific. You will be monitoring your communications for their effectiveness in keeping the interview on course, refocusing the client if the interview begins to drift away from its purpose, and possibly renegotiating a contract if that is indicated. When the purpose of the interview has been fulfilled, or just before the agreed time for ending the interview has been reached, the interview has reached the third stage.

During the termination stage, summarize what has happened during the interview. Agree on the next step (including the work to be done before the next interview and the purpose, time, and place of the next interview). Kadushin (1972) advises:

> In moving toward the end there should be a dampening of feeling, a reduction in intensity of affect. Content that is apt to carry with it a great deal of feeling should not be introduced toward the end of the interview. The interviewees should be emotionally at ease when the interview is terminated. (p. 208)

Usually it is appropriate to engage in a few minutes of social conversation as a transition out of the interview.

Sheafor, Horejsi, and Horejsi (2000) suggest some helpful guidelines for interviewing:

1. Be prepared to respond in an understanding way to the client's fears, ambivalence, confusion, or anger during the first meeting.

2. Be aware of your own body language. The way you are dressed, your posture, facial expressions, and hand gestures all send messages to the client. Try to send a message of respect and caring.

3. If you have only limited time to spend with a client, explain this at the beginning of the session so the things of highest priority will receive attention.

4. Give serious attention to the presenting problem, as described by the client, but realize that many clients will test your competency and trustworthiness before revealing the whole story or the "real" problem. Begin with whatever the client considers important and wants to talk about.

5. Adapt your language and vocabulary to the client's capacity to understand.

6. If you do not understand what the client is saying, ask for further clarification or an example.

7. When you do not know the answer to a question asked by the client, explain so in a nonapologetic manner and offer to find the answer.

8. Explain the rules of confidentiality that apply to your meeting, and be certain to inform the client if what he or she says cannot be held in complete confidence.

9. If the client is bothered by your note-taking, explain why [notes] are needed, what will happen with [them], and offer to show the notes you have taken. If the client still objects, cease note-taking. If you are completing a form or following an outline, give the client a copy of the form to follow along with you.

10. Before the interview ends, be sure that the client has your name and the agency phone number, and that you have the client's full name, address, and phone number. (pp. 197–198)

To these we add a few of our own guidelines that will make it easier for clients to trust and feel that you are professional:

1. Never lie to a client or pretend that you have experience that you do not.

2. Do not make promises that you may not be able to keep or promises on behalf of others.

3. Do not argue with clients.

4. Do not attempt to force a client to tell you something that he or she does not want to tell. (If either you or the client is making frequent use of the word *but*, then you are probably forcing some idea or line of questioning on the client. This will be experienced as more of an interrogation than an interview.)

5. Do not display (verbally or nonverbally) shock, surprise, or disbelief in response to what a client may tell you.

6. Do not talk down to a client or try to impress the client with your knowledge of clinical terms or jargon.

7. Although you may run out of time, do not rush the client. Realize that hesitation may be the result of anxieties or fears. Furthermore, do not finish sentences or supply words for clients in an effort to speed them up. If necessary, make a second appointment to complete the interview.

HOW DO I BEGIN TO HELP THE CLIENTS WHO ARE ASSIGNED TO ME?

Having acknowledged that you may feel a little insecure in your ability to help clients, let us quickly review what you should already know about the helping process:

1. The social worker makes use of self in helping clients. *Self* includes the knowledge acquired from the traditional academic environment, the common sense developed as a result of life experiences, and the social worker's personality. Social workers help clients to solve their problems through techniques such as listening, leading, reflecting, summarizing, confronting, interpreting, and informing. They support, explore alternatives, model behavior, teach, and sometimes refer. To help others, social workers should have self-awareness. They must know their own values, biases, strengths, and limitations. In reviewing the training of family therapists, Bagarozzi and Anderson (1989) discuss the sense of self as a primary vehicle for therapeutic change,

> often evidenced in less of a tendency to "do things to and for clients" or to "give clients an intervention" and more of an emphasis on "being with clients" or "responding" to clients with greater genuineness, honesty, openness and courage. (p. 284)

The necessary skills and knowledge to help clients are not easily specified—and probably reflect a constellation of abilities, knowledge, and experiences. Some social work students will be more aware of themselves than others; some will be more knowledgeable or more experienced. Many students can, however, make up for most real or presumed deficiencies in their expertise by being an active and interested participant in the helping process. Egan (1990) writes:

> The best helpers are active in the helping sessions. They keep looking for ways to enter the worlds of their clients, to get them to become more active in the sessions, to get them to own more of it, to help them see the need for action—action in their heads and action outside their heads—in their everyday lives. (p. 105)

2. The first step in helping any client is establishing a therapeutic relationship. How exactly do social workers go about establishing such relationships? More than 30 years ago, Carl Rogers identified empathy, respect, and genuineness as being necessary for the therapeutic relationship. When these are communicated to clients along with a nonjudgmental attitude and an unconditional acceptance of their individual worth, a relationship begins to develop. Without the social worker engaging the client or building rapport, the client is unlikely to share any personally important information. Patterson (1985) writes, "Counseling or psychotherapy is an interpersonal relationship. Note that I don't say that counseling or psychotherapy *involves* an interpersonal relationship—it *is* an interpersonal relationship" (p. 3).

3. Once the social worker establishes rapport, he or she begins to explore and assess the client's problem. The social worker needs to understand what kind of assistance the client seeks, when the problem began, what factors complicate solving the problem, what efforts have been made, and what resources are available to the client. During this phase, the social worker finds a place to start the problem-solving process. Both client and social worker must agree on and choose some aspect of the problem causing trouble for the client. Often social workers support and encourage clients by providing them with hope that their present situation can be improved.

4. When the client and the social worker reach an agreement on what needs to be done and what realistically can be done, a contract is developed. The contract, which can be either written or verbal, provides focus and clarification—it serves as a reminder of what the client wants to achieve as well as what can be expected from the social worker.

5. Implementation of the intervention or the actions covered in the agreement constitute the middle phase, or what Hepworth and Larsen (1990) call the "heart of the problem-solving process" (p. 33). They point out that "interventions should directly relate to the problems and to the consequent goals that were mutually negotiated with clients and that were derived from accurate assessment" (p. 33).

6. When the client and the social worker achieve the contract goals, the final step in the problem-solving process follows. This step involves termination of the therapeutic relationship and evaluation of its results. Either the client or the social worker may begin a discussion about termination when some or all of the agreed goals have been achieved. Judgment about the appropriateness of termination is perhaps the easiest when the intervention is time-limited, based on a set number of sessions, or revolves around specific tasks (such as acquiring or extinguishing certain behaviors). Because many factors affect the decision to terminate, clients commonly drop out of therapy or express an interest in termination before achieving all of the stated goals. It is often appropriate to indicate that clients can return should they express an interest at some future time.

WHAT IS PROCESS RECORDING?

Process recording is a detailed narration of what happened during a social worker's contact with a client. Historically it has been used to monitor service delivery and assist in the development of practice theory. Field instructors and faculty field liaisons sometimes require student interns to do a process recording so they can examine the dynamics of the client–student interaction. It is an excellent teaching device for learning and refining interviewing and intervention skills. Process recording can help the student to conceptualize and clarify the purpose of the interview or intervention, to improve written expression, to identify strengths and weaknesses, and to improve self-awareness. Although they are often written exercises, process recordings can also involve audio- or videotaping and live observation. (See Chapter 8 for more on audio- and videotaping.)

Many social work programs are rediscovering the importance of process recording as an invaluable learning tool. We know of at least one school that requires:

- BSW Juniors complete a minimum of one process recording.
- BSW Seniors do two process recordings.
- MSW Foundation students complete two process recordings.
- MSW Concentration (Interpersonal Practice) students do six process recordings.

A process recording usually contains:

1. At least first names of those involved in the session

2. The date of the session

3. A description of what happened

4. The social worker's observations of the client's actions and nonverbal communications

5. The social worker's assessment of what happened and why

6. A diagnostic summary that pulls together the social worker's overall thoughts on the entire session (in a paragraph or so)

7. A brief statement of goals or plans for further contact with the client

The actual description of what transpired can be written either with alternating lines for client and student intern or as a narrative. When written as a script, the process recording can be used for role playing in supervisory conferences.

Cohen (1988) developed a five-step format for process recording: (1) *preengagement*—the student records affective and cognitive preparation for the interview; (2) *narrative*—the student describes the details of what transpired during the interview (not a verbatim reconstruction but a summary of verbal interaction); (3) *assessment*—the student evaluates what transpired; (4) *plans*—the student describes the agreed-upon next steps; and (5) *questions*—the student records any questions about the content and process of the interaction. For format, Wilson (1981) suggests the use of three or four columns. The first column is for the supervisor's comments and is left blank. The second column is used by the student to describe the content of the interview. The third column is used for recording the student's feelings as the dialogue takes place. Wilson believes it is difficult to put one's feelings into writing and that students may tend to use the third column to comment on the client's responses. If that happens, a fourth column should be added to analyze the client's responses. The use of these columns should help the student to develop diagnostic skills by providing a place for recording interpretations while forcing a separation of feelings from professional assessments. Other educators have suggested that the third column can be used simply for student reflection.

If you are required to do process recording, you will benefit from the following suggestions:

1. The time lag between the interview and writing up the process recording should be as short as possible. Since the process recording demands that you describe everything that takes place in the interview, you are likely to forget material with the passage of time.

2. Whenever possible, try to do process recording in conjunction with audio- or videotaping. This will help you to identify significant omissions and to remember things that you might otherwise have forgotten. (Remember to obtain both the client's and agency's permission and be sure that the taping will not unduly inhibit the client or negatively affect the session.)

3. Keep in mind that the purpose of process recording is to help you learn how to be a sensitive, effective practitioner. If you severely edit portions of the interview instead of allowing it to be verbatim, you may be depriving yourself of beneficial feedback.

4. Select the most challenging cases for process recording. Because process recording is a time-consuming activity, it is likely that you will be

Engage, Assess, Intervene, Evaluate

Critical Thinking Question: How would you assess a suicidal client?

required to do this type of recording on only a few cases. Choose a case that has the greatest potential for learning.

5. Take pains to ensure that your process recording does not jeopardize the client's confidentiality. Use a fictitious name for the client or perhaps only the first letter (Mr. C.). Keep the written records in a secure place. Remember that a process recording is a teaching device only. It should never become a part of the formal record of the agency.

Background: This is the first contact with a four-year old patient in hospital. The purpose of this session is to establish rapport.

COMMENTS AND FEELINGS

Student: Good morning, Melissa. How are you today?

Melissa: *No response*

Student: Did you have breakfast yet?

Melissa: *Nods her head affirmatively*

Trying to find a question she would have to answer.

Student: Let me guess what you had. Was it a big ol' baked potato? Was it a tiny little hot dog? Okay, then. . . was it one corn flake and a whole bowl of raisins. No? Then what was it?

Thought I'd try a humorous approach.

Melissa: Scrambled eggs and toast. (*smiles*)

Student: Did you gobble them all up?

Melissa: *Nods her head affirmatively*

More humor because she had smiled back to me.

Student: Good. Do you want anything else?

Thought I'd open things up to see what Melissa wanted to talk about.

Melissa: Where's my Mommie?

A break-through!

Student: Well, after the wreck they took her to another hospital. Do you remember the wreck last night?

Wanted to give Melissa opportunity to ventilate about the wreck.

Melissa: *Nods with downcast eyes*

Student: Wrecks can be pretty scary. Can't they? Do you want to talk about the wreck you were in?

Another opportunity for ventilation.

Melissa: *Shakes her head "no"*

Student: Okay. Maybe later, if you want. Say, I know. Want to go for a wheel-chair ride? This floor of the hospital has a whole bunch of kids and you know what? Some of them have IV fluids dripping into their arms just like you! We might even find anoth-er little girl with a broken leg. Want to see if we can find one?

Since she doesn't want to talk, thought she might be reassured by seeing other children. It also gives her occa-sion to raise questions about medical procedures or how other kids are getting along with their injuries.

I didn't want to give her more informa-tion about her mother than she needed. At least, not until Mom's con-dition stabilizes a bit more.

Melissa: Un-huh.

Figure 7.1

Example of Process Recording

You may want to follow this order in your process recording:

1. Purpose of the interview
2. Observations about the client's physical and emotional status
3. Description of the interview
4. Impressions (but based on facts)
5. Reflection on skills and techniques used
6. A plan for future contact and activity

Although there are many ways in which to present a process recording, Figure 7.1 contains a streamlined example of one for you to visualize. This model does not separate out the student's feelings from his or her thoughts, although that can be a useful process, too.

Lastly, Vourlekis, Hall, and Rosenblum (1996) have developed a reliable and valid checklist for rating process-recorded interviews that can help field instructors to provide unbiased feedback to students on their interviewing skills.

I'M SELF-CONSCIOUS ABOUT MY ABILITY TO WRITE WELL. WILL THIS BE A PROBLEM?

Unfortunately, people who don't know us often form impressions about us on the basis of our written communications. Therefore, it is essential, if you want to be viewed as a competent professional, that your reports, memos, and progress notes show that you can communicate effectively and efficiently. This means your "formal" writing should be neat, free of misspellings and poor grammar, and should be punctuated correctly.

Look at the paragraph below to see what sense you get of the author:

> The accused, I think his name was Bobie Meson or somethin like that was halucinating as he drove the Metro Bus into the city garage. He and his wife bough some LSD from a freind and they told Bobbie that, it would be safe to drive as long as he didn't take to much at one time. Carefully driving, the bus between parked cars until the Little Man with a gun. "Later." He ran and sat at a lunch counter and ordered a stake. That's were the police found them. The clinical staff recommended a 72-hour hold; and I agree: you can't be to carefull in this type of situation and need to seperate the details out from the lyes.

If you know yourself to be a poor speller, always consult a dictionary. Even better, type everything you can on a computer that has a spell-check function. Even this will not protect you from choosing the wrong homophone (like stake and steak), which the computer may recognize as correct although it could be an inappropriate choice for the passage you had intended. If the document is very important, have someone else proofread the final draft for you.

In terms of grammar, you may need to take a refresher course in writing skills. It is essential that you know when to capitalize and how to punctuate. If you are not sure of the rules, or if your papers typically come back from instructors with lots of red ink on them, this is a pretty good indication that you could use some help. If you are loathe to take another English course, at least make a trip to the library or bookstore and look in the reference section for writing guides. Consult these guides whenever you are in doubt about pronoun agreement, dangling participles, run-on sentences, sentence fragments, and the like.

Finally, take pride in your work by reading and revising. Proofread everything before you release it. Revise. If necessary, do two or three revisions. One of the best things you can do to improve your writing is to edit what you write. Remove unclear and unnecessary words. Polish. Don't be afraid to try and find another, crisper way of expressing yourself. Find those in the agency who have a writing style you like, and then study it. Observe the points they make and how they make them. Don't hesitate to ask for help. Your communication skills are important.

Proofread everything before you release it.

WHAT DO I NEED TO KNOW ABOUT CHILD ABUSE?

1. Child abuse or child maltreatment is a social problem that has no boundaries. It occurs among all socioeconomic groups in all locations—rural, urban, and suburban and in all settings—children's homes, foster homes, childcare centers, and residential institutions. Its incidence is painfully astounding. Information from the Children's Bureau and the Child Welfare Information Gateway shows that during the federal fiscal year (FFY) 2009, there were approximately 3.3 million referrals for alleged mistreatment of about 6 million children. An estimated 1,770 children died as a result of abuse and neglect. This number is probably not reflective of the true picture of child fatalities due to child abuse and neglect. Many researchers and practitioners in the field believe that child fatalities are still underreported.

2. The major types of child abuse are (1) physical abuse, (2) sexual abuse, (3) emotional abuse, and (4) neglect. Other types of maltreatment include abandonment and congenital drug addiction. During FFY 2009, 78.3 percent of child abuse victims experienced neglect, 17.8 percent were physically abused, 9.5 percent were sexually abused, and 7.6 percent received psychological maltreatment. Although victims are categorized on the basis of the prominent symptoms of maltreatment, children experience a combination of various types of abuse. A physically abused child is emotionally abused as well, and a sexually abused child may also be neglected.

3. Child abuse and neglect can adversely affect a child's physical, intellectual, social, and psychological growth and development. In the words of Green and Roberts (2008),

> The effects of child sexual abuse may include fear, anxiety, depression, anger, hostility, inappropriate sexual behavior, poor self-esteem, substance abuse, and difficulty with close relationships. Effects of physical child abuse can include the immediate effects of bruises, burns, lacerations, and broken bones as well as longer-term effects such as brain damage, hemorrhages, and permanent disabilities. Physical trauma and abuse can also negatively affect children's physical, social, emotional, and cognitive development. Emotional abuse, also known as psychological maltreatment, can seriously interfere with a child's

cognitive, emotional, psychological, or social development. The effects of emotional abuse may include insecurity, poor self-esteem, destructive behavior, withdrawal, poor development of basic skills, alcohol or drug abuse, suicide, difficulty forming relationships, and unstable job histories. (p. 79)

4. Although no group of children and no class of adults are untouched by this problem, some children are at greater risk of being abused and some adults are more likely to be perpetrators of child maltreatment. Younger children are at greater risk. The rate of victimization was inversely related to the child's age group. For example, victimization rate for the *birth to 1 year* age group was 24.4 per 1,000 children of the same age group and that for the *1–3 years* age group was 14.2 per 1,000. African American, American Indian, and multiracial children had the highest rates of victimization at 19.8, 15.9, and 15.4 per 1,000 of the same racial or ethnic group, respectively. About one half (48.8 percent) of all victims were white, almost a quarter (22.8 percent) were African American, and 18.4 percent were Hispanic. Asian children had the lowest rate of 2.5 percent per 1,000. Children who were previously abused were 96 percent more likely to experience a recurrence than those who were not prior victims. Children who were reported as disabled were 54 percent more likely to be abused than those not disabled.

5. The reasons for child abuse are as many as there are people involved in abuse and their situations. Several theories explaining the causes and consequences of child abuse and models for intervention have been proposed. Tzeng, Jackson, and Karlson (1991) have described nine models of child maltreatment: (1) individual determinants, (2) offender typology, (3) family systems, (4) individual–environment interaction, (5) parent–child interaction, (6) sociocultural, (7) sociobiological, (8) learning/situational, and (9) ecological. Winton and Mara (2001) have listed 12 theories of child abuse and neglect and have classified those into the following three groups:

(1) Psychiatric/medical/psychopathology models
    Medical (biological) model
    Sociobiological/evolutionary theory
    Psychodynamic/psychoanalytic theory

(2) Social/psychological models
    Social learning theory
    Intergenerational transmission theory
    Exchange theory
    Symbolic interaction theory
    Structural family systems theory

(3) Sociocultural models
    Ecological theory
    Feminist/conflict theory
    Structural-functional/anomie/strain theory
    Cultural spillover theory

You may familiarize yourself with these models and theories. No theory can do justice to the complexity of a problem such as child abuse. However, theories do provide logical perspectives on a phenomenon. Theories that not only explain a problem but also prescribe how to intervene should be preferred.

HOW DOES ONE ASSESS FOR CHILD ABUSE?

The following are the signs and symptoms of the different types of child maltreatment. This material is from "Recognizing Child Abuse and Neglect: Signs and Symptoms, *Child Welfare Information Gateway*: Factsheet, June 2007*.

Physical Abuse: The child (1) may have unexplained burns, bites, bruises, broken bones or black eyes; (2) has fading bruises and other marks noticeable after an absence from school; (3) seems frightened of the parents and protests or cries when it is time to go home; (4) shrinks at the approach of adults; and (5) reports injury by a parent or another caregiver. The parent/other caregiver (1) offers conflicting, unconvincing or no explanation of the child's injury; (2) describes the child as "evil" or in another negative way; (3) uses physical discipline with the child; and (4) has a history of abuse as a child. It is at times impossible to tell physical abuse from accidental injury.

Neglect: The child (1) is frequently absent from school; (2) begs or steals food or money; (3) is consistently dirty and has severe body odor; (4) lacks weather-appropriate clothing; (5) lacks the needed medical and dental care; (6) abuses alcohol or other drugs; and (7) says that there is no one at home to provide care. The parent/other caregiver (1) seems to be indifferent to the child;(2) seems apathetic or depressed; (3) behaves irrationally or in a bizarre manner, and (4) is abusing alcohol or other drugs.

Sexual Abuse: The child (1) has difficulty walking or sitting; (2) suddenly refuses to change for gym or to participate in physical activities; (3) reports nightmares or bedwetting: (4) experiences a sudden change in appetite; (5) demonstrates bizarre, sophisticated, or unusual sexual knowledge or behavior; (6) becomes pregnant or contracts a venereal disease, particularly if under age 14; (7) runs away; and (8) reports sexual abuse by a parent or another adult caregiver. The parent or other adult caregiver (1) is unduly protective of the child or severely limits the child's contact with other children, especially of the opposite sex; (2) is secretive and isolated; (3) is jealous or controlling with family members.

Emotional Abuse: The child (1) shows extremes in behavior, such as overly compliant or demanding behavior, extreme passivity, or aggression; (2) is either inappropriately adult (e.g., parenting other children) or inappropriately infantile (e.g., frequently rocking or head-banging); (3) is delayed in physical or emotional development; (3) has attempted suicide;

---

*This information is available at:

1. http://www.childwelfare.gov/can/statistics/stat_/natl_state.cfm

2. http://acf.hhs.gov/programs/cb/pubs/cm09.pdf

and (4) reports a lack of attachment to the parent. The parent or other adult caregiver: (1) constantly blames, belittles, or berates the child; (2) is unconcerned about the child and refuses to consider offers of help for the child's problems; and (3) overtly rejects the child. Threats of harm are emotionally abusive.

Child abuse and neglect are defined by the federal law, the Child Abuse Prevention and Treatment Act (CAPTA)** of 1988 as "any recent act or failure to act on the part of a parent or caretaker, which results in death, serious physical or emotional harm, sexual abuse, or exploitation, or an act or failure to act which presents an imminent risk of serious harm" (http://www.acf.hhs. gov/programs/cb/ laws_policies/cblaws/capta/index.htm). The CAPTA definition of sexual abuse includes "the employment, use, persuasion, inducement, enticement, or coercion of any child to engage in, or assist any other person to engage in, any sexually explicit conduct or simulation of such conduct for the purpose of producing a visual depiction of such conduct; or the rape, and in case of caretaker or interfamilial relationships, statutory rape, molestation, prostitution, or other form of sexual exploitation of children, or incest with children."

All states and other administrative units of the United States such as District of Columbia, Puerto Rico, and Guam have laws that define the different types of child maltreatment as the basis for government intervention for the protection of children. Know what the law requires of social workers in your state and how abuse and neglect are defined.

Substantiating abuse of small children and in cases where indications of abuse are not obvious is a difficult task. The difficulty becomes worse in sexual abuse cases. The professionals involved in investigating and assessing cases of abuse must have highly developed interviewing skills. The child abuse allegations can have serious consequences for the alleged abusers and their families. The assessments and recommendations of those interviewers become the basis for rulings of the courts of law. Lamb and his associates (2007) have recommended the use of a structured interview protocol based on the results of several controlled studies showing improvement in the quality of information obtained. The protocol is called the National Institute of Child Health and Human Development (NICHD) Investigative Interview Protocol. You may like to study this protocol. It is appended to the Lamb et al. article.

Children can be abused not only by their parents and families but also by the so-called professional caregivers in day-care centers and residential care facilities. Abuse in these facilities can include (1) limitations on the children's ability to contact their parents for extended periods of time; (2) overuse of medication to control behaviors; (3) confiscation of children's shoes to prevent them from running away; and (4) use of physical restraints for hours at a time. The overuse of restraints led to the death of some children and youth. If you observe or suspect child maltreatment in a residential care/treatment center, discuss it with your field supervisor and, if needed, your field course instructor. They will come up with an appropriate response

---

**The Act was originally passed in 1974 and has been amended several times since then. It was most recently amended and reauthorized in 1996 by the Child Abuse Prevention and Treatment and Adoption Act Amendments of 1996 (P.L. 104-235).

to your concern. In the process, you may learn how to influence change in organizational behavior.

The purpose of child abuse assessment is not only to determine the presence or absence of abuse in suspected cases but also to plan a course of action if abuse or neglect is substantiated. Therefore, the assessment has to be comprehensive and multidimensional with the goal of understanding the child, child's parent or caregiver, child–parent/caregiver relationship, the child's family, and its setting and situation. It is desirable that the assessing professional's skills be supplemented with the use of standardized measures, if possible, such as the Beck Youth Inventories of Emotional and Social Impairment (2005), the Child Abuse Potential Inventory (Milner, 1986), and the Parenting Profile Assessment instrument (Anderson, 2000).

Social workers are a prominent part of the society's response to the problem of child maltreatment and adhere to the basic philosophy of child protective services that include these major tenets: (1) A safe and permanent home and family is the best place for children to grow up; (2) Most parents want to be good parents and, when adequately supported, they have the strength and capacity to care for their children and keep them safe; (3) Families that need assistance are diverse in terms of their structure, culture, race, religion, economic status, beliefs, values, and lifestyles; (4) Child Protective Service (CPS) agencies are held accountable for achieving outcomes of child safety, permanence, and family well-being; (5) Child protective efforts are most likely to succeed when clients are involved and actively participate in the intervention process; (6) When parents cannot or will not fulfill their responsibilities to protect their children, CPS agency has the right and obligation to intervene directly on the children's behalf; (7) When children are placed in out-of-home care because their safety cannot be assured, CPS should develop a permanency plan as soon as possible; and (8) To best protect a child's overall well-being, agencies involved should assure that children move to permanency as quickly as possible (DePanfilis & Salus, 2003).

HOW DO I REPORT POSSIBLE ABUSE?

The federal law (CAPTA) has made it obligatory for states to pass mandatory child abuse and neglect reporting laws in order to qualify for federal funds. All states require the reporting of suspected child abuse. In some states, this requirement applies to specific professionals (and health and human service institutions) such as providers of health and mental health care, teachers and other school personnel, social workers, day-care providers, and law enforcement personnel. In many states the reporting laws are much broader and require any person who suspects a child being abused to report. Some states exempt clergymen from reporting who receive information about abuse in the context of a sacred communication or confession. However, in the wake of the Catholic Church sex abuse scandal, many states have revised their mandatory reporting laws to include clergy as mandatory reporters (Smith, 2007). In most states, a person who reports suspected child abuse in "good faith" is immune from criminal and civil liability. You should remember that the state reporting laws vary and undergo changes. To know the current laws in your state in terms of their scope and other relevant practices, start with Child Welfare Information Gateway (www.childwelfare.gov).

All states require a report of child abuse or neglect to be made to either a law enforcement authority or the child protection agency. In some states, a toll-free number is listed in the telephone directory. The call goes to a central registry worker who records the information about the allegation and sets in motion an investigation if there is a reason to believe that a child is being abused or neglected or is at risk of abuse and neglect. The information is passed on to the appropriate law enforcement office or child protective agency. Reporting is easy. All it takes is looking up the toll-free number or the number for the local CPS agency or law enforcement authority and making the call. However, the reporting party must be calling from the same state where the child is allegedly being abused. For reporting abuse in another state, the toll-free number is **800-4-A-CHILD (800-422-4453).** While reporting, you should provide the following information.

All states require a report of child abuse or neglect to be made.

1. The name/s of the child/ren and parent/s or caregiver/s,
2. The address of the child/ren and parent/s or caregiver/s,
3. The type, extent, and duration of maltreatment and its consequences such as injuries and behavior changes,
4. The alleged perpetrator/s, and
5. Any other information that may help in the investigation.

As a private citizen reporting suspected abuse, under your state law, you may have the choice of remaining anonymous or giving your name and contact information. Similarly, you may or may not be required to send a written report of the allegation. In any case, your identity will not be revealed to the alleged abuser/s. It is wiser to provide your name and contact information so that you can give additional information if needed (Winton & Mara, 2001). Most allegations of abuse and neglect are investigated immediately or within a 24-hour period, but inadequate and incomplete information can cause delay in the investigation process. As a social work professional in the making, you have the advantage of the experience of your field instructor/supervisor and the resources and connections of your field agency. You need to discuss any suspicions of abuse or neglect with your instructor/supervisor.

Reporting suspected child abuse and neglect is a professional responsibility of health and human services personnel and, under reporting laws in many states, there are penalties for not reporting.

HOW DO I RECOGNIZE A CLIENT WHO IS SUICIDAL?

Most social work field placements are in health and human service agencies often based in locations where most serious social problems are found. Social workers deal with clients who are variously disadvantaged; some are disabled, dependent, defeated, or distressed. Others are delinquent or facing criminal charges, and still others are depressed, disorganized, and disoriented. Some clients contemplate suicide when they believe that they have no means of escaping from a difficult situation.

Every year approximately 33,000 Americans die of suicide, and more than 800,000 make nonfatal suicide attempts. Other facts to understand the problem better: There is a suicide about every 15.2 minutes, and in 2007 it was the 11th leading cause of death in the United States (www.suicidology.org). It is estimated that each suicide intimately affects several six other persons, including the spouse, children, parents, and friends. The *"prototypical* suicide is an older white male who is often depressed, alcoholic, socially isolated, cognitively rigid, failing in physical health, and increasingly hopeless" (Maris, Berman, & Silverman, 2000, p. 32). However, suicide is the third leading cause of death in adolescents aged 10–24 years (www.cdc.org). Predictors of suicide include the following:

▶ Mental disorder (substance abuse, affective disorders, schizophrenia, panic disorders)
▶ Age (persons 45 years of age or older are at greater risk)
▶ Gender (about four times more men kill themselves than women)
▶ Marital status (divorced, separated, widowed, and persons never married are more likely to commit suicide)
▶ Recent losses (resources, employment, relationships, status)
▶ Chronic physical illness
▶ Hospital discharge and apparent improvement
▶ Race (Native Americans and white men have higher suicide rates)
▶ Previous attempts

Symptoms exhibited:

▶ Thinking about or mentioning thinking about suicide
▶ Hopelessness, no reason for living or loss of sense of purpose
▶ Rage, uncontrolled anger
▶ Feeling trapped, like there's no way out
▶ Increased drug or alcohol use
▶ Withdrawing from friends, family, and society
▶ Anxiety, depression, unable to sleep or sleeping too much
▶ Dramatic mood changes
▶ Recklessness

The American Association of Suicidology has recommended this mnemonic to help remember the warning signs and symptoms: **IS PATH WARM?**

I=Ideation (Suicidal thoughts)
S=Substance abuse
P=Purposelessness
A=Anxiety
T=Trapped
H=Hopelessness
W=Withdrawal
A=Anger
R=Recklessness
M=Mood changes

Wollersheim (1974) has suggested using the following question to evaluate the patient: "You certainly seem to feel extremely depressed. Feeling this miserable, have you found yourself thinking of suicide?" There does not seem to be any evidence that talking directly about suicide will put ideas into the client's head. Instead, most clients would probably be relieved to have the opportunity to talk about suicidal thoughts (Sommers-Flanagan & Sommers-Flanagan, 1995).

Although it may not be unusual for most people to have at least considered the notion of suicide at some time in their lives, healthy individuals do not dwell on these thoughts. You should be concerned and mention to your supervisor any time that a client mentions suicidal ideation. Sometimes these are brief, passing thoughts; at other times they are recurrent and seriously considered notions. You should be especially concerned with any client who *frequently* has suicidal ideation, whose self-destructive thoughts are *intense*, or have significant *duration*.

Miller (1985) has recommended evaluating suicidal plans by assessing the four areas of **S**pecificity of plan, **L**ethality of method, **A**vailability of proposed method, and **P**roximity of social or helping resources. These dimensions compose the acronym **S-L-A-P**. The more specific the plan, the greater the lethality of the method, the quickness with which the patient could implement the plan, and the farther a patient is from helping resources, the greater the inferred risk of suicide.

Critical Thinking

Critical Thinking Question: How could a process recording help you to critique and analyze your work with a client?

Questions you can use to assess suicide risk:

1. In the past week including today, have you felt like life is not worth living?
2. In the past week including today, have you wanted to kill yourself?

   If they positively endorse the second question, then ask these questions:

   1. Have you ever tried to kill yourself?
   2. In the past week including today, have you made plans to kill yourself? (Wintersteen, Diamond, & Fein, 2007)

HOW CAN I PREPARE TO DEAL WITH SUICIDAL CLIENTS?

You can improve your ability to help suicidal clients by learning about the epidemiology, theories, and risk factors of suicide, as well as assessment and treatment of suicidal clients. A useful article to read is by Joiner et al. (2007). In the meantime, the American Association of Suicidology has recommended these ways of being helpful to someone threatening suicide.

- Be direct. Talk openly and matter-of-factly about suicide.
- Listen. Allow expression of feelings. Accept the feelings.
- Be nonjudgmental. Don't debate whether suicide is right or wrong or whether feelings are good or bad. Don't lecture on the value of life.
- Don't be shocked. (This will put distance between you.)
- Don't allow yourself to be sworn to secrecy. Seek support.
- Offer hope that alternatives are available but do not offer glib reassurance.
- Where possible, take action to remove guns, stockpiled pills, and so on.
- Get help from persons or agencies specializing in crisis intervention and suicide prevention.

Suggestions for Intervention with Suicidal Clients

The purpose of intervention with suicidal clients is (1) to assess the depth of psychic pain, sense of hopelessness and helplessness, and seriousness of suicide intent; (2) to use appropriate crisis control and management strategies to reduce distress; and (3) to help the client regain his or her problem-solving abilities and learn new coping skills. The following are some helpful suggestions.

1. *Overcome the taboo against talking about suicide.* Study the literature about suicide, and examine your own biases about it. How do you feel about suicide? Is it a sign of weakness? Is it illogical, a sin, a personal taboo? Remember that "the clinician's ability to calmly and matter-of-factly explore suicidal thought often provides a platform from which the patient's long-endured silence about suicide can be broken . . . . Suddenly, suicidal ideation is no longer a sin to be hidden; it is a problem to be solved" (Shea, 1999, pp. 110–111).

2. *Interpret clues about suicidal intention as "cries for help."* Most suicidal persons communicate clues that may be verbal, cognitive, affective, and behavioral (Fuse, 1997). To pick up these signals, you must be 100 percent present in the interview process. "If the patient feels that he or she is not being listened to, disengagement can occur with brutal swiftness" (Shea, 1999, p. 121).

3. *Modify your interviewing style to the developmental level of the client.* Hendren (1990) has provided a list of appropriate questions for suicidal assessment of children, adolescents, adults, and the elderly, exploring such areas as family functioning, family history, past attempts, suicidal intent, depression, associated risk factors, social supports, coping ability, and so forth.

4. *Try to fathom the depth of the client's feelings of hopelessness and helplessness.* See if you can weave into your interview the use of such instruments as Beck's Hopelessness Scale (Beck, Brown, & Steer, 1989).

5. *Use the interviewing technique of normalization.* Employ this technique as a gentle lead-in to a discussion of suicide. It may take the form of a question such as: "When people are feeling extremely upset, they sometimes have thoughts of harming themselves. Have you had any thoughts of wanting to kill yourself?" (Shea, 1999, p. 112).

6. *Treat answers such as "No, not really" as indications of suicidal ideation.* Gently ask, "What kind of thoughts have you had, even if just fleeting in nature?" (Shea, 1999, p. 121).

7. *Make an assessment of the risk of suicide.* This involves exploring areas of the client's life such as mentioned in item #3. There are several models and outlines available for guidance. Two are briefly explained in our answer to the next question.

8. *Employ crisis theory for intervention.* Such intervention has three basic components: (1) identifying the precipitant(s), (2) encouraging the client to tolerate and bear the psychic pain aroused by the crisis, and (3) specifying and implementing a plan of action (Doyle, 1990). The plan will depend on the seriousness of the intent and lethality of the method for suicide. It may involve alleviating the client's isolation, facilitating the removal of weapons and other means of suicide, developing or re-establishing his or her support system, identifying alternatives to the difficulties being experienced, and facilitating improved problem solving and coping. If medical evaluation or intervention is indicated, be reassuring in letting the person know how you plan to proceed (Johnson, 1997).

Research Based Practice

Critical Thinking Question:
What research-based information on suicidal clients informs your practice?

WHAT DO I DO IF I SUSPECT MY CLIENT PLANS TO ATTEMPT SUICIDE?

Once you have identified risk factors or signs or symptoms usually connected with suicidal ideation, your next step will be to ask the client directly if he or she is seriously considering suicide. Look the client in the eye, and do not be shy or hesitant—this is a serious matter. If you have a good rapport with the client, generally he or she will be candid. If the client answers in the affirmative, then ask the client to contract with you not to attempt suicide without giving you time to help. Try to understand the depth of the client's despair. Do not minimize it. At the same time, try to infuse hope. Discuss the progress that the client has made. Point out the client's strengths and positive characteristics. Be optimistic and enthusiastic about what the two of you have accomplished.

If the client admits to planning suicide, or even if the client denies it but you judge the risk of suicide to be severe, you will need to discuss immediate psychiatric hospitalization. If the client does not agree to the hospitalization, inform him or her that in a situation such as this the policy is to inform your agency supervisor, responsible people in the client's life, and possibly the police. Immediately involve your agency supervisor, if possible, while the client is still in your office. You and your supervisor together may then decide to contact a family member, friend, or some other significant person in the client's life. In an emergency such as a suicide attempt, do not worry about breaking client confidentiality. "The duty to save a human life would take precedence over the duty to keep information shared by a client confidential" (Reamer, 1982, p. 584). Depending on the seriousness of the threat, protective actions (e.g., inpatient hospitalization) or involvement of legal authorities may be required even if the client objects.

Additional measures can be taken to manage the suicidal crisis. For instance, the client can be informed of the national 24-hour suicide prevention lifeline at 1-800-273-TALK. You may also want to stress your availability to be reached by phone. This can be accomplished between agency visits by making telephone "appointments" when the client may call you in your office and talk for a brief period. Inform the client of the availability of emergency psychiatric services and crisis counseling hotlines when you cannot be reached in your office. Although practitioners will sometimes give out their home phone numbers in situations such as this, students generally are advised against this practice. If it is vital that the client reach you at home, then leave your number with the community's 24-hour crisis hotline or the agency's staff so that you can return the client's call.

Remember that any time you are dealing with a suicidal client or even a client you suspect may be suicidal, you must inform your field instructor or agency supervisor.

Case Example

In a new practicum you will be the case manager for five severely mentally ill persons. After a week of orientation and shadowing your agency supervisor, she hands you the files and asks that you contact the clients as soon as possible. With the first case, there has been no contact in three months with a 64-year-old woman with a record of seven hospitalizations over the past five years.

You try to reach the client by phone, and although it is a working number, no one answers. No one answers when you call again later in the morning and several times in the afternoon. The next day you make about six efforts to reach the client, but to no avail. There is no family member or close relative. You decide to make a home visit.

The client lives in a neighborhood where about every third house appears to have a junked and abandoned car in the yard. Wind-blown litter and trash is everywhere. The house where your client lives looks as if it should be condemned. The front porch is sagging badly and several of the floor boards are rotten. You knock on the front door, and for a moment you think you hear some movement inside. No one answers the door. You knock again louder, but with the same result.

Questions

1. Should you try to peek into one of the windows to see if you can see anyone or just terminate the case?
2. Should you go to the neighbors and ask them what they know about your client?
3. Should you call the police and ask them to assist you?

HOW DO I TRANSFER A CASE?

Despite your best efforts, sometimes clients will not improve. In fact, they may get worse. This might have happened whether you were assigned to them or not. In other words, it may have nothing at all to do with you: It could be part of a cyclical illness like bipolar disorder, a result of poor decisions the client has made, or environmental influences that you can't counteract. At other times, you may discover that there is something about a particular client that you dislike which makes it difficult for you to work with that person. If a client reminds you of someone like an abusive father, and you do not feel that you can be unbiased or provide the client with the same level of care you provide to others, then this is an argument for transferring the case.

Should you discover after a reasonable attempt and period of time that the client is not improving, you should at least discuss the possibility of transferring this case to someone else with your field instructor.

The staff person who is receiving the case may want to meet with you in order to go over the client's file and ask questions. Other staff may want you to arrange a meeting where you introduce the client and the new therapist.

The protocol for these meetings is for you to make the introductions, and to review the client's presenting problem, the strategies or steps the two of you have taken to address the problem, and what remains yet to be accomplished. If possible, point out any success or gains the client has made, and examples of changes the client has made—even if they are minor. Then, your role is to fade quietly into the background as the new therapist takes an active role and begins to raise questions of the client and to direct the remainder of the session. Do not answer questions for the client or take an active role after you have finished your summary. Take Rothman's (2000) advice and "Once disengaged, **stay that way**! Don't give in to the temptation to go back for a 'last goodbye,' or to make a lengthy phone call 'just to check on how it's going'" (p. 112).

Meeting a fundamental need.

Case Example

In transferring a client who had made little progress, Perry noticed that although he had used a cognitive approach with Sheila, the new therapist was primarily Gestalt-oriented. When the new therapist asked the client to describe her feelings about living with an alcoholic husband, Sheila looked at Perry with eyes that pleaded, "What's going on here? What have you done to me?" When he saw the tears in Sheila's eyes, Perry blurted out, "We've talked about this before, and Sheila doesn't want to leave her husband." Margot, Sheila's new therapist, glared at Perry and said, "Can I have a word with you out in the hall?"

Questions

1. Did Perry do anything wrong?
2. What should Perry have done?
3. Why would Margot try a theoretical approach so different from the one used by Perry?

HOW DO I TERMINATE SERVICES WITH A CLIENT?

Termination means the ending, limiting, or concluding of services. Not much has been written about termination in the helping process in social work literature. Possibly, this is because termination is an aspect of professional practice that resists precise definition.

Part of the problem in discussing the termination of services with a client comes from not knowing when a client will stop requesting services. Clients may decide not to appear for a scheduled second appointment or the planned final session. Premature and unilateral terminations by clients (i.e., terminations against professional advice) are often thought to represent unresolved resistance. Sensitive areas may have been opened up that the client is uncomfortable handling. This discomfort may result in strong denial or minimization of the problem.

There are many reasons that clients may prematurely terminate services.

Although students may be personally disappointed or feel that they have failed whenever they experience a premature termination, there are many reasons that clients may prematurely terminate services: The original problem may have actually improved in a short span of time; the client may have moved or be planning to move to another geographic area; there may have been major changes in the client's life (e.g., divorce from an abusing spouse or a prison term for that person). Other changes such as taking a new job, the birth of a child, or a serious illness of a close relative can make it difficult for clients to continue with a social service agency. If a student believes that a client needs further help, then the student may gently challenge the client's reasoning behind the decision to terminate, but ultimately he or she must respect the client's wishes. In such instances, it is advised that students inform clients that they can return to the agency if the need arises at some future time.

Termination of services also occurs when the social worker and client jointly agree to conclude the service agreement. This may come about whenever either party believes that the client should be referred to another agency (e.g., for detoxification) or to another professional (e.g., a therapist who specializes in working with incest survivors). Termination may also be scheduled because both the client and the social worker believe that the original goals have been met, because progress is not being made, or because the practitioner is departing (e.g., the semester is ending for the student intern). In addition to premature termination, Hepworth and Larsen (1990) identify four other types of termination:

1. Planned terminations determined by temporal constraints
2. Planned terminations with time-limited modalities
3. Planned terminations involving open-ended modalities
4. Terminations due to the departure of a practitioner (p. 597)

Schools, hospitals, youth camps, and similar institutions are examples of settings where temporal factors determine when termination will take place. In these settings, there is a reduced chance that clients will interpret the termination as being arbitrarily imposed and have feelings of desertion or abandonment. The predetermined ending time, however, may not be appropriate for every client, and in such cases students must deal with the feelings (the client's as well as their own) that result from untimely separation. Where necessary, students will make arrangements for their clients to receive additional services.

Planned terminations associated with time-limited modalities involve the client's knowing from the beginning how long the service will last. This reduces the degree of emotional attachment and dependency, and the feeling of loss that clients may experience as the result of termination. Nevertheless, even in time-limited modalities, clients do form attachments and experience some sense of loss. Student interns must be sensitive to these reactions and allow the client to express these feelings.

In agencies where open-ended modalities of service are used, students need to begin thinking about termination when they start to feel that the gains from continued service will be minor at best. If the client has experienced improvement, but now progress has slowed considerably, then the student and the client should discuss this. If both concur that little recent progress has been made, then the client's options are (1) to take a furlough from services, (2) to cease services altogether, or (3) to continue with another practitioner.

It is not uncommon for students to feel a little nervous when thinking about termination—especially when a strong working relationship has developed. If the student suggests that his or her assistance is no longer needed, will the client feel rejection? Could the client regress? Students sometimes fear great damage might occur to the client if the termination is handled badly, but that thinking probably is not realistic. According to Epstein (1980), "It is a rare client who truly becomes unhappy or adrift when termination occurs" (p. 257). Nevertheless, the ending phase of the helping process is the culmination of all of the energies and efforts previously applied and should be taken seriously. Termination can be conceptualized as a series of discrete tasks, which you can review to help plan for the concluding of services with a client:

1. Determine the most appropriate time to conclude services.
2. Anticipate the emotional reactions commonly experienced.
3. Recognize the conflict in being helped and needing to move away from it.
4. Discuss what the client has learned, his or her strengths, positive changes in the client's thinking or life since beginning therapy. Point out how the problem-solving experience can be transferred to future problems.
5. Plan for the stabilization of the client's gains and continued growth.
6. Evaluate the service provided and the achievement of goals.
7. Emphasize the agency's continued interest in the client's well-being, and suggest that he or she seek help again if needed.

The dynamics of each case will influence the way you actually approach termination with a client. Create in your mind a continuum for each of the concepts of emotional involvement, anxiety over termination, extent of problem resolution, and prognosis for future success. Different points on these continuums will characterize every client, and these positions will affect the way the client experiences termination.

Many authors have provided guidelines for effective termination. After reading this section, you may wish to consult several of the references at the end of the chapter for additional help with your termination efforts. But first we want to add a few guidelines from Egan (1990):

1. Plan for a termination in the helping process right from the beginning. (This can be accomplished in the client's service agreement or contract by setting an approximate ending date or the expected number of sessions.)

2. Be sensitive to any excessive dependency on the relationship that you or the client may have developed. Look for clues which suggest that the relationship has become more important than the problem management process.

3. State in the contract the degree of progress or change that would be sufficient for termination. End the helping process when it is clear that the goals have been accomplished.

Finally, with some clients who have become overly dependent, it is a good idea to take a gradual approach to termination by lengthening the time between sessions. During this process, make sure that the client is connected with other natural helpers, informal resources, or sources of social support. For clients who are terminating even though significant problems remain, you can suggest follow-up or booster sessions after official termination. Do everything to make a termination as positive an experience for the client as possible and to keep it from being abrupt or unexpected.

SUMMARY

This chapter was designed to help students feel less nervous about beginning to work with their clients by providing a brief refresher on topics usually covered in students' practice courses. Identifying child abuse and suicidal ideation were highlighted.

The Social Worker–Client Professional Relationship

1. What are the attributes of the professional relationship in social work?

   _____

   _____

   _____

   _____

2. How is the social worker–client relationship different from physician–patient, lawyer–client, and teacher–student relationships?

   _____

   _____

   _____

   _____

3. What are the factors that influence the social worker–client relationship?

   a. Of the factors identified earlier, which ones do/can you as the social worker have control over?

   _____

   _____

   _____

   b. What are the strategies appropriate for manipulating each of these factors?

   _____

   _____

   _____

4. Think about the kind of relationship you have/had with your clients.

   a. Have you had difficulty in establishing relationships or getting connected with some clients? (Describe)

   _____

   _____

   _____

   b. What do you attribute that difficulty to?

   _____

   _____

   _____

c. Using hindsight, what would you do/not do with a similar client with a similar problem in a similar situation?

_____

_____

_____

5. Have you had difficulty in maintaining appropriate boundaries between some clients and yourself? (Describe)

_____

_____

_____

a. Identify boundary-related issues involved in your work with your clients. How have these challenged you?

_____

_____

_____

b. How have you dealt with those challenges?

_____

_____

_____

c. Would you deal with them differently in the future?

_____

_____

_____

How?

_____

_____

_____

Why?

_____

_____

_____

Mastering the Interview Process

1. Think of the major factors that influence the interview process and create two lists:

   a. List of social worker–related factors

   _____

   _____

   b. List of client-related factors

   _____

   _____

   c. Underline or circle those factors in both lists that you have/can have control over and specify an appropriate way of manipulating each of those factors.

   _____

   _____

2. Based on your knowledge and skills, list at least three principles of interviewing such as "Start where the client is."

   _____

   _____

   _____

3. Rate your mastery of the following most common interview techniques.

Technique	None	Low	Adequate	High
Listening	❏	❏	❏	❏
Observing	❏	❏	❏	❏
Questioning	❏	❏	❏	❏
Probing	❏	❏	❏	❏
Inquiring	❏	❏	❏	❏
Uncovering	❏	❏	❏	❏
Drawing out	❏	❏	❏	❏
Commenting	❏	❏	❏	❏
Clarifying	❏	❏	❏	❏
Educating	❏	❏	❏	❏
Suggesting	❏	❏	❏	❏
Guiding	❏	❏	❏	❏
Focusing	❏	❏	❏	❏
Reassuring	❏	❏	❏	❏
Reframing	❏	❏	❏	❏

Technique	None	Low	Adequate	High
Paraphrasing	❑	❑	❑	❑
Confronting	❑	❑	❑	❑
Summarizing	❑	❑	❑	❑
Structuring	❑	❑	❑	❑
Advice giving	❑	❑	❑	❑
Seeking clarification	❑	❑	❑	❑
Reflecting feelings	❑	❑	❑	❑
Communicating feelings	❑	❑	❑	❑
Using silences	❑	❑	❑	❑
Self-disclosing	❑	❑	❑	❑

4. Based on your knowledge and skills, list at least three barriers to communication with a client who is:

   a. A child

   _____

   _____

   _____

   b. A person with a visible disability

   _____

   _____

   _____

   c. An abused woman

   _____

   _____

   _____

   d. An elderly person

   _____

   _____

   _____

   e. A convicted prisoner

   _____

   _____

   _____

Making Termination of Professional Activity and Relationship Easier

Termination can be more or less difficult for both the client and the social worker. Consider what issues may arise as you think about terminating with your clients.

1. How do you deal with endings and saying good-bye? Is it difficult for you? Explain what goes through your mind.

   _____

   _____

   _____

   _____

2. What factors and/or strategies may make termination with clients easier for you?

   _____

   _____

   _____

   _____

3. What questions do you have about terminating with your clients?

   _____

   _____

   _____

   _____

4. At the end of the semester/quarter, you may be saying good-bye not only to your clients but also to your field supervisor and other agency personnel. What difficulties do you anticipate in ending your placement?

   _____

   _____

   _____

   _____

5. What can you do to minimize any potential problems?

   _____

   _____

   _____

   _____

Exploring and Creating Other Learning Experiences

Listed here are a number of learning experiences that will enrich your social work knowledge and skills. Check those activities that you would like to engage in. Pencil in specific information as necessary.

_____ 1. Reading and discussing with your field supervisor journal articles related to skills or knowledge that you want to acquire. (List any specific topics or articles.)

_____

_____

_____

_____ 2. Gathering basic information about referral resources in the community. (List any specific agency.)

_____

_____

_____

_____ 3. Discussing with your field supervisor how a particular conceptual framework, theory, model, or perspective is applied within the agency. (List any specific theory or approach.)

_____

_____

_____

_____ 4. Reviewing closed cases from the agency's records for understanding the "how" and "why" of social work interventions.

_____

_____

_____

_____ 5. Reviewing any educational films, audiotapes, or videos used in training staff.

_____

_____

_____

_____ 6. Participating in agency continuing education programs.

_____

_____

_____

____ **7.** Attending professional conferences and workshops including NASW meetings.

_____

_____

_____

____ **8.** Role playing to rehearse professional approaches, skills, and techniques with other students in the field agency or school-based seminar group. (What skill or technique would you want to observe or role-play?)

_____

_____

_____

____ **9.** Making a home visit to a client that you are working with.

_____

_____

_____

____ **10.** Doing a process recording of a session with a client and receiving your field supervisor's feedback.

_____

_____

_____

____ **11.** Audio- or videotaping an interview session with a client and having your field supervisor review and discuss it with you.

_____

_____

_____

____ **12.** Shadowing for a day a social work practitioner who is recognized as an expert in a field of practice. (Which practitioner or field of expertise?)

_____

_____

_____

_____ **13.** Learning about and, if possible, participating in the grant writing process in the agency.

_____

_____

_____

_____ **14.** Observing and participating in an agency committee or task group meeting. (Which committee?)

_____

_____

_____

Succeed with **mysocialworklab**

Log onto **www.mysocialworklab.com** to access a wealth of case studies, videos, and assessment. (*If you did not receive an access code to* **MySocialWorkLab** *with this text and wish to purchase access online, please visit* www.mysocialworklab.com.)

1. **Watch the Core Competency video: "Assessment."** In the video Mrs. Davis reveals that she started using crack and heroin at a very young age. If we were to focus just on her alcohol use, how much, how frequent, or what indicators from the research literature might suggest when drinking becomes a significant problem and could be characterized by making poor decisions as a parent and putting her child at risk?

2. **Watch the Core Competency video: "Applying Critical Thinking."** In this video we learn that the husband's drinking may be a large contributor to violence in the home. As you think about your reading and the discussions you've had about domestic violence, what other factors contribute to the husband's behavior that aren't discussed in this video?

PRACTICE TEST The following questions will test your knowledge of the content found within this chapter.

1. Social workers must be able to assess child abuse they find in various contexts. Which statement does not reflect current research?
   a. Child abuse occurs primarily in rural areas.
   b. Children under one year of age are most at risk.
   c. Approximately half of the victims of child abuse are white.
   d. Children previously abused may experience a recurrence.

2. Good written communication skills are important in social work. Which suggestion was not made in this chapter?
   a. Use spell-check or consult a dictionary when in doubt about a word.
   b. Reading every third sentence is a good check for organization.
   c. If you need help with grammar, take a course or consult a reference.
   d. Proofread even if it means reading the document multiple times.

3. Consider the guidelines for interviewing discussed in this chapter. Which one was not recommended?
   a. Having an awareness of one's own body language.
   b. Adapting one's language and vocabulary to the client.
   c. Explaining the limits of confidentiality.
   d. Explaining agency policies before identifying the client's problem.

4. In getting started to help a new client assigned to you, which response would not be a good practice?
   a. Helping to establish a therapeutic relationship.
   b. Developing an agreement on the problem and how to address it.
   c. Creating either a verbal or written contract.
   d. Discussing one's training before establishing rapport.

Short Answer Question:
Juan is investigating possible child abuse. The mother is attractive, articulate, and a good housekeeper. There are no apparent injuries on the young child although the neighbors reported hearing screaming. The mother says she is a child abuse survivor. She loves this child and says she will never injure it. Juan wants to believe her. What additional information does he need in his investigation?

ASSESS YOUR COMPETENCE Use the scale below to rate your current level of achievement on the following concepts or skills associated with each competency practice behavior presented in the chapter:

1	2	3
I can accurately describe the concept or skill.	I can consistently identify the concept or skill when observing and analyzing practice activities.	I can competently implement the concept or skill in my own practice.

_____ know how to assess a suicidal client.

_____ use the written communication of process recording to analyze my practice with clients.

_____ obtain research-based information on how to intervene with a suicidal client.

Answers

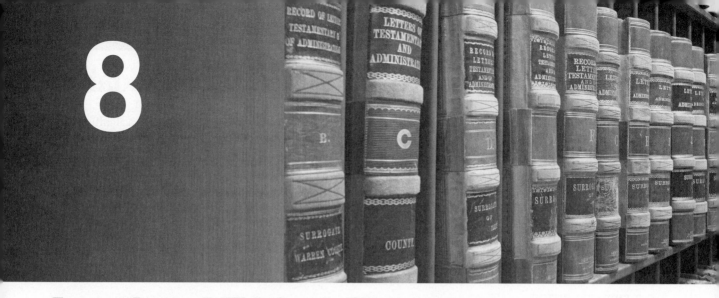

8

Legal and Ethical Concerns

Core Competencies in This Chapter (Check marks indicate which competencies are covered in depth)				
✓ Professional Identity	✓ Ethical Practice	☐ Critical Thinking	☐ Diversity in Practice	✓ Human Rights & Justice
☐ Research-Based Practice	☐ Human Behavior	☐ Policy Practice	☐ Practice Contexts	☐ Engage, Assess, Intervene, Evaluate

OVERVIEW

Social workers are called upon to testify in court to be expert witnesses and are involved in various legal proceedings to protect clients, their families, and the general public. Whether as a child protection worker or a therapist concerned about a client who is a harm to self or others, social workers need a basic knowledge of the legal system. It is also important to have a working vocabulary of legal terms. This chapter provides that and broadens the discussion to include professional boundaries, ethical responsibilities, and legal liability.

WHAT LEGAL TERMS SHOULD SOCIAL WORK STUDENTS KNOW?

Legal terms vary from state to state; however, some of the most commonly used throughout the United States are listed here. If you learn these definitions, you will feel better prepared and more confident when dealing with attorneys and courts of law.

1. *Civil proceeding*—includes all lawsuits other than criminal prosecutions.

2. *Conditional discharge*—allows a convicted criminal defendant to remain at liberty, under a suspended sentence of imprisonment and subject to certain conditions of behavior, but without the supervision of a probation officer.

3. *Contempt of court*—conduct that tends to bring in disrespect or disregard to the authority or administration of the law or court. The lines of division between civil and criminal contempt are indistinct but, basically, civil contempt is intended to compel compliance with a court order for the benefit of another, while criminal contempt is intended as punishment for the direct defiance of a court's power or disruption of the court's function.

4. *Criminal prosecution*—the filing of allegations that constitute a charge of crime, followed by the arraignment and trial of the defendant.

5. *Delinquency*—denotes behavior in a minor which, if the minor were an adult, would be criminal conduct.

6. *Dependency*—denotes the lack of proper parental care of supervision in a minor's life.

7. *Deposition*—recording a witness' testimony outside the courtroom.

8. *Felony*—a serious crime, for which the punishment may be imprisonment for longer than a year and/or significant fines.

9. *Indictment*—the report of a Grand Jury, charging an adult with criminal conduct.

10. *Misdemeanor*—a lesser category of crime for which the punishment usually is imprisonment in a county jail rather than state prison and/or a lesser fine of (usually) no more than $500.

11. *Parole*—pertains to the supervised release from incarceration of an adult criminal defendant prior to the completion of a term of

Social workers need a basic vocabulary of legal terms and knowledge of the legal system.

imprisonment. Parole does not affect the defendant's sentence, and the defendant is subject at any time to being returned to the penal institution for breach of the conditions of release.

12. *Persistent felony offender* (PFO)—an adult who stands convicted of a felony after previously having been convicted of one or more felony offenses.

13. *Petition*—the document filed in juvenile or family court at the beginning of a neglect, abuse, or delinquency case.

14. *Plea bargaining*—settlement of a criminal prosecution, usually by the reduction of the charge and/or the penalty, in return for a plea of guilty. The judge need not adhere to the plea bargain agreement reached between a prosecutor and a defendant, although as a practical matter most judges usually do so.

15. *Probation*—allowing a convicted criminal defendant or juvenile found to be delinquent to remain at liberty, under a suspended sentence of imprisonment, generally under the supervision of a probation officer, and usually under certain conditions.

16. *Status offense*—denotes behavior in a minor, who if an adult, would not be criminal conduct (e.g., truancy and waywardness).

17. *Subpoena*—a document issued by a court clerk requiring that person to appear at a certain court at a certain day and time, to give testimony in a specified case.

18. *Summons*—a document issued by a court clerk notifying that person of the filing of a lawsuit against him or her. A summons does not require the attendance at court of any person.

19. *Violation*—an offense, other than a traffic violation, that generally is punishable only by a fine.

20. *Warrant*—a document issued by a judge, authorizing the arrest or detention of a person, or the search of a place and seizure of specified items in that place.

WHAT SHOULD SOCIAL WORK STUDENTS KNOW ABOUT TESTIFYING IN A COURT OF LAW?

The Do's and Don'ts of Courtroom Testifying: A Few Simple Rules

- BE RESPECTFUL OF THE JUDGES: <u>*Always*</u> address the judge as "Your Honor"; never as "Sir" or "Madame"; of the attorneys; of other workers; of the clients.
- DO NOT GIVE AN OPINION ABOUT SOMETHING FOR WHICH YOU ARE NOT QUALIFIED: Give information only relative to your education, expertise, and training.
- STATE IF INFORMATION IS SECOND-HAND: For example, say, " 'so and so' worker told me that . . ."; if the Judge has ruled that what you have said is hearsay and not to repeat it, do <u>not</u> repeat it; always admit if you are not fully informed.
- DON'T GET ANGRY: Attorneys will try to wear you down; remember the practice rules for handling criticism in Chapter 6.

- ALWAYS GIVE THE ENTIRE TRUTH EVEN IF IT WILL HURT YOUR CASE: You have a duty to the court, to present the evidence as you know it.
- HAVE DISPOSITION REPORTS TO THE ATTORNEY THREE WORKING DAYS AHEAD OF TIME: Tardiness on reports can have an adverse effect on the attorney's ability to present a well-thought-out and clear presentation of the case to the court.
- DRESS APPROPRIATELY: Do not wear jeans and a T-shirt; khakis and a shirt are fine; do not wear clothing cut too low or too-short shorts/skirts.
- DON'T COMMIT TO SERVICES YOUR AREA CANNOT PROVIDE: Let the court know exactly which services are available, and which would have to be provided elsewhere.

WHAT HAPPENS IF I MAKE A MISTAKE IN MY PRACTICUM?

Generally, small mistakes are not legal issues. It is hard to go through life (or maybe even a week) without making some kind of a blunder. What happens if you make a mistake in your practicum? First, let's examine several examples of small mistakes:

1. You have promised a client that you would obtain information about a community resource and you forgot to do so.
2. While interviewing a client, you forget an important question you had intended to ask.
3. You fail to get a client's signature on a necessary form.

These problems are not serious because each can be easily resolved by a phone call or at the time of the client's next visit.

Most mistakes that you make as a student probably will not involve legal or ethical considerations. However, some mistakes are more serious than others. For example, you might inadvertently disclose confidential information about a client to someone who should not have that information. Or, you might not take action to protect someone threatened by the client you counsel twice a week. In instances where something you have done or failed to do results in harm or could have resulted in injury, where a complaint could or might be filed against the agency, inform your field instructor as soon as possible.

Minor mistakes may cause some inconvenience (e.g., a client having to make another trip to the agency to sign a form), but major mistakes violate rights or have the potential to cause harm. Always inform your field instructor about major mistakes, but it is not necessary to mention every little oversight. When in doubt, it is better to inform your field instructor than to treat the mistake as a secret.

Ethical Practice

Critical Thinking Question: If you experience an ethical dilemma, what steps would you take to resolve it?

Case Example

Carrie was assigned to escort a nursing home patient with dementia through a series of diagnostic tests at a large university hospital. While waiting for the lab to draw the patient's blood, Carrie momentarily left Mr. Jones in a wheelchair to make a phone call. When she returned, the patient was gone. Three hours later the patient was found huddled in a corner of the hospital's basement. Because he was unhurt, Carrie doesn't think she needs to inform the nursing home staff about the patient's disappearance.

Questions

1. Does Carrie have an obligation to inform the nursing home?
2. Would Carrie have less of an obligation to inform the nursing home if the patient had been lost for only 45 minutes?

WHAT IS MALPRACTICE?

Malpractice is defined as an act of commission or omission by a professional that falls below accepted standards of care and results in or aggravates an injury to the client. Students in field placements are acting in a professional role that involves the responsibility to uphold the same professional, legal, and ethical standards as other practicing social workers. Clients expect students to perform in a competent manner. However, students are vulnerable to the extent that they lack professional skills.

Zakutansky and Sirles (1993) have listed several examples of situations that can lead to civil or criminal action against a student. These include:

> misrepresenting qualifications, such as failing to inform the client of student status; providing treatment without obtaining proper consent; keeping inaccurate or inadequate records; administering inappropriate or radical treatment; failing to consult with or refer to a specialist; failing to seek proper supervision; failing to take action to prevent a client's suicide; and failing to warn third parties of potential harm. (p. 340)

DO I NEED LIABILITY INSURANCE?

The United States is a very litigious society. Social workers and social work agencies are not immune from being sued for malpractice. Kurzman (1995) has given several reasons for this including (1) in all 50 states social work has gained legal stature, and its practice is regulated by law; (2) courts are less likely to grant protection from liability; (3) there is an easy availability of negligence attorneys willing to work on a contingency basis; and (4) there are important changes in liability associated with managed care.

Although the chances of a social work student being sued are small, the expense of defending against even a preposterous charge can quickly go beyond the resources of most students. Having liability insurance does not protect you from being sued. However, if you are sued, the insurance will be greatly appreciated.

Only a few social work programs provide liability insurance for students. Some programs require, or give option to, their students to purchase this insurance. Should you buy liability insurance if it is not required? The best argument for buying the insurance is that the National Association of Social Workers Insurance Trust offers it at a relatively inexpensive rate.

Another argument for purchasing the insurance would be if you are placed in an agency where there have been recent suits against staff members or where you feel that conditions are right for a suit against an employee or the agency. On the other hand, you may be provided some protection by the agency's or even the university's liability policy. However, you cannot always count on this. You can be sued as an individual. Protection that you think you have under the agency's policy might evaporate if attorneys for the agency argue that you were not a bona fide employee. If you can spare the cash, purchasing liability insurance is worthwhile, although it is unlikely that you will ever use it.

CAN CONFIDENTIAL CLIENT MATERIAL EVER BE SHARED?

Most social work students, by the time they are ready to start a practicum, have been well drilled on the importance of respecting confidentiality. From the NASW Code of Ethics, students have learned to hold in confidence information obtained in the course of professional service. You've learned that you need explicit written permission from clients to share information about them with anyone other than the professional staff of the agency. And you've learned that the NASW Code of Ethics states that clients should have access to records concerning them; that care should be taken to protect the confidences of others contained in those records; and that the social worker should obtain the informed consent of clients before taping, recording, or permitting third-party observation of their activities.

By the start of the practicum, students have also learned that the term *confidentiality* in a social service agency generally refers to relative confidentiality, not absolute confidentiality. The Federal Privacy Act of 1974 makes it clear that information about clients and staff may be shared with officers and employees of the agency who need such records in the performance of their duties. That information revealed by a client can be subpoenaed for use in court also helps students understand the concept of relative confidentiality.

Unquestionably, there are times when information obtained from clients should be shared with others. The client's right to confidentiality, for instance, does not extend to the abuse or harm of children. All 50 states have statutes that require professionals to report any suspected child abuse or neglect. In some states, professionals are also required to report elder abuse. Similarly, if a client makes a serious threat of suicide, or harm to others, this information should be shared with other professionals and family members even if it violates confidentiality.

Guidelines for violating the client's confidentiality are not well defined. For instance, if a client threatens to commit a criminal act (e.g., a man says he is going to beat his partner), professionals must weigh the seriousness of the crime and abandon the principle of confidentiality to prevent serious harm. Using this criterion, illegal activities such as buying or selling marijuana do not justify breaking confidentiality. Engaging in prostitution does not either, unless the individual is infected with AIDS. When confronted with a dilemma about breaching a client's confidentiality, it is always important to discuss your next course of action with your agency supervisor. Certainly, disclosure without a client's permission should take place only under the most extreme circumstances and only as a last resort (Reamer, 1991).

Relative confidentiality can also be seen in the way that researchers, evaluators, and quality assurance personnel read case records or parts of these records to determine which clients are benefiting from intervention, and the

When a client's confidentiality must be breached, always discuss your plan with your agency supervisor.

characteristics of clients enrolled in selected programs. Generally, clients must give their permission in order to participate in a research or evaluation project. However, if the nature of the research or evaluation relies on closed cases or historical data, then client permission generally is not sought, provided that personal identifying information (e.g., the client's name, address, or phone number) is not recorded and that the research methodology does not involve contacting clients directly.

Occasionally, social work students may be asked to make a case presentation to one of their classes or seminars. In such situations, sharing details of a case is not a violation of the client's confidentiality if you do not give out any personal identifying information. However, do not describe clients in such a way that they can be recognized. Instead, be somewhat general in your description and try to change a few personal details. You might say, for instance, that the client is a 40-year-old mother of four with a professional career, who has been referred from the courts for a first-time shoplifting offense. If you find it necessary to refer to the client by a name, make one up or refer to the client by some initial (e.g., "Mrs. B").

Descriptions that could fit any number of people in the community because they do not identify the client are not a violation of clients' confidentiality when used within a professional or educational context. However, the more times you repeat a description, the greater the likelihood that someone might recognize your client. For this reason, professionalism requires that even brief, general descriptions of clients not be shared at parties and social occasions.

The same discretion is expected if you should identify a client from another student's presentation. Occasionally during classes or seminars, a client who receives services from more than one agency will be recognized by one or more students who know each other. Whenever this happens, you are bound by the same principle of confidentiality as is the student assigned the case and making the presentation.

Confidentiality is a complex subject that can be covered only superficially in this section. You may want to consult additional resources such as Schwartz (1989); Millstein, Dare-Winters, and Sullivan (1994); Dickson (1998); Strom-Gottfried (1998); or Rock and Congress (1999). Most agencies have written policies addressing the issue of confidentiality. These policies generally have components mandated by law. However, policies may not be current or may not address such issues as electronic records and managed care organizations' access to those records. Ask your field instructor about the agency's policies and what you should tell clients about protecting their confidential information. Clients should be informed about the limits of confidentiality before, rather than after, they disclose information that could create additional problems for them.

MAY I AUDIO- OR VIDEOTAPE CLIENTS?

As part of your course work, it may be required or desirable to reproduce one of your sessions with a client. Graybeal and Ruff (1995) have noted, "Audiotapes provide evidence of how much or little students talk, the modulation, tenor, and emotion of voice, and pace of interactions. Students and instructors can pick up on tones, attitudes, and subtleties not available in the written record" (p. 275). Videotape is even better because students and instructors can see body language and movement in the room as well as hear the dialogue with all its inflections.

Taping saves you the arduous task of remembering everything that happened in a session. If you are required by your faculty field liaison to tape a session with a client, do not assume that your agency supervisor will know about it. Discuss your need to audio- or videotape a client with your agency supervisor. The two of you can then begin the necessary planning and client selection. Keep in mind, though, that you must *always* obtain the client's permission before you begin to audio- or videotape—even if the client's identity will not be known to your audience or identifiable characteristics can be obscured by editing. Most agencies require that clients indicate their agreement to taping by signing a written release or consent form. This is a good idea even if the agency does not have a prepared form. Most clients will not mind being taped and may be glad to help if you approach them in a straightforward, honest, and relaxed manner. When you are interested in taping children, obtain permission from their parents or guardians.

Once permission has been secured, it is a good idea to test the equipment and make sure that you know how to operate the video or audio recorders. Experiment with the placement of the microphone or camera to ensure that you get the best possible recording. Have everything arranged so there will be minimal distraction or attention given to the equipment once the clients arrive. Do not remind clients to look toward the camera. Try to keep the equipment as unobtrusive as possible. Remember that the process of recording should be less important than what you and your clients achieve together in the session.

Afterwards, listen to or watch the tape critically. Analyze the material in terms of your feelings, thoughts, and the theoretical concepts you were employing. Make notes for discussion with your instructor. You may want to play back portions of the tape for the client to enable both parties to examine the helping process and to give the client an opportunity to comment on the intervention process.

Points to Remember about Confidentiality

▶ You cannot release client information (either orally or in writing) without the explicit written permission of the client.

▶ Clients must give permission for taping or recording of their sessions.

▶ Be careful not to leave charts, records, and information that is personally identifying on your desk where sensitive information could be viewed by other clients or unauthorized persons.

▶ You may break a confidence if the client is threatening to harm someone else or himself or herself. You are legally required to report any evidence or suspicions of child abuse.

▶ In general, do not talk about cases unless it is with your supervisor, field instructor, faculty field liaison, legal authority, or other agency staff who has a need to know.

▶ When calling a client at work or at home, be careful not to reveal too much information to any parties other than your client. For instance, you may wish to leave only your name and phone number and not indicate that you are associated with the Comprehensive Mental Health Center.

WHAT IS AN ETHICAL DILEMMA?

An ethical dilemma is when you must make a choice among arguably correct but conflicting courses of action. Dilemmas also usually involve negative repercussions either for you or the client. The following list from Blumenfield and Lowe (1987) identifies situations where ethical dilemmas may be experienced. Such circumstances include:

Ethical dilemmas require making a choice among arguably correct but conflicting courses of action.

▶ Conflict between one's personal and professional values
▶ Conflict between two values/ethical principles
▶ Conflict between two possible actions, each with reasons strongly favorable and unfavorable
▶ Conflict between two unsatisfactory alternatives
▶ Conflict between one's values/principles and one's perceived role
▶ Conflict between the need to act and the need to reflect

To further illustrate how it is possible to be caught in an ethical dilemma, consider the following example:

You are interning as a school social worker, and on your first day in the school your field instructor is out sick. The principal is juggling several crises and asks you to help out by meeting with a nine-year-old who has been crying since arriving at school that morning.

The child is very reluctant to talk, but you coax and encourage. Finally, the child says that she'll tell you, but only if you promise to tell no one else what she reveals. In your haste to learn what has been troubling her, you agree. The child then divulges a history of abusive treatment by her stepmother.

By law you are required to report known or suspected incidents of child abuse. Furthermore, the principal and the child's homeroom teacher are both interested in her welfare and want you to share what you have learned. However, you made a promise. Do you break your promise and inform the child protection authorities and the principal? If you break your promise, will that destroy the rapport you have established with the child? If the abuse cannot be substantiated by child protection services (CPS), will the nine-year-old receive worse treatment at home as a result of your reporting the stepmother?

CAN ETHICAL DILEMMAS BE AVOIDED?

The social work intern in the previous scenario created a difficult situation by promising to hold the nine-year-old's story confidential. The dilemma could have been avoided if the social work student had not promised to safeguard the nine-year-old's account. A better way to have handled this would have been to show concern, reiterate to the child that no one has a right to hurt or threaten her, and communicate that you want to help *but* that the law requires you to share information with other people under certain circumstances. In other words, you would inform the client early on, before anything important has been revealed, of your professional obligation to report child abuse.

At the same time, it is entirely possible that informing a child of the necessity to report any abuse may result in the child clamming up and not talking any further with you. The child may need to meet with you on several occasions before she trusts you enough to reveal anything important.

So, while the ethical dilemma might have been avoided in this first example, it is very unlikely that you will be able to practice social work without encountering others. For instance, suppose you are running a self-esteem group in a high school. During an especially productive session, a 16-year-old student reveals that since he broke up with his girlfriend, he has been smoking pot and doing other drugs. He wants help, but he also does not want his parents to know. His father is the chief of police.

Is the student the only client? Should the parents also be viewed as the client system? Should they be informed that their son is breaking the law? Does the principal have a right to know that the student is bringing marijuana onto school property and may be selling it to classmates?

Because most students are minors, it is unclear in many situations whether information about a child should be transmitted to the parents or kept confidential. In this second scenario, however, the intern should urge the client to stop bringing illegal drugs onto campus and to disclose to his parents his need for substance abuse counseling. Many social workers feel that confidentiality should extend to minors as well as to adults; they also believe that advising them to disclose important information is consistent with the social work value of client self-determination.

Because of advances in technology and its ability to sustain life of those in frail health, social workers in medical settings can also expect to have to deal with complex ethical problems. In these settings the social worker may discover conflicts when multiple parties (the patient's family, the hospital, and even society—which wants scarce medical resources justly allocated) each have different visions of what is best for the patient.

A study of hospital social workers (Proctor, Morrow-Howell, & Lott, 1993) found that the majority of ethical conflicts they reported consisted of a clash between the client's self-determination and what social workers judged not to be in the client's best interest. For example, the patient wants to be discharged, but he or she would not accept the amount of in-home help needed to live independently. In 61 percent of the social workers' cases, there was some disagreement among parties about discharge destination.

Can ethical dilemmas be completely avoided? Probably not. It is best to prepare yourself for them by examining your own values from time to time and learning all you can about how past ethical problems in your practicum setting were resolved.

HOW DO I AVOID RUSHING INTO ETHICAL DILEMMAS?

Two actions are helpful in keeping ethical dilemmas at arm's length: First, develop a working knowledge of the NASW Code of Ethics. The Code of Ethics provides general guidelines for ethical behavior. These standards may not, however, suggest what you should do in every instance. By necessity they cannot be specific to every possible ethics violation. At the same time, some behaviors will almost always be viewed as unethical. These include such behaviors as:

- Sexual intimacy with clients
- Libeling or slandering a client
- Sharing confidences without compelling professional reasons
- Assaulting, causing physical injuries, or placing clients in danger
- Dishonesty, fraud, or misrepresentation
- Discriminatory practices
- Withdrawing services precipitously (abandoning a client)
- Failure to warn and protect the victim of a violent crime
- Failure to exercise reasonable precautions with a potentially suicidal client
- Promising "cures" for problems

Second, you can avoid ethical dilemmas by anticipating likely trouble spots before they occur. If, for instance, your practicum is in a school, you should give prior thought to how you would respond if a child reveals abuse or neglect. Find out how your field instructor wants you to handle these situations. What information does the school expect you will share with concerned teachers? The principal?

Additionally, be alert to areas where your values may collide with the clients' best interest. For example, if you believe that keeping families together is the most important thing you can do as a social worker, you may not be as quick to recognize the emotional damage occurring within a family when an abuser lives there and doesn't cooperate with counseling. In one real-life situation a father with explosive anger kicked in his ten-year-old child's bedroom door because the parent wanted to punish his son for coming home a few minutes late for supper. When the worried mother got on the phone and called the "family counselor," he did not encourage her to call the police or the child protection authorities—actions that would have resulted in greater protection of the child and the mother and probably would have provided the motivation for the father to participate in therapy.

Case Example

Retta is an undergraduate student in a practicum at a large, multiservice agency with strict eligibility standards based on income. Retta has a client, Tonya, a single mother with four small children, who is struggling to get by on her welfare check. Tonya also receives a small amount of assistance with her large utility bill from the agency. However, Retta receives a phone call from Tonya's neighbor informing her that Tonya has been working part time and not reporting her income.

Questions

1. Should Retta just forget about this piece of information and allow Tonya to provide more income for her family?
2. Should Retta reduce the amount of assistance by the income the neighbor reported? What would you do?
3. Could the "correct" response for Retta to make be in opposition to the most ethical course of action?

HOW DO I RESOLVE ETHICAL DILEMMAS?

The first step in resolving an ethical dilemma is to recognize the problem and identify the source of the conflict. For instance, is it a clash between professional and personal values? Between professional values and agency policy? It may be useful to write down the problem as you understand it and then to gather relevant information. How has this problem been handled in the past?

You must also keep all parties informed of your legal and ethical obligations. Engage clients or involved parties in dialogue, and brainstorm the "best" course of action. Make sure you are constantly keeping in mind the mission of the profession and observing the client's right to self-determination. If you are still unclear about what to do, discuss the situation with your field instructor or faculty liaison. Protect the identity of the client if necessary, and present the situation as a "hypothetical" case.

Lowenberg and Dolgoff (1996) have suggested an approach for ordering social work values that might help you get off the "horns of a dilemma." For instance, they say that protection of life should always take precedence over lower-ranked values, such as privacy and confidentiality, or even truthfulness (as when you have to break a promise). Their priority ranking of ethical principles is as follows:

1. Protection of life
2. Equality

3. Autonomy and freedom

4. Least harm

5. Quality of life

6. Privacy and confidentiality

7. Truthfulness and full disclosure

How do you know when you are doing the right thing? It is not always possible to know, but there is a greater chance that you can feel good about the decision you have to make if you go through a deliberate process where you examine your values, seek additional information, and consult others.

Joseph (cited in Garrett, 1994) has outlined a decision-making model that requires these steps:

1. definition of the dilemma;

2. looking at all the relevant facts and developing valid arguments for various courses of action;

3. consideration of practice wisdom, personal beliefs and values, and how these might influence the final decision;

4. developing options, exploring compromises, evaluating alternatives in an attempt to find a course of action with the least negative effects; and

5. choosing a position that you can defend.

Other decision-making models have been discussed by Lowenberg and Dolgoff (1996) and Tymchuck (1992). When you have conscientiously gone through such a process to resolve ethical dilemmas, then you have done all that can be done.

Professional Identity

Critical Thinking Question: After accidentally breaking a client's confidentiality, how could you reflect upon the experience to avoid making the mistake again?

Case Example

Freda and Holly are placed in a large agency where their field instructor is so busy that she scarcely has time to see them each week. Mrs. Morgan, the field instructor, had agreed to accept the two students before she learned that she would be given responsibility for managing a new branch office miles from town. Because she is frequently unavailable to them, Freda and Holly have been using their time in the practicum setting to do their homework and catch up on reading for their other courses. After the first month, Freda and Holly have yet to see a client, and they have only been given some basic clerical assignments like answering the phones and finding files.

Freda wants to inform their faculty liaison that they are not being used appropriately and are not learning any social work skills. Holly says, "Why ruin a good thing?" She clearly communicates that she will be most unhappy if Freda speaks to their faculty liaison.

Questions

1. Should Freda take the chance that things will eventually settle down for Mrs. Morgan and that she will find some meaningful assignments for them before the semester is out?

2. Should Freda go against her friend's wishes and speak to Mrs. Morgan or their faculty liaison? What are the arguments for each position?

3. Besides speaking to Mrs. Morgan or their faculty liaison, what else could Freda do to enrich her own experience within the agency?

MAY I ACCEPT A GIFT FROM A CLIENT?

Sometimes clients are so appreciative that they want to give their favorite social worker a gift. Some agencies have policies on receiving gifts; others do not. Check with your agency supervisor if a client hints that he or she will be bringing you a present. The client's giving of a small gift may be a demonstration of simple gratitude for being helpful or for simply accepting something that the client said or did. But the gift may also be an attempt to ask the therapist to like the client more, or to manipulate the therapist (Gabel, Oster, & Pfeffer, 1988). This would be particularly true with expensive or extravagant gifts. In the absence of an agency policy, you may want to devise one of your own— such as not accepting gifts valued at more than $10. Generally, small tokens of appreciation such as cookies or a cake that could be shared with others in the agency can be graciously accepted. Here's a situation that actually happened to one of our students:

> Cynthia received a birthday card from a client who had heard a couple of staff talking about taking her out for lunch. When Cynthia opened the card, she found a $50 bill in it. That night in her practicum group she revealed that she didn't know what to do. The client was on probation and she was afraid that if she told her field instructor, the client would get into trouble. She wanted to return the money quietly without informing her supervisor. Without exception, her classmates strongly urged her not to keep it secret but to advise the field instructor. Otherwise, they reasoned, the client might accuse Cynthia of taking a bribe or soliciting favors.

Once in a while, a client will want to give a special student a gift even after a case has been transferred or closed. Generally when this happens, there is some dependency on the client's part, and the client may be trying to keep the student involved in the case. If it is a small gift, it may be possible to accept it. However, you may want to have the client leave the gift at the agency or with another worker, so that you can pick it up without becoming entangled again.

IS IT EVER PERMISSIBLE TO DATE CLIENTS OR COWORKERS?

Students should not date clients or socialize with them outside of the agency. Although one date may not lead to romantic involvement, in any dating situation where there is physical attraction the potential for sexual involvement exists. And it is never permissible for helping professionals to engage in sexual activities with their clients. The NASW Code of Ethics (1999) states, "Social workers should under no circumstances engage in sexual activities or sexual contact with current clients." Further, social workers are prohibited from engaging in sexual activities with clients' relatives or other individuals with whom clients maintain close personal relationships when there is risk of harm to the client. In fact, because of its destructive consequences for clients, all of the major mental health professions have explicit prohibitions against therapist–client sexual involvement. In some states legislation has been passed making therapist–client sexual intimacy a criminal offense.

If you find that you are strongly attracted to a client, the advised course of action is to speak to your agency supervisor about arranging a transfer of this client to another staff member. Romantic involvement jeopardizes professional objectivity. The social worker's judgment about what is best for the client may be clouded as the social worker becomes overprotective and over involved.

Confine relationships with patients to the office, except when specific interventions are needed elsewhere. When would it be appropriate to see a client outside of the office? An example would be when it is impossible to talk or hear in your office (e.g., because of remodeling or construction), and it is convenient to walk to the corner restaurant and talk over coffee or a soft drink. In such instances, inform at least one other person in the agency (e.g., your agency supervisor) of your whereabouts. Although it is clear that, given a choice, some clients may prefer not to meet in the office, the use of an office within an established agency lends an air of propriety. Requests from clients to meet outside of the office may indicate an interest in manipulating or undercutting progress being made.

Social workers must behave in a trustworthy manner.

It is also not a good idea to date staff members within the agency as long as you are a student there. When there are breakups, relationships have a way of causing hard feelings. Former soulmates can turn vindictive or uncooperative. Even if the relationship doesn't turn sour, you might not be able to maximize your learning in an agency where your relationship becomes a prime topic of conversation and office relationships are extremely difficult to keep secret. Finally, the NASW Code of Ethics (1999) states:

> Social workers who function as supervisors or educators should not engage in sexual activities or contact with supervisees, students, trainees, or other colleagues over whom they exercise professional authority.

WHAT DO I DO IF I OBSERVE SOMETHING ILLEGAL OR UNETHICAL?

It is possible that you will observe or overhear something in an agency that strikes you as illegal or unethical. Consider this example: A student intern observes an employee apparently stealing an assortment of office supplies. Should the student report this to her field instructor? Probably not. The employee may be working at home on agency-related work and plans on bringing the unused materials back to the office the next morning. It is not the student's role to police other employees.

However, if you were to observe someone in the agency misappropriating client funds, fondling a client, or snorting drugs, then you would have a responsibility to report these much more serious accusations to your field instructor. The NASW Code of Ethics (1999) requires social workers who have a direct knowledge of a social work colleague's impairment due to personal problems, substance abuse, or mental difficulties to take action through appropriate channels.

Sometimes it is very difficult to know whether some action should be reported. One student was told not to use the agency phone for personal calls, yet observed a staff member who tied up a phone line for 45 minutes on a call to her boyfriend. This was not fair, and the student wanted to complain to her field instructor. In fact, she did complain. The field instructor took no action. The staff member was a personal friend of the field instructor, and there was no disciplinary action. But the student was viewed as a malcontent who was always complaining. Her final evaluation was much lower than her midterm evaluation.

The best advice is to consider the seriousness of the offense or charge. Is someone harmed or likely to be harmed? Contemplate what the consequences would be if you are wrong. What if you were mistaken and the 45-minute call was not to a boyfriend but to a legitimate client who was falling apart and needed 45 minutes of the social worker's time? If you are sure that you are right and the charge is serious enough to be unethical, illegal, or unprofessional, discuss the incident in private with your field instructor or your faculty field liaison, and the two of you can decide what the next step should be.

Case Example

For your first practicum you are assigned to a residential facility for persons with developmental disabilities and mental retardation. After the second week, a friend stops by, and since you are not busy at the time, you take about 15 minutes to give your friend a tour of the facility. Later, the agency director makes it clear that you are not to invite friends and family members to the facility. You explain that you had not invited your friend; she had just shown up, and you were merely being polite. Your feelings are a little hurt.

The next weekend, the interior of the facility is being painted and all but about four clients go home for a visit. Jim, a long-time employee of the facility, has a visit from his girlfriend on Saturday afternoon. They go into the office and keep the door closed for about two hours. During this time Jim does not answer the phone or attend to any agency business that you can observe.

Questions

1. Should you inform your agency supervisor of Jim's activities?
2. Should you let Jim know that you felt that he was violating the rules?
3. Should you cover for Jim?

HOW DO I HANDLE AGENCY SECRETS?

Once in a while students learn of transactions or behaviors within an agency that are not common knowledge. For instance, the treasurer may have been accused of embezzling a sum of money or the director may have been sued for palimony. Because the agency is not your client, you are not obligated to keep this information confidential in the same way as you have to safeguard sensitive material that clients share with you. However, you would be well advised to be very discreet in revealing these agency secrets.

For one thing, the allegations could turn out to be completely false and the result of vicious rumor. It would be embarrassing (if not irresponsible) if you were to spread such gossip throughout the community. Could you be guilty of slander in this situation? Furthermore, the personal affairs of agency officials may not interfere with their administrative abilities within the agency. Airing an agency's secrets in public could contribute to the agency's loss of reputation in the community and do a disservice to the many fine, hard working, and unselfish staff members.

If you feel that the private information that you have about the agency has or could have a direct effect on the quality of services to clients or the learning in your practicum, report this information to either your field instructor or your faculty field liaison. Also report this information if you think it might prevent future students from being placed in the agency. Otherwise, whom you tell about the agency's secrets depends on your own discretion.

HOW DO I HANDLE SEXUAL HARASSMENT?

Sexual harassment is unwanted verbal or physical conduct of a sexual nature. This harassment includes compliments of a very personal or sexual nature; pressure for dates or sexual contact; jokes with suggestive themes; unwelcome notes; or physical activities such as touching, brushing against, unsolicited back rubs; or blocking passage with one's body. The few studies available on sexual harassment of social workers have shown that human service agencies are not immune from this problem and that almost 30 percent of social workers have experienced some form of sexual harassment.

Human Rights & Justice

Critical Thinking Question:
What argument could you make to advocate for a sexual harassment policy if an agency didn't have one?

When does a hug or a touch become sexual harassment? Sexual harassment is one-sided. There is no reciprocity involved; the offender's behavior is unwelcome and almost always repetitive. A single incident usually is not sexual harassment unless a serious threat or assault is involved.

Another aspect of sexual harassment is that the offender may use clout or power of position to insinuate that the victim has much to lose by not going along with the offender's requests. Sexual harassment exists when you fear a loss of position or status, or negative evaluation, because you rejected sexual advances. Both men and women can be victims of sexual harassment.

If you feel that you are being subjected to sexual harassment, you should immediately inform your primary supervisor. If the person harassing you is the supervisor, or if you do not feel comfortable discussing the matter with this person, by all means contact your faculty field liaison. Often, the situation will not improve until someone—the victim—decides to take a stand. One of our graduate students, placed in a psychiatric setting, was repeatedly subjected to derogatory comments from a male physician about the nature of her work. These comments were completely unfounded and sexist in nature. When the student discussed this situation with her field instructor, a great deal of support was generated for her, and the result was that a letter of disciplinary action was placed in the physician's personnel folder.

Do not be silent just because you are a student or because you don't have much longer in the placement. If you are feeling sexually harassed, it is likely that the same offender is harassing others. There are laws to protect you against sexual harassment. One way to avoid becoming a victim is to familiarize yourself with your agency's policies for complying with sexual harassment laws. Dhooper, Huff, and Schultz (1989) found that 54 percent of social workers surveyed were ignorant of the applicable laws.

SUMMARY

This chapter has aimed to provide some beginning information about the legal system and to prepare you for handling such thorny problems as resolving ethical dilemmas, handling mistakes, and gives guidance for some common problems that might be encountered.

Understanding the Interaction of Personal and Professional Values

1. Just as everyone else, you have a set of values that guide your personal and social life. As a social worker, your professional behavior should be guided by the NASW Code of Ethics. But what are the values that constitute your personal ethical "code"?

   a. _____

   _____

   _____

   b. _____

   _____

   _____

   c. _____

   _____

   _____

   d. _____

   _____

   _____

2. Have any of your personal values changed because of your exposure to a world of diverse people, ideas, and experiences, or your education for a professional career? Which values and how?

   _____

   _____

   _____

3. Is there any conflict between your personal values and social work professional values? Where do they clash?

   _____

   _____

   _____

4. How do you plan to resolve the conflict between your personal and professional values?

   _____

   _____

   _____

The Ethical and Legal Bases of Professional Behavior

1. Compare the NASW Code of Ethics with the American Psychological Association's Ethical Principles of Psychologists and Code of Conduct (see www.apa.org/ethics/code2002.html).

   a. List 2–3 commonalities found in the NASW and APA codes.

   _____

   _____

   _____

   b. List 2–3 differences in the two codes.

   _____

   _____

   _____

2. Study the NASW Code of Ethics, and identify one absolute ethical standard that allows for no exception or qualification and that every social worker in every practice setting must observe.

   a. What is that standard?

   _____

   _____

   _____

   _____

   b. What sets that one apart from all others?

   _____

   _____

   _____

   _____

   c. Why is that so?

   _____

   _____

   _____

   _____

3. Among the legal issues involved in human services are:

   a. Clients' right to privacy

   _____

   _____

   _____

b. Clients' right to privileged communication

_____

_____

_____

c. Clients' right to confidentiality

_____

_____

_____

d. Disclosure of information

_____

_____

_____

Make a list of the questions you have about how these issues are handled in your agency, and discuss them with your agency supervisor.

_____

_____

_____

_____

_____

_____

_____

The Ethical and Legal Dimensions of Social Work Practice

Having gained some micropractice experience, listened to case presentations of human service practitioners at the agency staffings, and participated in classroom discussions, what have you learned about:

1. Practice activities that are prohibited by law?

_____

_____

_____

_____

_____

_____

_____

_____

_____

2. Practice activities that are considered ethically unacceptable?

_____

_____

_____

_____

_____

_____

_____

_____

_____

3. Think of all the activities that are disallowed either by law or by a professional code of ethics.

    a. Identify a practice activity that is ethically forbidden but is not illegal.

    _____

    _____

    _____

    b. How would you deal with a coworker or friend involved in such an activity? What is your responsibility in terms of reporting?

    _____

    _____

    _____

4. Again think of all the possible activities that are either illegal or morally indefensible.

    a. Can you identify a practice activity that is illegal but ethically permissible?

    _____

    _____

    _____

    b. How would you deal with a coworker or friend in such an activity? What is your responsibility?

    _____

    _____

    _____

More about Dealing with Ethical and Legal Challenges

1. Interview your field supervisor or another practitioner in the agency about the type of ethical dilemmas encountered by the agency's professional staff and how these are generally resolved. List one recent dilemma.

   a. How did the agency resolve the dilemma?

   _____

   _____

   _____

   b. When you consider the agency's response, which factor seemed to be most influential? (Possible legal repercussions, commitment to professional ethics, pragmatic considerations, or some other reason?)

   _____

   _____

   _____

2. Approach a social worker in your field agency or elsewhere who often has to appear in court, and arrange to observe that worker's testimony.* Make sure that you get answers to such questions as:

   a. What is the social worker's role and function in the court?

   _____

   _____

   _____

   b. How does a worker prepare for a court appearance?

   _____

   _____

   _____

   c. What types of questions are generally asked by attorneys?

   _____

   _____

   _____

   d. What written documents does the social worker provide the court?

   _____

   _____

   _____

*This exercise is based on a suggestion from Horejsi and Garthwait (2002).

e. What legal and/or ethical issues can pertain to a social worker's advocacy for his or her client in court? Testimony on behalf of one client against another? What about participation in involuntary treatment of clients? Select one issue and discuss the ethical challenges.

_____

_____

_____

Succeed with PEARSON mysocialworklab

Log onto **www.mysocialworklab.com** to access a wealth of case studies, videos, and assessment. (*If you did not receive an access code to* **MySocialWorkLab** *with this text and wish to purchase access online, please visit* www.mysocialworklab.com.)

1. **Watch the Core Competency video: "Keeping Up with Shifting Contexts."** The special transportation service provided to clients with Alzheimer's disease will be stopped due to budget cuts. The social worker is shown shaking her head in disagreement. Since she is strongly opposed to the budget cuts, is this an ethical issue for which she should resign her position to protest and force the agency to find another solution?

2. **Watch the Core Competency video: "Providing Leadership to Promote Change."** In this video the social worker informs the client's son about an elder advocacy group so he can speak to the legislature about funding. Can you make a case for it being appropriate for social workers to be directly involved as advocates for this type of thing because it advances human rights and economic justice, or should it always be left to the clients?

PRACTICE TEST The following questions will test your knowledge of the content found within this chapter.

1. Which term means a legal document requiring a court appearance on a specific day and time, to give testimony:
   a. Subpoena
   b. Indictment
   c. Summons
   d. Warrant

2. Court room testifying has certain rules. To which rule must social workers adhere?
   a. If needed circumvent the truth
   b. Commit to needed services
   c. Furnish information relative to your expertise
   d. Emphasize third-party information

3. *Relative confidentiality* refers to:
   a. Giving a client's close relative information
   b. Researchers obtaining secondary data
   c. Gaining written permission from clients' relatives
   d. Obtaining informed consent from each client

4. Students may be vulnerable to a malpractice action if they:
   a. Inform clients of their student status
   b. Keep detailed records
   c. Fail to seek proper supervision
   d. Warn third parties of potential harm

Short Answer Question:

After many months, Selina has gained the trust of Mrs. Smith. However, recently Mrs. Smith let it slip that she puts her elderly father with dementia to bed without supper whenever he soils himself. Selina doesn't want to contact Adult Protection because the father sits in the waiting looking cheerful. If reported, Mrs. Smith might get angry and drop out of treatment. What should Selina do?

ASSESS YOUR COMPETENCE Use the scale below to rate your current level of achievement on the following concepts or skills associated with each competency practice behavior presented in the chapter:

1	2	3
I can accurately describe the concept or skill.	I can consistently identify the concept or skill when observing and analyzing practice activities.	I can competently implement the concept or skill in my own practice.

_____ apply the NASW Code of Ethics (or international codes).

_____ use self-assessment and supervision to improve my practice.

_____ advocate for clients who are sexually harassed.

Answers

Key: 1) a, 2) c, 3) b, 4) c

9

Pragmatic Concerns

Core Competencies in This Chapter (Check marks indicate which competencies are covered in depth)				
✓ Professional Identity	☐ Ethical Practice	✓ Critical Thinking	☐ Diversity in Practice	☐ Human Rights & Justice
☐ Research-Based Practice	☐ Human Behavior	☐ Policy Practice	☐ Practice Contexts	✓ Engage, Assess, Intervene, Evaluate

OVERVIEW

This chapter contains practical advice regarding situations and topics not covered elsewhere in the book. It provides answers to several miscellaneous questions that may arise during the social work practicum.

WHAT DO I DO IF I GET SICK OR AM RUNNING LATE AND MISS MY APPOINTMENTS?

It is probably inevitable that at some time during a practicum you will become ill, have car trouble, or experience another problem that may cause you to miss scheduled appointments. Once you know that you will be late or will miss an appointment, the professional course of action is to call the agency. Ask the secretary to contact your clients, your agency supervisor, and other involved parties to inform them of your absence. If you have an infectious illness (e.g., the flu), it is much kinder to miss an appointment or two than to infect coworkers and clients. Appointments can be rescheduled when you are feeling better. If you are too ill to go to work, do not feel obligated to contact clients from home and provide routine counseling over the phone. If your car breaks down, and you do not have access to a cell phone, all you can do is to call the agency at the first opportunity. Once you are back in the agency, reschedule all missed appointments as soon as possible.

Case Example

Your car is undependable, and it is particularly difficult to start in the morning after it has been idle for eight or ten hours. You have taken the car to many repair shops, but no one can find the problem. You cannot afford to buy a new car now, and public transportation is not available within a reasonable walking distance of you.

Since beginning your practicum, problems with starting your car have made you late on three occasions. Once you were only 20 minutes late. The second time you were about 45 minutes late. On the third occasion, your agency supervisor sternly advised you to find another means of transportation because she had to see your client for you. After four frustrating weeks, you have just learned that your supervisor lives just a little over a mile from your apartment.

Questions

1. Should you ask if you can car pool with your agency supervisor?
2. What other options are available to you?

WILL I BE ASKED TO SHARE A DESK OR OFFICE?

When sharing an office or desk, show consideration for others.

Student interns do not always have their own private offices. Often, they must share space with another student or students. Ideally, however, students should have their own desks and phones. When an office is shared with others (and it may be the field instructor), you should show consideration for others.

If you use a desk that is shared with another student or staff person, keep it tidy. Ensure that the working surface of the desk is clean before you leave each day. If you share an office, try not to monopolize it or the phone with loud conversation when your office-mate is working. Do not transform the office into your personal habitat. It is probably best if you do not bring in radios, televisions, or expensive personal effects to entertain you or to decorate the office.

If you share an office and you need private space for counseling, the agency should have a vacant office for either you or your office-mate to use. Sometimes this space must be scheduled in advance. Be sure to learn the procedures for this before you find yourself with a client and no space suitable for interviewing. If the agency is critically short of space and on more than one occasion you and a client have to use an unsuitable area (such as a vacant corner of the waiting room), report this to your faculty field liaison. The agency may not be well suited for the training of students. It is especially critical that the space or rooms utilized for working with clients not jeopardize their confidentiality by others overhearing or observing emotional responses.

HOW DO I KEEP TRACK OF TIME IN THE PRACTICUM?

You can keep track of the amount of time spent in your practicum placement by one of several methods. It may be simple enough to remember that you spend all day on Tuesdays and Thursdays and half of each Friday—for a total of 20 hours each week. Such a crude accounting system does not provide any description of *how* you spent your time. If asked about your major activities last week, could you recall them without the aid of some notes? Therefore, it is important to keep a record of the hours you spend in an agency as well as the variety of experiences to which you are exposed. Reviewing this record from time to time can help you and your agency supervisor monitor your progress toward your learning objectives and your development as a social worker.

A convenient way to determine what you have been learning in the agency is to review how you have spent your time. Agencies and social work programs use different procedures and forms to keep track of students' use of time. If, however, none is mandated and you are looking for a quick reporting scheme, see Figure 9.1 for an illustration of one that you could create for your own use.

Another variation would be to use a blank sheet of paper for each day you are in the practicum. Write down any cases, events, problems, or interesting situations you want to know more about. At the end of each week, you might want to write a summary of what you have learned. This information might be useful to you later when you prepare to enter the job market and need to create a résumé. But educationally, it is sound too. Students often don't realize how much they have learned until they reflect back over their experiences.

Finally, if you find that you are accumulating more hours in the agency than is required, you might want to discuss this with your faculty field liaison. If you are doing two placements in the same agency back-to-back, carrying over of your excess hours may not be allowed. However, having a few hours of comp time "in the bank" is a good idea and may be beneficial in case of illness, when your car breaks down, or if you need to take off some time to study for an exam.

Professional Identity

Critical Thinking Question: What might you learn about your use of time if you kept an hour-by-hour accounting?

		Date _____	

Student's Name _____   Agency _____

Hours Interned This Week _____   Cumulative Hours _____

Hour	Monday	Wednesday	Friday
8:00 8:30	Team meeting	Supervision with Field Instructor	Agency Research Project (Cont.)
9:00 9:30	Counseling Mrs. J	Staff Inservice	Preparation for Case Presentation
10:00 10:30	Writing Progress Notes and Treatment Plan		Counseling Mr. M
11:00 11:30	Preparation for Afternoon Group	↓	Interview Children's Services Coordinator
12:00 12:30	Lunch	Lunch	Lunch
1:00 1:30	Observation Marital Therapy	Intake Desk	Staffing Crisis Phone Line
2:00 2:30	Counseling Jim C.	Intake Desk	Staffing Crisis Phone Line
3:00 3:30	Writing Progress Notes and Reading on Tourettes'	Counseling Ms. W.	Emergency Room Visit
4:00 4:30	Self-Esteem Group Session (6 Kids)	Agency Research Project (Reviewing Files)	Consultation with Jim C.'s Teacher
5:00			

Figure 9.1

Practicum Reporting Form

Cooper, W. E. (1982). Time management techniques for clinicians. In P. A. Keller & L. G. Ritt (Eds.), *Innovations in clinical practice: A source book* (pp. 177–183). Sarasota, FL: Professional Resource Exchange.

HOW DO I LEARN TO LEAVE MY WORK AT THE AGENCY?

Do not take client and agency problems home with you.

For your own mental health and well-being, do not take client and agency problems home with you. Concern yourself with clients' problems only when you are on duty at the agency. When you are at home or in the classroom, you need to give your attention to your family, friends, or schoolwork. Although it sounds a little callous, you do not own your clients' problems. You cannot "make" anyone get better. Although you will do your best to help, clients' problems are *their* problems. If you find yourself not sleeping or being preoccupied with a client's difficulties when you are at home or school, you are probably overinvolved. If you suspect this might be true, a discussion with your field instructor or faculty field liaison would be in order.

It will not always be easy to leave client problems at the agency at the end of the day. If you were not concerned about people, you probably wouldn't have chosen the career of social work. However, separating your work life from your leisure is a mental discipline that you must practice. To help you with this, make a personal rule to not bring paperwork from the agency home with you. Although it might be tempting to catch up on your progress notes or other work-related assignments at home, this is not advised. To do this type of work, client files or charts are usually needed, and students should never take agency files or confidential material out of the office without permission of the agency supervisor or field instructor. In one horror story, a student took several files home one evening only to have her briefcase containing the files stolen from her car. In another case, a physician was taking home medical files, and the files actually blew out the window of his car and across the interstate highway.

WHAT DO I DO IF I AM GIVEN TOO MUCH OR TOO LITTLE RESPONSIBILITY?

Too much responsibility can be frightening! Overwhelming! A couple of years ago a student confided that in her placement, interns were assigned six or more cases the first day after orientation and told to schedule the appointments. They were expected to handle themselves as professionals and, if they needed, ask for help. No help was given unless it was sought. Although the student's initial reaction was "poor me," by the end of his or her two semesters there he or she had been asked to remain as a paid employee. If, however, you feel as though you are being given too much to do, you probably need to talk to your field instructor. Should that not work, talk with your faculty field liaison.

If you are mildly concerned about what you perceive to be your unproven ability to help others, this probably would not be seen as a serious problem. On the other hand, if you are experiencing tremendous stress (e.g., insomnia, indigestion, panic attacks), you are likely being given more responsibility than you can handle. In this instance, it is appropriate to inform your field instructor of what you are experiencing.

The problem of being given too little responsibility was addressed in Chapter 4. Briefly, students should expect to be occupied in direct service at least half of the time that they are in their placement. If this is not happening, talk first with the field instructor. If additional responsibilities are not given, share your concerns with the faculty field liaison. All three participants in the learning contract (the student, the faculty field liaison, and the field instructor) need to be involved should problems arise in the practicum. Do not feel that you have to solve major problems in your field instruction by yourself.

WHAT DO I DO WHEN I AM HAVING A "DOWN" DAY?

Sometimes the severity of clients' problems (e.g., child sexual abuse, adolescent suicide attempts, domestic violence) can cause students to experience "down" days—especially when a favorite client takes a turn for the worst (e.g., attempts suicide again or gets re-arrested). Although intellectually students

Talk about the problems
you experience in the
agency.

Critical Thinking

Critical Thinking Question:
If your practicum
experience is not going
well, how could you use
your communication skills
to improve it?

can tell themselves that it will be impossible to help every client, they are still
likely to feel some pain when clients make bad choices for themselves.

It is important for you not to become depressed because of an action that a
client freely chose. Do not label yourself as a failure if a client becomes dys-
functional. Almost always, clients have some problems in everyday functioning or they would not be requesting services from a social service agency. With
problems such as substance abuse, it is expected that clients will "fall off the
wagon" on one or more occasions even though they may later successfully
maintain sobriety. One therapist's technique for avoiding depression when his
clients had relapses was to think about the clients' strengths and then envision
them using these assets at some future time to live successfully.

If you find yourself more than a little depressed or depressed fairly frequently
because of the cases you have been assigned, tell your faculty field liaison. You
may need therapy—particularly if these cases are close to some trauma you have
personally experienced. If you find it too difficult to handle the emotional pain
shared and experienced in the practicum setting, you may be better suited for research or administrative social work than direct practice with clients.

WHAT DO I DO WHEN THINGS ARE NOT GOING WELL?

If agencies can be personified as people we know, some would be dynamic—
fast-moving, attractive, decisive. Others would have a frumpy appearance and
would be slow-moving and ponderous. Not every student can be placed in a
dynamic agency. For one thing, there are probably too few of them and too
many students. You know this intellectually and yet you are unhappy in your

placement. When should you ask for another placement? Here are some suggested guidelines:

- When you are not getting adequate supervision (and you have repeatedly sought and requested it)
- When you are not being given anything to do, or when the work being given to you is clerical and you have made numerous requests for additional responsibility
- When you are being harassed or feel in danger
- When you discover that you cannot be empathic with persons you are assigned to counsel because of personal or traumatic experiences with this problem
- When you are required to be in the agency at a time when you are expected to be in class or at a field seminar, and the agency is inflexible in its demands
- When there is a significant personality clash between you and your agency supervisor (e.g., the supervisor gives the impression that you can do nothing right)
- When unethical or illegal practices are common occurrences (discussed in detail in Chapter 8)

Asking for another placement is not a decision to be taken lightly. This is especially true after you have spent four or five weeks in an agency. Some social work programs allow the student only one "replacement" in another setting. Nonetheless, some problems are so serious that students really ought to seek a new assignment—even if it means losing credit for the month spent in the first agency. Keep in mind, though, that it is not uncommon for students to experience a slow start—for field instructors give very few assignments the first few weeks until they get to know the student and the student's capabilities. Sometimes the student feels that the first several weeks of a placement are spent reading with very little client contact.

There are logical explanations for this. Supervisors may want students to become more knowledgeable in a given area (e.g., the disease model of alcoholism) and may request completion of specific readings or observations before they assign clients. Supervisors may want to screen clients to ensure that the student is matched with one who can realistically show progress by the semester's end. Or, they may want to avoid assigning overly complicated cases to a student. Supervisors may want to wait for the "right" family before involving the student as a cotherapist. Furthermore, students may have to wait for sufficient clients to be recruited or identified before they can become involved as a group leader or coleader. Often there is little planning or recruiting for a new group until the student is established in the agency. So, expect some delays. Although it is frustrating, your agency supervisor will not always be available on a moment's notice. But none of these situations are by themselves good reasons for changing a practicum.

More serious concerns are when an agency is seriously mismanaged or understaffed, or when unethical practices are tolerated. In our program, a student interning in a group home for adolescents was made responsible for helping the residents prepare their meals over the weekend, but the only food left for her was a single can of lasagna. This event by itself was insufficient reason to remove a student, but it had been preceded by other indications of poor management. Hearing the student's account of this experience and then learning that the police were investigating one staff member for an illegal practice convinced

Engage, Assess, Intervene, Evaluate

Critical Thinking Question: What might you do to prevent a fellow student from becoming depressed by clients' problems in your agency?

us that the student would not have the type of experience that we had hoped. We moved the student to another agency.

Students should advocate for themselves—to try to rectify unhappy situations to the best of their abilities. When sincere (and usually repeated) effort has been made, it is up to the faculty field liaison to decide the next course of action. Do not decide to leave an assignment without the approval of the faculty member who placed you there—this could result in a failing grade. What may seem to be an insurmountable problem to a student often turns out to be resolvable when a conscientious faculty member becomes involved.

If you spent a semester in a lackluster agency, or had a field instructor who contributed little to your educational experience, one way to feel better about this would be to discuss with your faculty field liaison the development or adoption of a student feedback form on field instructors, if one is not being used in your program. Feedback from students can improve the supervision and quality of future students' learning experiences by documenting when a particular field instructor performs unsatisfactorily.

Even if unhappy, do not leave your practicum agency without first securing approval.

HOW DO I PLAN FOR MY NEXT PRACTICUM?

If you find yourself in a setting where your learning opportunities have been severely limited and you strongly feel that you need another practicum placement in a similar agency, discuss this with your faculty field liaison. It would be to your advantage to give some thought to the areas of deficiency in this practicum setting and to the type of agency or program that could help you to develop needed skills. At some point in your practicum, you may learn of highly recommended agencies or field instructors from students who are farther along in the program than you are. Advocate for yourself sufficiently ahead of time so that your faculty field liaison can assign you to these agencies or with these field instructors.

SHOULD I CONSIDER DOING A PRACTICUM ABROAD?

More and more bachelor and masters students are considering the benefits of studying abroad. They hope to take advantage of immersing themselves in a totally different culture, meeting fascinating people, and visiting picturesque lands. Immersion into other cultures has a way of helping us gain a better understanding of diverse peoples and political systems and forcing us to examine our own biases and values. Travel abroad can promote personal growth and self-confidence. See, for example, the Web site http://www.transitionsabroad.com/publications/magazine/0403/benefits_study_abroad.shtml.

If you decide to travel and study abroad, here is a checklist that may be helpful. Before you leave the United States you should have several documents and should have completed certain information. Listed here are a few of the things you should do before you leave the country.

▶ **Have your passport picture taken.** You will need at least two photographs for your passport and two for your International Student Identification Card (ISIC). It is also a good idea to take at least four passport size photos to your destination country. Most professional photographers, post offices, and copy offices will take a passport photo. Make sure you specify that you want passport photos.

- **Obtain your passport and necessary visas.** You can apply for a passport at the USPS Passport Agents in your city. You can find locations on the State Department's Web site. Passport acceptance facilities will have the necessary forms, or they can be downloaded from the Internet at http://travel.state.gov. Apply for your passport as soon as you decide to go abroad. It can take several months for your documents to arrive. If your passport is lost or stolen while you are abroad, report this to the nearest U.S. embassy as soon as possible. Before you travel abroad, make a copy of the identification page of your passport so that it will be easier for you to get a new one.
- **Obtain an International Student Identification Card.** You can purchase an ISIC card from the Office of International Affairs on your campus.
- **Letter from sponsoring university.** You should take a letter from the U.S. or foreign university that is sponsoring your study abroad experience. The letter should state that you have been accepted as a full-time student with the university.
- **Financial aid.** Talk to the people at your sponsoring school and the university you attend. Make sure that your financial aid, scholarships, and tuition payments have been satisfactorily met.
- **Health insurance.** Check with your current health care provider to make sure that you will be covered should you become sick or injured during your time abroad. Some providers require you to take out an additional policy during your time abroad.
- **Vaccinations.** It is important that all of your vaccinations be up to date before you travel. Check with your local health department to find out what vaccinations you should have before traveling to certain foreign countries. You will probably require a tuberculosis screening. Have your doctor fill out an international vaccination card and take it with you.
- **Living expenses.** Make sure that you have a sufficient fund to support yourself during your time abroad. Unless you receive special permission, you will not be allowed to work. In addition, it is important to remember that you may lose money when your American dollars are changed into the currency of your host country. If you are living in a large city, keep in mind that it may be significantly more expensive than if you currently reside in a small town. You will also need extra money for traveling and sight-seeing. Overall, expect to spend at least $1,000 per month in living expenses.
- **Other financial information.** Take some currency of your host country when you travel. Depending on your destination, you will probably be able to get this currency at a local bank. It is also important to check with your bank to ensure that you will be able to access your account with an ATM in a foreign country. You can also bring traveler's checks. You will probably not be able to cash personal checks. It is also a good idea to take a credit card with a limit of at least $1,000 in case of an emergency.
- **Other items to bring.** Make sure you bring clothes that are suitable for not only your country of primary destination but also the other places you will travel. This may include warm clothes, gloves, waterproof clothes, hiking shoes, and so on. If you are planning on bringing electrical equipment, check and see if you will need an adapter. In many countries, you

will need a special attachment to plug your item into the outlet. Clearly label your luggage, and make sure that you are able to carry it without assistance. Remember that if something is inexpensive it might be better to buy a new one when you arrive in your country of destination.

Completing a practicum abroad can be one of the most exciting experiences of your college life. Often the tuition and books cost no more than if you stayed in the United States. If you know you cannot be away for an entire semester because of family/friendship commitments, financial concerns, safety concerns, or you are very close to graduation, you may want to consider a two- or three-week program. These shorter experiences hold a lot of promise and can fulfill some of your most important educational goals.

AM I CUT OUT FOR SOCIAL WORK?

From time to time even most seasoned professionals wonder if they have chosen the right vocation. Should you, too, be having some doubts, that is okay. Seldom does anyone have to make an immediate decision about a career choice. If your first practicum did not go well, this may not be a reflection on you. Perhaps your supervisor was too often unavailable or too critical. Maybe staff members just did not reach out to you because of internal strife or poor morale within the agency (e.g., frustration over lack of a pay raise). Despite your faculty field liaison's efforts, maybe your experience was not a pleasant one. Do not take this personally. Especially if you are not at the end of your social work program, most students will have another practicum to test whether social work is the right career.

Sometimes even a relatively unpleasant practicum yields useful learning about yourself or a certain population of clients. For instance, if you tend to be very trusting of people, you may have learned not to display that trait to drug addicts who are not very far along in their recovery process. Maybe this experience will direct you to another population (e.g., hospice patients) with whom you will build excellent rapport because of the same trait.

The purpose of the practicum is to provide you with the opportunity to learn experientially. Maybe there are some things you would do differently now. You do not have to consider changing careers even if you made a few mistakes in your practicum. (Of course, if these were serious mistakes, and you made several of them, this is a different matter.) Sometimes talking with your adviser or your faculty field liaison can help you evaluate the advantages and disadvantages of changing majors or careers.

Finally, if you felt that you did good work with your clients, be reassured by that. We do not always get recognized for a job well done. In fact, you are more likely to get recognition if you create a serious problem than if you handle your assignments effectively and efficiently.

SUMMARY

This chapter has presented practical advice regarding situations and topics not covered elsewhere in the book. It provided answers to questions regarding several professional and pragmatic issues that may arise during the social work practicum.

Understanding and Evaluating the Field Agency as a Human Service Organization

1. Drive around the community from which most of your field agency's clients come. Drawing on your knowledge of macro social work practice and through an observation of the community, make an informal assessment of the community's needs and problems.

   a. What needs do you observe?

   _____

   _____

   _____

   b. Think of the agency's major programs and services in relation to the community's needs and problems. To what extent do those programs and services seem to be dictated by the community's needs?

   _____

   _____

   _____

   c. Find out if there has been a formal survey of the community needs in recent years. If yes, compare your impressions with the findings of the formal survey.

   _____

   _____

   _____

   d. If there is nothing to compare your findings with, to what extent does your supervisor agree with your assessment of community needs and the agency's responsiveness to those needs?

   _____

   _____

   _____

2. The changing economic, political, and social conditions are creating for human service agencies such challenges as reduced resources, increased demands, competing needs, and higher expectations for accountability. Your field agency is no exception. On the basis of your understanding of your agency, list the ways in which it is dealing with the situation.

   a. _____

   _____

   b. _____

   _____

   c. _____

   _____

d. _____

_____

e. _____

_____

f. How have the changes affected the agency's

Goals?

_____

_____

_____

Programs?

_____

_____

_____

Organizational Structure

_____

_____

_____

Personnel?

_____

_____

_____

Clients?

_____

_____

_____

3. Contrast the formal structure and functioning of your field agency as described/reflected in its policy manual and organizational chart with its informal structure, unwritten rules, and values—the way it really works. What differences do you see?

a. _____

_____

_____

b. _____

_____

_____

c. _____

_____

_____

d. _____

_____

_____

4. "One who pays the piper calls the tune." How do the following funding sources affect your field agency—positively and/or negatively?

a. Federal and state governments

_____

_____

_____

b. Local county and/or city authority

_____

_____

_____

c. United Way

_____

_____

_____

d. Insurance companies

_____

_____

_____

e. Self-paying clients

_____

_____

_____

5. Identify the major stakeholders in the agency and the ways the agency demonstrates its accountability to them.

a. _____

_____

_____

b. _____

_____

_____

c. _____

_____

_____

d. _____

_____

_____

6. Given your field agency's goals, philosophy, programs, personnel, professionalism, and overall climate, would you want to work for this agency as a qualified and credentialed social worker? Why or why not?

_____

_____

_____

_____

Taking Stock of Your Gains as a Learner

1. Read over your journals, logs, and other fieldwork-related written assignments this term in order to relive your experience in the field agency thus far. What are the most remarkable things you have learned about

   a. Your clients?

   _____

   _____

   _____

   b. Working with clients?

   _____

   _____

   _____

   c. The agency?

   _____

   _____

   _____

   d. The larger human service community?

   _____

   _____

   _____

   e. Yourself?

   _____

   _____

   _____

2. Review *your* learning experiences in the field agency and describe significant experiences in terms of

   a. Fields of social work practice observed.

   _____

   _____

   _____

   b. Major interventions used.

   _____

   _____

   _____

c. Social work professional roles played.

_____

_____

_____

d. Involvement in social work professional activities.

_____

_____

_____

e. Social work professional skills acquired.

_____

_____

_____

f. Social work practice wisdom learned.

_____

_____

_____

g. Ethical dilemmas encountered.

_____

_____

_____

3. Given the learning you have acquired, what would you do differently if you were entering your field agency for the first time?

_____

_____

_____

_____

_____

4. Based on the information you've provided in this exercise, would it make sense to update your résumé? What skills or abilities are you now comfortable in highlighting?

_____

_____

_____

Log onto **www.mysocialworklab.com** to access a wealth of case studies, videos, and assessment. (*If you did not receive an access code to **MySocialWorkLab** with this text and wish to purchase access online, please visit* www. mysocialworklab.com.)

1. **Watch the Core Competency video: "Applying Critical Thinking."** As a social worker employed by a shelter for women experiencing domestic violence, what would you do to truly "suspend judgment" about the client when she is caught between minimizing her partner's actions and needing to protect her children?

2. **Read the MySocialWorkLibrary case study: "Dan."** For Dan, the therapist in this case often represented his biological father, foster family, or even mother. With a complex case like this, why might it be important for the social worker to engage in self-reflection about their previous work together before agreeing to take the client again?

PRACTICE TEST

The following questions will test your knowledge of the content found within this chapter.

1. If clients' problems caused a student intern to feel depressed, what would *not* be a good strategy for handling the problem?
   a. Remembering that clients with substance abuse often have relapses
   b. Thinking about clients as children who need "consequences"
   c. Thinking about clients' strengths and envisioning them getting better
   d. Talking with the faculty field liaison if clients' problems become too much

2. Sometimes practicum placements aren't ideal and don't work out as planned. Under what circumstances should you seek another placement?
   a. Supervisor is thorough and demands accountability.
   b. Supervisor is expecting too much knowledge.
   c. You've made a mistake or been sick a lot.
   d. You're expected to ignore unethical or illegal practices.

3. You are asked to share a desk with a person who wasn't born in America. How should you show self-awareness of the culture?
   a. By personalizing the space with photos of loved ones and pets
   b. Locking the drawers where you keep snacks and drinks
   c. Providing hand sanitizer in the middle of the desk
   d. Cleaning the working surface before you leave each day

4. In planning your next practicum, what self-assessment might be the most important consideration?
   a. Your boy or girlfriend's interest in the same agency
   b. The prestige of the agency
   c. The potential for development of new skills
   d. The cleanliness of the agency's clients

Short Answer Question:
Jack's practicum has had lots of crises and challenges. Clients have disappeared and dropped out of treatment. He feels he's a failure but knows he needs to do some self-reflection and examination of the skills he's acquired and those that he hasn't. What else should he consider as he tries to assess whether social work is the right career for him?

ASSESS YOUR COMPETENCE

Use the scale below to rate your current level of achievement on the following concepts or skills associated with each competency practice behavior presented in the chapter:

1	2	3
I can accurately describe the concept or skill.	I can consistently identify the concept or skill when observing and analyzing practice activities.	I can competently implement the concept or skill in my own practice.

_____ use my time productively to allow for self-reflection and self-correction.

_____ appraise the multiple sources of information to understand my level of functioning, if given contradictory messages about my performance.

_____ design a plan for prevention for a specific problem that I might encounter in an agency setting.

Answers

Key: 1) b, 2) d, 3) d, 4) c

Appendix A:
Problem-Oriented
Recording

Record keeping today involves a complex series of decisions in which social work agencies have to balance the costs of detailed reporting systems against their benefits. How much information and what information should become part of the official record? What information is pertinent, and what is immaterial? More comprehensive records generally allow greater accountability but are costlier to maintain and may provide less protection of the client's confidentiality.

Information in ongoing records must be organized in some logical, coherent manner, and social service agencies have tackled this problem in several ways. One approach, the problem-oriented record (also known as the problem-oriented medical record, the problem-goal-oriented record, the problem-oriented system, or Weed system), has been widely adopted by agencies in health and human service settings. This approach has been described as having a "remarkable concurrence with and support of social work principles and functions" (Biagi, 1977, p. 212).

The problem-oriented record has four components: (1) a database that contains relevant information about the client, (2) a problem list that includes a statement of initial complaints, (3) an assessment and a plan related to each identified problem, and (4) progress notes about what was done and the outcome of each activity.

There are several variations of the problem-oriented record. Perhaps the most often used form is **SOAP** (*subjective, objective, assessment, plan*). For each identified problem, the social worker records *subjective* information (the client's perception of the problem), *objective* information (the facts of the case; information that can be verified), the *assessment* (the professional's conclusions about the nature of the problem), and the *plan* for intervention. Another variation is **PAP** (*problem, assessment, plan*), in which the client's subjective complaint and the objective information pertaining to the problem are brought together. The assessment and plan portions of PAP remain the same as in SOAP.

Tremendous diversity exists in social service agencies, particularly in how they are organized and run. In fact, the way in which your practicum agency wants you to record client data in its files may not look at all like the SOAP or PAP systems. Sometimes other organizational schemes form the basis for documenting pertinent client information in the agency's records. For instance, some of the data may be organized using Perlman's (1957) *4-Ps* (*person, problem, place,* and *process*) or Doremus's (1976) *4-Rs* (*roles, reactions, relationships,* and *resources*). You may discover many variations of these schemes as you are placed in different social service agencies.

To help you visualize what the problem-oriented record would look like, we have taken the same case example and presented it first in a SOAP format, then in a PAP framework.

EXAMPLE OF PROBLEM-ORIENTED MEDICAL RECORD USING SUBJECTIVE AND OBJECTIVE INFORMATION, ASSESSMENT, PLAN (SOAP)

Data Base

Mrs. B., a 60-year-old widowed female, was admitted reporting headaches, dizziness, unsteady gait, double vision, and episodes of forgetfulness. She was diagnosed as having an aneurysm. After surgery, she had partial right eye vision loss and right side paralysis. Patient has a tenth-grade education and has worked as a hotel maid until recently. She has no children or close relatives. She says that her religion is very important to her.

Problem #1: Anxiety about Disability

Subjective

"I'm so nervous; my nerves are shot—worrying about how I'm going to manage with one good arm and leg. I've got so many questions rattling around inside of me sometimes I think I'm going to explode. I can't get a straight answer out of them doctors."

Objective

The ruptured aneurysm and resulting surgery have left Mrs. B. with serious disabilities that will likely keep her from working again. Medical staff might have presented too optimistic a picture prior to surgery and not prepared her sufficiently for the condition in which she now finds herself.

Assessment

Patient is having a difficult time adjusting to her partial paralysis. She is concerned that she might not be allowed to return to her own home. Additionally, patient will be unable to work and will experience a loss of income. Both of these fears are well founded in reality, although if patient makes good progress in physical therapy there is no reason she can't return home, although she may require some assistance, at least initially.

Plan

1. Encourage Mrs. B. to ventilate her feelings.
2. Provide Mrs. B. with emotional support and help her use her religious faith in dealing with the situation.
3. Involve medical staff in clarifying her physical status and prognosis.
4. Encourage patient to continue with physical therapy and make plans for the future.
5. Help client apply for disability.

Problem #2: Need for Post-Hospital Care

Mrs. B. will not be able to live independently in her apartment in her present condition and does not want to go to a nursing home, even temporarily.

Subjective

"There's no way I could get up into bed by myself, or go down into the basement to wash a load of clothes. Why, I've never used my left hand for anything—now I'm going to have to use it for everything. How am I going to tie my shoes?"

Objective

Patient does not ambulate at this time but seems to be making good use of her left hand to feed self, answer the phone, and so on. A rehab hospital can help patient with her walking and introduce her to appliances that will facilitate her living independently. Whether she will regain use of her right hand is questionable.

Assessment

Patient needs intensive physical therapy at a rehab hospital to learn how to live with significant disabilities. Her concerns about self-care are real. Patient's physician agrees that Mrs. B. can benefit from intensive rehabilitation and has requested a consult from Cardinal Valley Hospital.

Plan

1. Discuss with patient the need for a referral to a rehab hospital.
2. Arrange for the patient to visit the rehab hospital.
3. Prepare the patient psychologically for changes in her life caused by the paralysis.
4. Talk with Mrs. B. about other alternatives (in-home assistance) in the event that she can't get into the rehab hospital immediately.
5. Complete the discharge plan and application process to rehab hospital.

EXAMPLE OF PROBLEM-ORIENTED MEDICAL RECORD USING PROBLEM, ASSESSMENT, PLAN (PAP)

Database

Mrs. B., a 60-year-old widowed female, was admitted reporting headaches, dizziness, unsteady gait, double vision, and episodes of forgetfulness. She was diagnosed as having an aneurysm. After surgery, she had partial right eye vision loss and right side paralysis. Patient has a tenth-grade education and has worked as a hotel maid until recently. She has no children or close relatives. She says that her religion is very important to her.

Problem #1: Anxiety about Disability

Mrs. B. worries about her inability to get around and feels that she has been given ambivalent messages about the extent of recovery she can expect.

Assessment

Patient is having a difficult time adjusting to her partial paralysis. She is concerned that she might not be allowed to return to her own home. Additionally, patient will be unable to work and will experience a loss of income.

Plan

1. Encourage Mrs. B. to ventilate her feelings.
2. Provide Mrs. B. with emotional support and help her use her religious faith in dealing with the situation.
3. Involve medical staff in clarifying her physical status and prognosis.
4. Encourage patient to continue with physical therapy.
5. Help patient apply for disability.

Problem #2: Need for Post-Hospital Care

Mrs. B. will not be able to live independently in her apartment in her present condition and does not want to go to a nursing home, even temporarily.

Assessment

Patient needs intensive physical therapy at rehab hospital and must learn to adjust to life with a significant disability.

Plan

1. Discuss with patient the need for a referral to a rehab hospital.
2. Arrange for the patient to visit the rehab hospital.
3. Prepare the patient psychologically for changes in her life caused by the paralysis.
4. Talk with Mrs. B. about other alternatives (in-home assistance) in the event that she can't get into the rehab hospital immediately.
5. Complete the discharge plan and application process to rehab hospital.

Appendix B: Example of a Student Intern Evaluation Form

UNIVERSITY OF KENTUCKY COLLEGE OF SOCIAL WORK
*FIELD PLACEMENT EVALUATION FORM**

SW 640 _____ Semester_____ 20 _____

Student Name: _____

Agency: _____

Agency Address/Phone: _____

_____

_____

Field Instructor: _____

Seminar Instructor: _____

Duties and Responsibilities: (Briefly describe the kinds of learning experiences the student completed. The types and number of cases assigned should be included.)

_____

_____

_____

_____

_____

Use of evaluation form: This form should be completed twice, once at mid-term of the semester and once at the end of the semester. **If you rate a student at either level 1 or 5, you must comment in the space provided.** Ratings are as follows:

NA = **No opportunity to observe practice behavior**

   1 = **Consistently fails to meet basic requirements of practice behavior**

   2 = **Inconsistently meets basic requirements of practice behavior**

(Continued)

_____

Note: This form is an excerpt from a longer version and draws from the Council of Social Work Education's new (2008) Educational Program Accreditation Standards (epas).

3 = Consistently meets basic requirements of practice behavior

4 = Consistently meets basic requirements of practice behavior and occasionally exceeds expectations

5 = Consistently exceeds basic requirements of practice behavior

2.1.4. Engages diversity and difference in practice.	Mid-Term Semester Rating	End of Semester Rating
1. Recognizes personal biases and values to remove their influence in working with diverse groups.	NA ⌊1⌋2⌋3⌋4⌋5⌋	NA ⌊1⌋2⌋3⌋4⌋5⌋
2. Recognizes the extent to which a culture's structure and values may oppress, marginalize, alienate, or create or enhance privilege or power.	NA ⌊1⌋2⌋3⌋4⌋5⌋	NA ⌊1⌋2⌋3⌋4⌋5⌋
3. Recognizes and communicates their understanding of the importance of differences (diversity) in the shaping of the meaning of an individual's life experiences.	NA ⌊1⌋2⌋3⌋4⌋5⌋	NA ⌊1⌋2⌋3⌋4⌋5⌋
4. Views self as learner and engages with clients to understand their lives, culture, and experiences.	NA ⌊1⌋2⌋3⌋4⌋5⌋	NA ⌊1⌋2⌋3⌋4⌋5⌋

Comments:

2.1.6. Engages in research-informed practice and practice-informed research.	Mid-Term Semester Rating	End of Semester Rating
1. Uses practice experience to inform scientific inquiry.	NA ⌊1⌋2⌋3⌋4⌋5⌋	NA ⌊1⌋2⌋3⌋4⌋5⌋
2. Uses research evidence to inform practice.	NA ⌊1⌋2⌋3⌋4⌋5⌋	NA ⌊1⌋2⌋3⌋4⌋5⌋

Comments:

2.1.9. Responds to contexts that shape practice.	Mid-Term Semester Rating	End of Semester Rating
1. Continuously discovers, appraises, and attends to contextual changes (example current events, changing locales, populations, scientific and technological development, and emerging societal trends to provide relevant services).	NA ⌊1⌋2⌋3⌋4⌋5⌋	NA ⌊1⌋2⌋3⌋4⌋5⌋

2. Provides leadership in promoting sustainable changes in service delivery and improves the quality of social services.   NA |1|2|3|4|5| NA |1|2|3|4|5|

Comments:

2.1.10. Engages, assesses, intervenes, and evaluates with individuals, families, groups, organizations, and communities.	**Mid-Term Semester Rating**	**End of Semester Rating**

Engagement

1. Substantively and effectively prepares for action with clients.   NA |1|2|3|4|5| NA |1|2|3|4|5|
2. Uses empathy and other interpersonal skills.   NA |1|2|3|4|5| NA |1|2|3|4|5|
3. Develops a mutually agreed-upon focus of work and desired outcomes.   NA |1|2|3|4|5| NA |1|2|3|4|5|

Assessment

1. Collects, organizes, and interprets client data.   NA |1|2|3|4|5| NA |1|2|3|4|5|
2. Separates fact from opinion in data presentation.   NA |1|2|3|4|5| NA |1|2|3|4|5|
3. Assesses client's strengths and limitations.   NA |1|2|3|4|5| NA |1|2|3|4|5|
4. Develops mutually agreed-upon intervention goals and objectives.   NA |1|2|3|4|5| NA |1|2|3|4|5|
5. Selects appropriate intervention strategies.   NA |1|2|3|4|5| NA |1|2|3|4|5|

Intervention

1. Initiates action to achieve organizational goals.   NA |1|2|3|4|5| NA |1|2|3|4|5|
2. Implements prevention interventions that enhance client capacities.   NA |1|2|3|4|5| NA |1|2|3|4|5|
3. Helps clients resolve problems.   NA |1|2|3|4|5| NA |1|2|3|4|5|
4. Negotiates, mediates, and advocates for clients.   NA |1|2|3|4|5| NA |1|2|3|4|5|
5. Facilitates transitions and endings.   NA |1|2|3|4|5| NA |1|2|3|4|5|

Evaluation

1. Critically analyzes and evaluates interventions.   NA |1|2|3|4|5| NA |1|2|3|4|5|

References

Abbott, A. A. (1986). The field placement contract: Its use in maintaining comparability between employment-related and traditional field placements. *Journal of Social Work Education, 22*(1), 57–66.

Anderson, C. L. (2000). Revisiting the Parenting Profile Assessment to screen or child abuse. *Journal of Nursing Scholarship, 32*(1), 53.

Appelbaum, P. (2002). Privacy in psychiatric treatment: Threats and responses. *American Journal of Psychiatry, 159,* 1809–1818.

Austin, D. M. (1986). *A history of social work education.* Austin, TX: University of Texas at Austin, School of Social Work.

Bagarozzi, D. A., & Anderson, S. A. (1989). *Personal, marital, and family myths: Theoretical formulations and clinical strategies.* New York: W. W. Norton.

Beck, A. T., Brown, G., & Steer, R. A. (1989). Prediction of eventual suicide in psychiatric inpatients by clinical ratings of hopelessness. *Journal of Consulting and Clinical Psychology, 57,* 309–310.

Beitin, B. K. & Allen, K. R. (2005). Resilience in Arab American couples after September 11, 2001: A systems perspective. (2005). *Journal of Marital & Family Therapy, 31*(3), 251–267.

Biagi, E. (1977). The social work stake in problem-oriented recording. *Social Work in Health Care, 3*(2), 211–221.

Black, B. M., Oles, T. P., & Moore, L. (1996). Homophobia among students in social work programs. *Journal of Baccalaureate Social Work, 2,* 23–41.

Blumenfield, S., & Lowe, J. I. (1987). A template for analyzing ethical dilemmas in discharge planning. *Health and Social Work, 12*(1), 47–56.

Brendel, R. W., & Bryan, E. (2004). HIPAA for psychiatrists. Harvard Review of *Psychiatry, 12,* 177–183.

Browning, C. H., & Browning, B. J. (1996). *How to partner with managed care.* Los Alamitos, CA: Duncliff's International.

Brueggemann, W. G. (2002). *The practice of macro social work.* Belmont, CA: Brooks/Cole.

Coffey, R. M., Ball, J. K., Johantgen, M., Elixhauser, A., Purcell, P., & Andrews, R. (1997). The case for national health data standards. *Health Affairs, 16,* 58–72.

Cohen, M. (1988). Suggested outline for process recording. Unpublished manuscript as quoted by C. T. Graybeal & E. Ruff. (1995). Process recording: It's more than you think. *Journal of Social Work Education, 31*(2), 169–181.

Colby, I. & Drziegielewski (2001). *Introduction to social work: The people's profession.* Chicago: Lyceum.

Cooper, W. E. (1982). Time management techniques for clinicians. In P. A. Keller & L. G. Ritt (Eds.), *Innovations in clinical practice: A source book* (pp. 177–183). Sarasota, FL: Professional Resource Exchange.

Corcoran, K., & Fischer, J. (1994). *Measures for clinical practice: A sourcebook.* New York: Free Press.

Corey, M. S., & Corey, G. (1998). *Becoming a helper.* Pacific Grove, CA: Brooks/Cole.

Council on Social Work Education. (2008). *Educational policy and accreditation standards.* Alexandria, VA: Council on Social Work Education.

Crisp, B. R. (2004). Evidence-based practice and the borders of data in the global information era. *Journal of Social Work Education, 40,* 73–86.

D'Augelli, A. R. (1989). Homophobia in a university community: Views of prospective resident assistants. *Journal of College Student Development, 30,* 546–552.

Dana, R. H. (1998). *Understanding cultural identity in intervention and assessment.* Thousand Oaks, CA: Sage.

Davidson, J. R., & Davidson, T. (1996). Confidentiality and managed care: Ethical and legal concerns. *Health & Social Work, 21,* 208–215.

Davidson, T., Davidson, J. R., & Keigher, S. M. (1999). Managed care: Satisfaction guaranteed . . . Not! *Health & Social Work, 24,* 163–168.

Deal, K. H. (1999). Clinical social work students' uses of self-disclosure: A case for formal training. *Arete, 23*(3), 33–45.

DePanfilis, D., & Salus, M. K. (2003). *Child Protective Services: A guide for caseworkers.* Washington, DC: U.S. Department of Human Services, Administration for Children and Families.

Dhooper, S. S. (1997). *Social work in health care in the 21st century.* Thousand Oaks, CA: Sage.

Dhooper, S. S., Huff, M. B., & Schultz, C. M. (1989). Social work and sexual harassment. *Journal of Sociology and Social Welfare, 16*(3), 125–138.

Dhooper, S. S., & Moore, S. E. (2001). *Social work practice with culturally diverse people.* Thousand Oaks, CA: Sage.

Dickson, D. (1998). *Confidentiality and privacy in social work.* New York: Free Press.

Dillard, J. M. (1983). *Multicultural counseling.* Chicago: Nelson-Hall.

Doremus, B. (1976). The four R's: Social diagnosis in health care. *Health and Social Work, 23*(July), 296–299.

Doyle, B. B. (1990). Crisis management of the suicidal patient. In S. J. Blumenthal & D. J. Kupfer (Eds.), *Suicide over the life cycle: Risk factors, assessment, and treatment of suicidal patients* (pp. 381–423). Washington, DC: American Psychiatric Press.

Egan, G. (1990). *The skilled helper: A systematic approach to effective helping.* Pacific Grove, CA: Brooks/Cole.

Epstein, L. (1980). *Helping people: The task-centered approach.* St. Louis: Mosby.

Faria, G., Brownstein, C., & Smith, H. Y. (1988). A survey of field instructors' perceptions of the liaison role. *Journal of Social Service Education, 24*(2), 135–144.

Feld, A. (2005). The Health Insurance Portability and Accountability Act (HIPAA): Its broad effect on practice. *American Journal of Gastroenterology, 100,* 1440–1443.

Ferguson, H. (2003). Outline of a critical best practice perspective on social work and social care. *British Journal of Social Work, 33,* 1005–1024.

Flaherty, C. & Collins, Camargo, C. & Lee, E. (2008). Privatization of child welfare services: Lessons learned from experienced states regarding site readiness assessment and planning. *Children and Youth Services Review, 30*(7), 809–820.

Flores, J. A. (2005). HIPAA: Past, present and future implications for nurses [electronic version]. *Journal of Issues in Nursing, 10*(2), 1–9.

Fuse, T. (1997). *Suicide, individual and society.* Toronto: Canadian Scholars' Press.

Gabel, S., Oster, G., & Pfeffer, C. R. (1988). *Difficult moments in child psychotherapy.* New York: Plenum Medical.

Gambrill, E. (2008). Evidence-informed practice. In William Rowe and Lisa A. Rapp-Paglicci (Eds.), *Comprehensive handbook of social work and social welfare: Social work practice* (pp. 3–28). New York: John Wiley & Sons.

Garrett, K. J. (1994). Caught in a bind: Ethical decision making in schools. *Social Work in Education, 16*(2), 97–105.

Goldstein, E. G. (1997). To tell or not to tell: The disclosure of events in the therapist's life to the patient. *Clinical Social Work Journal, 25*(1), 41–58.

Gray, J. A. M. (2001). The origin of evidence-based practice. In A. Edwards & G. Elwyn (Eds.), *Evidence-informed client choice* (pp. 19–33). New York: Oxford University Press.

Graybeal, C., & Ruff, E. (1995). Process recording: It's more than you think. *Journal of Social Work Education, 31,* 169–181.

Green, D. L., & Roberts, A. R. (2008). *Helping victims of violent crime: Assessment, treatment and evidence-based practice.* New York: Springer.

Greene, R. R., & Sullivan, W. P. (2001). Managed care and the ecological perspective: Meeting the needs of older adults. In N. W. Veeder & W. Peebles-Wilkins (Eds.), *Managed care services: Policy, programs, and research* (pp. 163–186). New York: Oxford University Press.

Guyatt, G., & Rennie, D. (Eds.). (2000a). *Users' guide: Manual for evidence-based clinical practice.* Chicago: American Medical Association Press.

Guyatt, G., & Rennie, D. (Eds.). (2000b). *Users' guides to medical literature: Essentials of evidence-based clinical practice.* Chicago: American Medical Association Press.

Harlan, K. B. (2004). Compassion fatigue and Masters level social workers in direct mental health service delivery. *Dissertation Abstracts International, A: Humanities and Social Sciences, 65*(2), pp. 698–A.

Hendren, R. L. (1990). Assessment and interviewing strategies for suicidal patients over the life cycle. In S. J. Blumenthal & D. J. Kupfer (Eds.), *Suicide over the life cycle: Risk factors, assessment and treatment of suicidal patients* (pp. 235–252). Washington, DC: American Psychiatric Press.

Hepworth, D. H., & Larsen, J. A. (1990). *Direct social work practice.* Belmont, CA: Wadsworth.

Hepworth, D. H., Rooney, R. H., & Larsen, J. A. (2002). *Direct social work practice: Theory and skills.* Pacific Grove, CA: Brooks/Cole.

Hepworth, D. H., Rooney, R. H., Rooney, G. D., Strom-Gottfried, K., & Larsen, J. (2006). *Direct social work practice: Theory and skills* (7th ed.). Belmont, CA: Thomson Higher Education.

Higgs, J., & Jones, M. (2000). Will evidence-based practice take the reasoning out of practice? In J. Higgs & M. Jones (Eds.), *Clinical reasoning in health professionals* (2nd ed.) (pp. 307–315). Oxford: Butterworth Heineman.

Kagle, J. D. (1984). *Social work records.* Homewood, IL: Dorsey.

Jenkins, L. E., & Sheafor, B. W. (1982). An overview of social work field instruction. In B. W. Sheafor & L. E. Jenkins (Eds.), *Quality field instruction in social work.* White Plains, NY: Longman.

Joiner, T., Kalafat, J., Draper, J., Stokes, H., Knudson, M., Berman, A. L. et al. (2007). Establishing standards for the assessment of suicide risk among callers to the National Suicide Prevention Lifeline. *Suicide and Life-Threatening Behavior, 37*(3), 353–365.

Johnson, L. C. (1995). *Social work practice: A generalist approach.* Boston: Allyn & Bacon.

Johnson, S. L. (1997). *The therapist's guide to clinical intervention: The 1-2-3's of treatment planning.* San Diego, CA: Academic Press.

Kadushin, A. (1972). *The social work interview.* New York: Columbia University Press.

Kendall, K. A. (2002). Council on Social Work Education: Its antecedents and first twenty years. Alexandria, VA: Council on Social Work Education.

Kirst-Ashman, K. K., & Hull, G. H. (1993). *Understanding generalist practice.* Chicago: Nelson-Hall.

Knight, C. (1999). The implications of BSW students' experiences with danger in the field practicum. *Journal of Baccalaureate Social Work, 4*(2), 133–149.

Kurzman, P. A. (1995). Professional liability and malpractice. In *Encyclopedia of Social Work* (19th ed.) (pp. 1921–1927). Washington, DC: National Association of Social Workers.

Lamb, M. E., Orbach, Y., Hershkowitz, I., Esplin, P. W., & Horowitz, D. (2007). A structural forensic interview protocol improves the quality and informativeness of investigative interviews with children: A review of research using the NICHD Investigative Protocol. *Child Abuse & Neglect, 31,* 1201–1231.

Lance, L. M. (1992). Changes in homophobic views as related to interaction with gay persons: A study in the reduction of tensions. *International Journal of Group Tensions, 22,* 291–299.

Lowenberg, F. M., & Dolgoff, R. (1996). *Ethical decisions for social work practice.* Itasca, IL: Peacock.

Managed Mental Health Care: What to ask? What to look for? (1996). Rockville, MD: Center for Mental Health Services, U.S. Department of Health and Human Services.

Maris, R. W., Berman, A. L., & Silverman, M. M. (2000). *Comprehensive textbook of suicidology.* New York: Guildford Press.

Maslow, A. (1970). *Motivation and personality.* New York: Harper & Row. (Originally published 1954.)

McNeece, C. A., & Thyer, B. A. (2004). Evidence-based practice and social work. *Journal of Evidence-Based Social Work, 1,* 7–25.

Mesbur, E. S. (1991). Overview of baccalaureate field instruction: Objectives and outcomes. In D. Schneck, B. Grossman, & U. Glassman (Eds.), *Field instruction in social work: Contemporary issues and trends.* Dubuque, IA: Kendall/Hunt.

Miller, J., & Rodwell, M. K. (1997). Disclosure of student status in agencies: Do we still have a secret? *Families in Society, 78*(1), 72–83.

Miller, M. (1985). *Information Center: Training workshop manual.* San Diego: Information Center [As cited in Sommers-Flanagan and Sommers-Flanagan (1995)].

Millstein, K., Dare-Winters, K., & Sullivan, S. (1994). The power of silence: Ethical dilemmas of informed consent in practice evaluations. *Clinical Social Work Journal, 22*(3), 317–329.

Milner, J. S. (1986). *The Child Abuse Potential Inventory: Manual* (2nd ed.) Webster, NC: Psytec.

Munson, C. E. (1987). Field instruction in social work education. *Journal of Teaching in Social Work, 1*(1), 91–109.

National Association of Social Workers (1999). *Code of Ethics.* Washington, DC: National Association of Social Workers.

National Association of Social Workers (2003). *Social Work Speaks.* Washington, DC: Author.

Olinde, J. F., & McCard, H. (2005). Understanding the boundaries of the HIPAA preemption analysis. *Defense Counsel Journal, 72,* 158–169.

Patterson, C. H. (1985). *The therapeutic relationship: Foundations for an eclectic psychotherapy.* Pacific Grove, CA: Brooks/Cole.

Perlman, H. (1957). *Social casework: A problem-solving process.* Chicago: University of Chicago Press.

Pfeiffer, J. W., & Jones, J. E. (1972). Criteria of effective goal-setting: The SPIRO model. In *The 1972 annual handbook for group facilitators.* La Jolla, CA: University Associates.

Philp, E. P., & Berkman, B. (2001). Biotechnology and managed care: Effects on health care cost, clinical practice, and education of health care professionals. In N. W. Veeder & W. Peebles-Wilkins (Eds.), *Managed care services: Policy, programs, and research* (pp. 31–49). New York: Oxford University Press.

Pollio, D. E. (2002). The evidence-based group worker. *Social Work with Groups, 25,* 57–70.

Proctor, E. K., Morrow-Howell, N., & Lott, C. L. (1993). Classification and correlates of ethical dilemmas in hospital social work. *Social Work, 38*(2), 166–177.

Raines, J. C. (2004). Evidence-based practice in school social work: A process in perspective. *Children & Schools, 26,* 71–85.

Reamer, F. G. (1991). AIDS, social work, and the "duty to protect." *Social Work, 36*(1), 56–60.

Reamer, F. G. (1982). Conflicts of professional duty in social work. *Social Casework, 63*(10), 579–585.

Rey, L. D. (1996). What social workers need to know about client violence. *Families in Society, 77*(1), 33–39.

Richardson, M. A., Simons-Morton, B., & Annegers, J. F. (1993). Effect of perceived barriers on compliance with antihypertensive medication. *Health Education Quarterly, 20,* 489–503.

Rock, B., & Congress, E. (1999). The new confidentiality for the 21st century in a managed care environment. *Social Work, 44*(3), 253–262.

Rompf, E., Royse, D., & Dhooper, S. S. (1993). Anxiety preceding agency placement: What students worry about. *Journal of Teaching in Social Work, 7*(2), 81–95.

Rosen, A. (2003). Evidence-based social work practice: Challenges and promise. *Social Work Research, 27,* 197–208.

Rothman, J. C. (2000). *Stepping out into the field: A field manual for social work students.* Boston: Allyn & Bacon.

Royse, D. (1999). Single system designs. In *Research methods for social workers.* Belmont, CA: Brooks/Cole.

Royse, D., Thyer, B. A., Padgett, D. K., & Logan, T. K. (2001). *Program evaluation: An introduction.* Belmont, CA: Brooks/Cole.

Sackett, D. L., Rosenberg, W., Gray, J. A. M., Haynes, R. B., & Richardson, W. S. (1996). Evidence-based practice: What is and what it isn't. *British Medical Journal, 312,* 71–72.

Sarkisian, N., Gerena, M. & Gerstel, N. (2006). Extended family ties among Mexicans, Puerto Ricans, and whites: Superintegration or disintegration? *Family Relations, 55*(3), 331–344.

Schwartz, G. (1989). Confidentiality revisited. *Social Work, 34*(3), 223–226.

Shea, S. C. (1999). *The practical art of suicide assessment: A guide for mental health professionals and substance abuse counselors.* New York: John Wiley & Sons.

Sheafor, B. W., Horejsi, C. R., & Horejsi, G. A. (2000). *Techniques and guidelines for social work practice.* Boston: Allyn & Bacon.

Siporin, M. (1975). *Introduction to social work practice.* New York: Macmillan.

Smith, S. K. (2007). Mandatory reporting of child abuse and neglect. At http://www.smith-lawfirm.com/mandatory_reporting.htm.

Sommers-Flanagan, J., & Sommers-Flanagan, R. (1995). Intake interviewing with suicidal patients: A systematic approach. *Professional Psychology, 26*(1), 41–47.

Strom-Gottfried, K. (1998). Informed consent meets managed care. *Health & Social Work, 23*(1), 25–33.

Theriot, M. T., Johnson, T. K., Mulvaney, M., and Kretzschmar, J. A. (2006). Does slow and steady win the race? The impact of block versus concurrent field on BSW student's professional development and emotional well-being. *Journal of Baccalaureate Social Work, 12,* 203–217.

Thyer, B. A. (2003). Evidence–based practice in the United States. In B. A. Thyer & M. A. F. Kazi (Eds.), *International perspectives on evidence-based practice in social work.* Birmingham, UK: Venture Press.

Tolson, E. R., & Kopp, J. (1988). The practicum: Clients, problems, interventions, and influences on student practice. *Journal of Social Work Education, 24*(2), 123–134.

Tymchuck, A. J. (1992). Strategies for resolving value dilemmas. *American Behavioral Scientist, 26*(2), 159–175.

Tzeng, O. C. S., Jackson, J. W., & Karlson, H. C. (1991). *Theories of child abuse and neglect.* New York: Praeger.

Urbanowski, M. L., & Dwyer, M. M. (1988). *Learning through field instruction: A guide for teachers and students.* Milwaukee: Family Service America.

Vourlekis, B., Hall, G., & Rosenblum, P. (1996). Testing the reliability and validity of an interviewing skills evaluation tool for use in practicum. *Research on Social Work Practice, 6*(4), 492–503.

Wagner, E. R. (2001). Types of managed care organizations. In P. R. Kongstvedt (Ed.), *The managed care handbook* (pp. 33–45). Gaithersburg, MD: Aspen Press.

Walker, R. (1994). Risk assessment and risk management: For mental health, mental retardation, and substance abuse clinicians. Unpublished manuscript.

Watson, M. E. (1994). *Compliance with referral recommendations from an employee assistance program.* Columbia University Ph.D. Dissertation.

Weissman, A. (1976). Industrial social services: Linkage technology. *Social Casework, 57*(January), 5–57.

Weston, K. (1997). *Families we choose: Lesbians, gays, kinship.* New York: Columbia University Press.

Wilson, S. (1981). *Field instruction: Techniques for supervisors.* New York: Free Press.

Wintersteen, M. B., Diamond, G. S. & Fein, J. A. (2007). Screening for suicide risk in the pediatric emergency and acute care setting. *Current Opinion in Pediatrics, 19*(4), 398–404.

Winton, M. A., & Mara, B. A. (2001). *Child Abuse & Neglect: Multidisciplinary approaches.* Boston: Allyn & Bacon.

Wisniewski, J. J., & Toomey, B. G. (1987). Are social workers homophobic? *Social Work, 32*(5), 454–455.

Wollersheim, J. P. (1974). The assessment of suicide potential via interview methods. *Psychotherapy, 11,* 222–225.

Zastrow, C. (1995). *The practice of social work.* Pacific Grove, CA: Brooks/Cole.

Photo Credits

Index